Anger Management Solutions for Parents

I0559976

Quick, practical strategies for parents to manage
emotions, handle triggers, improve communication
and create
lasting connections in family life.

By
Agnes Blake

Table of Contents

Introduction 1

Chapter 1: Understanding Parental Anger 4
"Compassion Begins With \You Unpacking Anger Without
Judgment" 4
The Emotional Rollercoaster Of Parenting............................4
Identifying Your Anger Triggers 6
The Impact Of Childhood Experiences On Parenting..................7
The Science Behind Anger: What Happens In Your Brain...........9
Recognizing Early Warning Signs Of Anger 10
The Cost Of Unmanaged Anger On Family Dynamics.............12

Chapter 2: Mindfulness And Stress Reduction Techniques 14
"Finding Calm In The Chaos: Mindful Tools For Everyday
Parenting" 14
Introduction To Mindfulness For Parents............................14
Daily Deep-Breathing Exercises For Immediate Calm 16
Quick Meditation Techniques For Busy Parents 17
Developing A Mindfulness Routine......................................19
Using Visualization To Reduce Stress 21
Incorporating Mindfulness Into Family Activities.....................23

Chapter 3: Practical Anger Management Strategies 25
"Tools That Work: Real-Life Techniques To Keep Your Cool" 25
The "Pause And Breathe" Technique.....................................25
Creating A Calm-Down Corner At Home..............................27
Using The S.T.O.P. Method (Stop, Take A Breath, Observe,
Proceed)..29
Implementing Timeouts For Parents....................................31
The Power Of Journaling For Emotional Regulation..................32
Quick Physical Exercises To Release Tension 34
Summary..36

Chapter 4: Emotional Self-Reflection And Personal Growth ..37
"From Reaction To Reflection:
Growing Alongside Your Child"...37

Journaling Prompts For Self-Reflection..37
Understanding Your Emotional Triggers 39
Breaking Negative Cycles From Your Own Upbringing..............41
The Role Of Self-Compassion In Anger Management................43
Setting Personal Boundaries For Emotional Health 45
Building Emotional Resilience As A Parent 47
Summary 49

Chapter 5: Effective Communication With Children..............50
"Speak With Heart: Connecting Through Calm, Not Conflict"..50
The Basics Of Reflective Listening..50
Validating Your Child's Emotions 52
Using "I" Statements To Express Feelings 53
Role-Playing Scenarios To Improve Communication...................55
Navigating Difficult Conversations With Empathy 57
The Importance Of Consistent Communication...........................59
Summary 61

Chapter 6: Strategies For Reconnecting After Conflict...........62
"Healing Together: Rebuilding Trust And Strengthening Bonds"
....62
Steps To Rebuild Trust After An Outburst...................................62
The Art Of Apologizing To Your Child...64
Engaging In Shared Activities For Reconnection.........................65
Using Reconciliation Rituals To Heal...67
Creating A Family Reconnection Plan 68
Power Of Play In Strengthening Parent-Child Relationships 70

Chapter 7: Building A Support System 73
"You're Not Alone: Finding The Support Every Parent
Deserves"...73
Identifying Potential Support Networks 73
Leveraging Online Communities For Support...............................75
Building Supportive Relationships With Other Parents 77
Utilizing Local Resources And Groups...78
Communicating Your Needs To Your Support System................80
The Benefits Of Professional Counseling And Therapy 82

Chapter 8: Consistency And Long-Term Success...................85

"Staying The Course: Building Habits That Last A Lifetime" 85
Creating A Personal Action Plan For Anger Management 85
Setting Realistic Goals And Tracking Progress 87
Dealing With Setbacks And Staying Motivated............................89
Integrating Anger Management Strategies Into Daily Life..........90
Encouraging Family-Wide Emotional Health 92
Celebrating Success And Continued Growth................................94

Chapter 9: Practical Exercises And Worksheets 96
"Your Personal Parenting Toolkit: Hands-On Support For Daily
Growth" 96
Daily Reflection Worksheets..96
Family Meeting Agendas And Worksheets 101
Progress Tracking Tools For Long-Term Success 103

Conclusion..**106**
References **109**
Appendix: **113**
We'd Love Your Feedback! **114**

PART -II..**115**

Introduction **117**

Chapter 10: Understanding Anger And Its Roots 119
The Science Of Anger: What Happens In Your Brain 119
Interactive Element: Hormonal Journal Prompts 126

Chapter 11: Developing Emotional Intelligence 139
Interactive Element: Trigger Reflection Exercise........................ 140
Interactive Element: Personal Values Reflection......................... 148
Interactive Element: Daily Gratitude Prompt 159
Interactive Element: Reflection And Feedback Session 167

Chapter 12: Practical Strategies For Managing Anger 172
Breathing Techniques: Instant Calm For Intense Moments...... 172
Interactive Element: Daily Breathing Practice Checklist 173
Physical Outlets: Channeling Anger Into Activity...................... 179
Interactive Element: Physical Activity Exploration Chart......... 180

Creative Expressions: Art As An Emotional Outlet 181

Digital Detox: Balancing Online And Offline Worlds 184

Conflict   Resolution: Turning Arguments Into Discussions.186

Interactive Element: Conflict Resolution Role-Play 188

Humor And Anger: Laughing It Off..191

Chapter 13: Strengthening Relationships............................. 194

Interactive Element: Active Listening Role-Play Exercise 195

Effective Communication: Saying What You Mean.....................197

Empathy In Relationships: Walking In Their Shoes....................198

Interactive Element: Perspective-Taking Reflection...................200

Trust Building: The Foundation Of Strong Bonds.....................203

Apology And Forgiveness Exercise 204

Setting Boundaries: Respecting Yourself And Others.................207

Repairing Relationships: After The Storm.................................208

Chapter 14: Navigating Social And Academic Pressures 211

Interactive Element: Personal Study Space Checklist 212

Social Media Savvy: Navigating Online Interactions 216

Interactive Element: Online Self-Reflection Exercise 217

Peer Approval Vs. Self-Approval: Finding Balance....................221

Extracurricular Overload: Prioritizing Passions.........................222

Handling Bullying: Standing Up For Yourself............................224

Future Focus: Planning Without Panic 226

Chapter 15: Building Resilience And Confidence.................. 228

Interactive Element: Resilience Reflection Exercise 229

Positive Self-Talk: Rewriting Your Inner Dialogue 230

Interactive Element: Affirmation Creation Exercise...................231

Setting Realistic Goals: Steps To Success..................................236

Celebrating Small Wins: Building Momentum 237

Interactive Element: Daily Success Tracker 239

Learning From Failure: Embracing Mistakes 239

Support Systems: Leaning On Your Squad.................................241

Chapter 16: Engaging Parents And Guardians 244

Interactive Element: Generational Perspective Exercise.............245

Family Meetings: Creating A Safe Space For Dialogue 250

Negotiation Skills: Finding Middle Ground...............................251

Joint   Activities: Building Bonds Through Shared Experiences 253

Encouraging Independence: Trusting Your Teen 255

Professional Help: When To Seek Counseling 256

Chapter 17: Sustaining Emotional Growth 261

Interactive Element: Personal Growth Plan Template 263

Personal Growth Plan: Enhancing Emotional Skills 263

Reflective Practices: Regular Check-Ins With Yourself.............. 267

Interactive Element: Reflective Journaling Prompts 269

Giving Back: Helping Others Manage Their Emotions 275

Staying Inspired: Finding Motivation In Others 278

Adapting To Change: Embracing New Challenges 279

Crafting Your Narrative: Owning Your Story 281

Family Games 283

Conclusion 287

References 290

Leave A Review! 294

Introduction

One evening, after a long day of work and endless chores, I found myself in a familiar scene. My two young children were fighting over a toy, and the noise level was rising fast. I could feel my anger bubbling up, ready to spill over. My heart was racing, and my patience was wearing thin. In a moment of frustration, I yelled at them to stop. The look on their faces broke my heart. I felt an immediate wave of guilt wash over me. I wondered, "Why can't I control my anger? Why does parenting have to be so hard?"

If you've ever felt this way, you're not alone. Many parents struggle with managing their emotions, especially anger. This book aims to provide you with practical, easy-to-implement strategies for managing your emotions, improving communication, and creating lasting connections with your family. Consider this book a hands-on guide designed to fit into your busy life and offer real solutions.

Parenting is a rewarding journey, but it's also filled with challenges. One of the biggest struggles is dealing with anger. Anger can make you feel overwhelmed and out of control. It often leads to feelings of guilt and shame. Many parents worry about the impact their anger has on their children. They struggle with maintaining consistent discipline and fear they are not doing a good job.

Research indicates that nearly 70% of parents experience emotional overwhelm at least once a week. Guilt and shame often follow these emotional outbursts, making it even harder to manage anger in the future. This book aims to break that cycle by offering straightforward, easy-to-read content that addresses these challenges effectively.

My vision for this book is to provide you with the tools you need to navigate the emotional landscape of parenting. Each chapter is designed to offer practical exercises and interactive worksheets to help you apply the strategies in your daily life. The goal is to make these tools as accessible and effective as possible.

Here's what you can expect to gain from reading this book:

- Mindfulness and Stress-Reduction Techniques: Learn how to stay calm and focused, even in the most challenging situations.

- Understanding and Managing Emotional Triggers: Identify what sets off your anger and how to respond more constructively.

- Improved Communication with Your Children: Discover ways to talk to your kids that foster understanding and cooperation.

- Building a Supportive Network: Find out how to create a community of support among friends, family, and other parents.

The book is divided into several chapters, each focusing on a different aspect of anger management:

- Chapter 1: Understanding Anger - Explore what anger is and why it shows up in parenting.

- Chapter 2: Identifying Triggers - Learn how to recognize the situations that trigger your anger.

- Chapter 3: Mindfulness Techniques - Discover simple exercises to stay present and calm.

- Chapter 4: Effective Communication - Find ways to talk to your children that reduce conflict.

- Chapter 5: Consistent Discipline - Gain strategies for maintaining consistent and fair discipline.

- Chapter 6: Building Support Systems - Learn the importance of a support network and how to create one.

I am passionate about helping parents with young children. I have seen firsthand how effective anger management can transform family dynamics. My goal is to share this knowledge with you in a way that is easy to understand and apply.

As you read this book, I encourage you to engage actively with the exercises and reflect on your progress. Consistent practice and dedication will lead to lasting positive changes. Remember, managing anger is a journey, not a destination. It takes time, patience, and commitment. But the rewards are worth it—a happier, more harmonious family life.

You are not alone in this journey. Together, we will explore strategies that work, and you will find the support you need to create lasting connections with your family. Let's take this first step together. The journey to better managing your emotions and improving your family life starts here.

Chapter 1:
Understanding Parental Anger

"Compassion Begins with \You Unpacking Anger Without Judgment"

O ne Saturday morning, you might find yourself in a scene that feels all too familiar. The baby is crying for a bottle, the toddler is demanding attention, and the older child is arguing over screen time. You're running on only a few hours of sleep, and the laundry pile seems to be growing by the minute. Your partner is out running errands, and you're left juggling it all. As the noise level rises and your patience thins, you can feel the anger building inside you. You wonder, "Why do I feel this way? Why can't I just stay calm?"

This chapter aims to explore the emotional rollercoaster of parenting, a journey filled with highs and lows that can leave even the most patient parent feeling overwhelmed. Understanding these emotions is the first step toward managing them effectively.

The Emotional Rollercoaster of Parenting

Parenting is a complex mix of joy, frustration, anxiety, and guilt. The joy of witnessing your child's first milestones, like their first smile or first steps, fills your heart with unparalleled happiness. These moments make all the sleepless nights and endless diaper changes seem worth it. However, the frustration of dealing with tantrums can quickly overshadow these joyful moments. When your child throws themselves on the floor in the middle of a grocery store, screaming at the top of their lungs, it can be incredibly challenging to remain calm.

Managing daily responsibilities adds another layer of anxiety. Balancing work, household chores, and parenting can feel like an impossible juggling act. The constant worry about whether you're doing enough for your children, whether they're eating healthy, getting enough sleep, or doing well in school, can weigh heavily on your mind. This anxiety often leads to a heightened state of stress, making it easier for anger to surface.

Feeling anger towards your child can bring a profound sense of guilt. You love your children more than anything, but in those moments of anger, you might wonder if you're failing as a parent. The guilt can be overwhelming, leading to a cycle of self-doubt and further stress. But it's important to understand that these emotions are normal. You're not alone in feeling this way.

Many parents share similar experiences. One mother shared, "Sometimes, I feel like I'm walking on a tightrope. One wrong move, and I lose my balance. The guilt of yelling at my kids eats me up inside." According to a study, nearly 70% of parents report feeling overwhelmed by their emotions at least once a week. These statistics validate that these struggles are common and shared by many.

Sleep deprivation and constant stress further amplify these emotional responses. Lack of sleep can significantly affect your mood and patience. When you're running on empty, it's much harder to keep your cool. A study from the National Institutes of Health found that mothers with poor sleep quality exhibited more stress and less positive parenting behaviors. The link between sleep and emotional regulation is clear: the less sleep you get, the harder it is to manage your emotions effectively.

Stress also plays a significant role in emotional volatility. Daily stressors, whether from work, finances, or household responsibilities, can build up and make you more prone to anger. A study during the COVID-19 pandemic revealed that each additional stressor increased the likelihood of parents using aggressive discipline by 1.3 times. This highlights how situational stress can exacerbate emotional responses, making anger more likely.

Given these challenges, it becomes crucial to learn emotional regulation techniques. Emotional regulation involves understanding and managing your emotional responses to maintain healthy relationships and well-being. For parents, this means finding ways to stay calm and composed, even in the face of stress and frustration. The benefits of emotional regulation are immense. It not only helps you feel more in control of your emotions but also sets a positive example for your children. When you manage your emotions well, your children learn to do the same, leading to a more harmonious family dynamic.

Understanding and managing your emotions is the first step toward creating a happier, more balanced family life. This chapter will delve into the highs and lows of parenting, helping you recognize the normalcy of these emotions and the importance of emotional regulation. By acknowledging these feelings and learning to navigate them, you can foster a more positive and supportive environment for your family.

Identifying Your Anger Triggers

Recognizing what triggers your anger is crucial for managing it effectively. Think about the moments that make you see red. Is it when your child talks back or when siblings bicker endlessly? These situations can set off a cascade of emotions that seem uncontrollable. Disrespect and disobedience are common triggers. Your child refusing to follow instructions can feel like a direct challenge to your authority, igniting frustration and anger. Sibling fights, with their incessant noise and unresolved tension, can push you over the edge. It's essential to identify these triggers and understand why they provoke such strong reactions in you.

Understanding your triggers can pave the way for proactive anger management. When you know what sets you off, you can prepare yourself to respond more calmly. Consider the case of a mother who used to lose her temper whenever her children argued. By identifying this as a major trigger, she started using a trigger journal to keep track of these incidents. Over time, she noticed patterns. She realized that her anger was often rooted in her own childhood experiences of sibling rivalry, where conflicts were never resolved peacefully. Armed with this insight, she began to implement strategies to manage her reactions, such as taking deep breaths and calmly intervening in her children's disputes.

To help you recognize your own triggers, practical tools and methods can be very effective. Start with a trigger identification worksheet. This tool allows you to document specific situations that provoke your anger, along with your emotional and physical reactions. Over time, you'll notice patterns that can help you anticipate and manage your responses. Self-reflection questions can also be beneficial. Ask yourself, "What exactly about this situation made me angry?" and "How did I feel physically and emotionally?" Daily situations that might serve as triggers include morning rushes, mealtime battles, and bedtime routines. By consistently reflecting on these moments, you can gain deeper insights into your triggers.

Our past experiences often play a significant role in shaping our current reactions. Unresolved issues from childhood can influence how we respond to our children's behavior. For instance, if you grew up in a household where disobedience was met with harsh punishment, you might find yourself reacting strongly to any form of defiance. Addressing these past issues can mitigate your current triggers. Techniques like journaling about your childhood experiences and discussing them with a therapist can be incredibly helpful. By understanding the roots of your anger, you can begin to reframe your reactions and develop healthier ways to cope.

Understanding and managing your triggers is a process that requires patience and self-reflection. But by taking the time to identify what sets you off and why, you can pave the way for more effective anger management. This not only benefits you but also creates a more harmonious environment for your children. As you become more aware of your triggers and learn to manage them, you'll find that you can respond to challenging situations with greater calm and clarity. This journey of self-discovery and growth is essential for fostering a positive and supportive family dynamic.

The Impact of Childhood Experiences on Parenting

Our childhood experiences significantly shape how we approach parenting and respond emotionally to our children. Many of the disciplinary methods we use are inherited from our own parents. For instance, if you were raised in a household where strict discipline was the norm, you might find yourself defaulting to similar methods, even if they don't align with your current beliefs. This automatic response is deeply ingrained, often a result of years of conditioning. It's essential to recognize these inherited patterns to break free from them and adopt more positive parenting practices.

Consider the story of a father who grew up in a home where yelling was the primary mode of discipline. He noticed that he often resorted to shouting when his children misbehaved, despite his desire to be a more patient parent. Through self-awareness and reflection, he recognized this pattern and sought to change it. He started by acknowledging his behavior and understanding its roots. With time and effort, he began to implement calmer, more constructive disciplinary methods, breaking the negative cycle he had inherited.

Self-awareness is a crucial step in avoiding the repetition of negative patterns. By understanding your childhood experiences and how they influence your current behavior, you can make conscious choices about how you want to parent. One mother shared that she used to react harshly whenever her child spilled something, a response linked to her own experiences of being scolded for accidents as a child. Through journaling and therapy, she became aware of this trigger and learned to respond with empathy and patience instead. Tools like reflective journaling and mindfulness exercises can help you gain insights into your past and its impact on your parenting style.

Anger and emotional responses are often passed down through generations, a concept known as intergenerational transmission. When parents express anger in unhealthy ways, children learn to imitate these behaviors. Research shows that children of parents who frequently exhibit anger are more likely to develop similar emotional responses. Breaking this cycle requires a conscious effort to model positive behaviors. For example, a parent who grew up in an environment where anger was met with aggression might choose to practice deep-breathing exercises and teach these techniques to their children, thereby promoting a healthier way to handle anger.

To break free from the negative influences of your past, it's essential to adopt new, positive parenting habits. Start by setting clear goals for the kind of parent you want to be. Create a list of specific behaviors you wish to change and develop a plan to address them. Journaling exercises can be particularly beneficial, as they provide a space for you to reflect on your past influences and set new goals. Write about your childhood experiences, how they shaped your current behavior, and what steps you can take to create a more positive environment for your children.

For instance, if you tend to raise your voice when stressed, practice mindfulness techniques to stay calm. When you feel the urge to yell, take a few deep breaths and count to ten. Over time, these new habits will replace the old, negative ones, leading to a more harmonious family dynamic. Consider setting aside time each week to reflect on your progress and adjust your strategies as needed. The journey of breaking negative cycles is ongoing, but with dedication and self-awareness, you can create a healthier, more positive environment for your family.

The Science Behind Anger: What Happens in Your Brain

Understanding the neurological basis of anger can provide valuable insights into why we react the way we do. At the heart of our emotional responses lies the amygdala, a small, almond-shaped cluster of nuclei located deep within the brain. The amygdala acts as the brain's alarm system, responsible for detecting threats and initiating emotional reactions. When you perceive a situation as threatening or frustrating, the amygdala sends an immediate distress signal, triggering the emotional response of anger. This rapid reaction bypasses rational thought, making it challenging to control our emotions in the heat of the moment. The prefrontal cortex, located at the front of the brain, plays a crucial role in decision-making and self-control. When functioning optimally, it can help regulate the emotional responses triggered by the amygdala. However, during moments of intense anger, the prefrontal cortex's ability to exert control is often diminished. This is why you might find yourself saying or doing things in anger that you later regret. The amygdala's alarm has gone off, and the prefrontal cortex struggles to regain control.

The body's natural fight-or-flight response further complicates matters. This physiological reaction, evolved to protect us from danger, is triggered by the amygdala's distress signal. When you face a stressful or threatening situation, your body prepares to either confront the threat or flee from it. In parenting scenarios, this response can be triggered by something as simple as a child's defiance or a sibling argument. Your heart rate increases, muscles tense, and adrenaline floods your system, preparing you for action. Recognizing this response is the first step in controlling it. Take a moment to pause and breathe deeply, allowing your body to calm down before reacting. Techniques such as deep breathing and mindfulness can help manage this response, providing a buffer between the trigger and your reaction.

Hormones and neurotransmitters also play a significant role in how we experience and express anger. Adrenaline, released during the fight-or-flight response, heightens physical reactions, making your heart race and your muscles tighten. This hormone prepares your body for immediate action, but it can also make it difficult to think clearly. Cortisol, another stress hormone, impacts your mood and long-term stress levels. High cortisol levels over extended periods can lead to chronic stress, making you more prone to anger. On the flip side, neurotransmitters like serotonin help regulate mood and emotional responses. Low levels of serotonin are often linked to increased irritability and aggression. Understanding these chemical influences can help you develop strategies to manage your emotions better. For instance, regular exercise and a balanced diet can help maintain healthy serotonin levels, promoting a more stable mood.

The concept of neuroplasticity offers hope for those struggling with anger. Neuroplasticity refers to the brain's ability to reorganize itself by forming new neural connections throughout life. This means that with consistent practice, you can retrain your brain to respond differently to anger triggers. For example, parents who practice mindfulness and deep-breathing exercises regularly can create new neural pathways that promote calm responses instead of anger. Techniques such as meditation, cognitive-behavioral therapy, and even practicing gratitude can help rewire your brain, fostering a more balanced emotional state. Imagine a parent who used to react with immediate anger when their child misbehaved. Through consistent practice of mindfulness and deep breathing, they can train their brain to pause and respond calmly, breaking the automatic cycle of anger.

Understanding the science behind anger equips you with the knowledge to manage it more effectively. By recognizing the roles of the amygdala and prefrontal cortex, the fight-or-flight response, and the impact of hormones and neurotransmitters, you can take proactive steps to regulate your emotions. Embracing the concept of neuroplasticity allows you to retrain your brain, creating new pathways for healthier responses. This knowledge, combined with practical techniques, can empower you to navigate the challenges of parenting with greater emotional control and resilience, fostering a more harmonious family environment.

Recognizing Early Warning Signs of Anger

Recognizing the early warning signs of anger is crucial for managing it effectively. These signs often manifest physically, emotionally, and cognitively. Physical signs include increased heart rate, muscle tension, and a flushed face. You might notice your fists clenching or your jaw tightening. These bodily reactions are your body's way of gearing up for a potential threat, even if the "threat" is just your child refusing to put on their shoes. Emotional signs like irritability and frustration often accompany these physical changes. You may find yourself snapping at minor inconveniences or feeling a surge of impatience over trivial matters. Cognitive signs are equally telling. Negative thoughts, blaming others, and a general sense of being overwhelmed can cloud your judgment. You might catch yourself thinking, "Why do they always have to act up when I'm in a hurry?" Recognizing these signs early can prevent anger from spiraling out of control.

Early recognition of these warning signs plays a pivotal role in managing anger effectively. By catching these signs early, you can take proactive steps to address them before they escalate. Consider a father who used to lose his temper whenever his children argued. He began to notice that his heart rate would increase, and his muscles would tense up in these moments. By recognizing these physical signs, he started taking a few deep breaths and stepping away for a moment, which helped him regain his composure. Early intervention can significantly improve family dynamics, fostering a more peaceful and supportive environment. When parents manage their anger effectively, children feel more secure and less anxious, knowing that conflicts will be handled calmly.

Practical tools and strategies can help you monitor these warning signs. An anger monitoring chart can be a valuable resource. This chart allows you to track your physical, emotional, and cognitive signs of anger over time. By documenting these signs, you can identify patterns and triggers, making it easier to anticipate and manage your reactions. Daily self-check-in exercises are another effective tool. Set aside a few minutes each day to reflect on your emotional state. Ask yourself questions like, "How am I feeling right now?" and "Have I noticed any signs of rising anger today?" These exercises can help you stay attuned to your emotions and catch early warning signs before they escalate.

Once you recognize these warning signs, it's essential to know how to respond effectively. Taking a timeout is one of the most straightforward and effective techniques. When you notice the early signs of anger, step away from the situation for a few minutes. This break allows you to calm down and approach the situation with a clearer mind. Deep-breathing exercises can also be incredibly beneficial. When you feel anger rising, take several slow, deep breaths. This simple act can help lower your heart rate and reduce muscle tension, making it easier to stay calm. Cognitive reframing techniques can shift your perspective and reduce negative thoughts. Instead of thinking, "Why does this always happen to me?" try reframing it to, "This is challenging, but I can handle it." This shift in perspective can make a significant difference in how you respond to stressful situations.

Monitoring your warning signs and responding effectively can transform your approach to parenting. By recognizing the early signs of anger and using practical tools and techniques, you can manage your emotions more effectively. This not only benefits you but also creates a more positive and supportive environment for your children. As you become more adept at recognizing and responding to these signs, you'll find that you can navigate the challenges of parenting with greater ease and resilience. Recognizing early warning signs of anger is not just about preventing outbursts; it's about fostering a healthier, more harmonious family dynamic.

The Cost of Unmanaged Anger on Family Dynamics

Unmanaged anger can have profound effects on a child's emotional well-being and behavior. When children are exposed to frequent parental anger, they often develop anxiety or aggressive behaviors. Imagine a household where yelling and harsh words are common. Children in such environments may become anxious, fearing the next outburst. This anxiety can manifest in various ways, from trouble sleeping to difficulties in school. On the other end of the spectrum, some children may mimic these aggressive behaviors, believing that anger is the appropriate response to frustration. Studies show that children who witness frequent parental anger are more likely to exhibit behavioral issues, such as defiance and aggression, in their interactions with peers and authority figures (Source 1).

Unmanaged anger doesn't just affect children; it strains relationships with partners and other family members. Constant tension and conflict can create a toxic atmosphere, making it difficult for family members to communicate effectively. Marital strain is a common consequence of unmanaged anger. Partners may feel constantly on edge, leading to misunderstandings and resentment. For example, a couple might find themselves arguing over trivial matters, not because of the issues at hand, but because the underlying anger has eroded their ability to communicate constructively. However, there's hope. Many couples have reported improved relationships after learning anger management techniques. By addressing their anger, they were able to communicate more openly and supportively, fostering a healthier relationship dynamic.

Unmanaged anger often creates a cycle of reactive behavior within the family. One person's anger can trigger defensive or equally angry responses from others, leading to escalating conflicts. Imagine a scenario where a parent's frustration over a messy room results in yelling, which then causes the child to respond with defiance. This, in turn, fuels the parent's anger further, creating a vicious cycle. Breaking this cycle requires conscious effort and strategy. Techniques such as taking a timeout can help de-escalate conflicts. By stepping away from the situation momentarily, both parent and child can cool down and approach the issue with a clearer mind.

To mitigate the impact of anger on family dynamics, several actionable strategies can be employed. For de-escalating conflicts, consider using calming techniques such as deep breathing or counting to ten before responding. These methods can help diffuse tension and prevent the situation from escalating. Communication strategies play a vital role in repairing relationships. Practicing active listening and using "I" statements can foster understanding and reduce defensiveness. For instance, instead of saying, "You never listen," try saying, "I feel frustrated when I don't feel heard." This approach shifts the focus from blame to expressing emotions, making it easier for the other person to understand and respond empathetically.

Self-care practices are also crucial for reducing overall stress and improving emotional regulation. Engaging in regular physical activity, maintaining a balanced diet, and ensuring adequate sleep can significantly enhance your ability to manage stress and regulate emotions. Mindfulness practices, such as meditation or yoga, can provide a sense of calm and improve emotional resilience. By prioritizing selfcare, you equip yourself with the tools needed to handle the inevitable stresses of parenting more effectively.

The cost of unmanaged anger on family dynamics is high, but with awareness and effort, it is possible to make meaningful changes. By understanding the impact of anger on your children and relationships, recognizing the cycle of reactive behavior, and employing strategies to mitigate anger's impact, you can create a more harmonious and supportive family environment. Remember, the journey to better anger management is ongoing, but every step you take brings you closer to a healthier, happier family life.

Chapter 2:
Mindfulness and Stress Reduction Techniques

"Finding Calm in the Chaos: Mindful Tools for Everyday Parenting"

One morning, as you juggle getting the kids ready for school, preparing breakfast, and dealing with another unexpected mess, you might notice your stress levels rising. You feel the tension in your shoulders, and your patience starts to thin. Suddenly, your child spills their juice all over the table. In that split second, you feel the anger welling up, ready to overflow. But what if, instead of reacting, you could take a moment to breathe and stay calm? This chapter introduces mindfulness, a powerful tool to help you manage stress and anger, enhancing your overall well-being.

Introduction to Mindfulness for Parents

Mindfulness is the practice of being fully present in the moment, aware of your thoughts, feelings, and surroundings without judgment. It's about tuning into the present moment, rather than worrying about the past or future. For parents, mindfulness can be a game-changer. It helps you pause and respond thoughtfully, rather than reacting impulsively. By practicing mindfulness, you can reduce stress, improve emotional regulation, and create a more harmonious family environment. Imagine navigating the chaos of parenting with a sense of calm and clarity. That's the potential of mindfulness.

A growing body of research supports the benefits of mindfulness. Studies have shown that mindfulness can significantly reduce cortisol levels, the hormone associated with stress. Lower cortisol levels mean less stress and a greater ability to handle challenging situations calmly. Brain scans of individuals who practice mindfulness regularly show increased activity in the prefrontal cortex, the part of the brain responsible for decision-making and emotional regulation. This means that mindfulness can help you think more clearly and manage your emotions more effectively, even in the midst of intense situations.

Starting a mindfulness practice doesn't have to be overwhelming. You can begin with simple exercises that fit into your daily routine. Mindful breathing exercises are a great starting point. Find a quiet moment, close your eyes, and focus on your breath. Feel the air entering and leaving your body. If your mind wanders, gently bring your attention back to your breath. This practice can be done in just a few minutes and can help you feel more centered and calm. Another easy entry point is mindful observation. Take a moment to observe your surroundings without judgment. Notice the colors, shapes, and textures around you. This simple practice can help you feel more present and grounded.

Short body scan meditation is another effective way to practice mindfulness. Lie down or sit comfortably and close your eyes. Slowly bring your awareness to different parts of your body, starting from your toes and moving up to your head. Notice any sensations, tension, or discomfort without trying to change anything. This practice helps you tune into your body and release built-up tension. These exercises can be done anytime, whether you're taking a break at work, waiting for your child's soccer practice to end, or winding down before bed.

There are common misconceptions about mindfulness that can deter people from trying it. Some believe that mindfulness is time-consuming or only for the "spiritual." In reality, mindfulness can be practiced in just a few minutes a day and is accessible to everyone, regardless of spiritual beliefs. You don't need to sit cross-legged on a cushion or spend hours meditating. Mindfulness can be as simple as paying attention to your breath while doing the dishes or taking a mindful walk around the block. The key is to integrate mindfulness into your daily activities in a way that feels natural and sustainable.

Mindfulness is not about achieving a state of constant calm or eliminating stress altogether. It's about developing a greater awareness of your thoughts and emotions, allowing you to respond to them more skillfully. By practicing mindfulness, you can cultivate a sense of inner peace and resilience, even in the midst of parenting challenges. Imagine being able to handle your child's tantrums with patience, communicate with your partner more effectively, and create a more loving and supportive family environment. That's the promise of mindfulness for parents.

Visual Element: #### Reflection Exercise

Take a moment to reflect on a recent stressful parenting situation. Write down the following:

1. Describe the situation in detail.

2. What were your immediate thoughts and emotions?

3. How did your body react (e.g., tense muscles, increased heart rate)?

4. How did you respond to the situation?

5. How might you apply mindfulness techniques to respond differently in the future?

This exercise can help you become more aware of your reactions and explore how mindfulness can positively impact your life. Practice this regularly to deepen your mindfulness practice and enhance your emotional regulation skills.

Daily Deep-Breathing Exercises for Immediate Calm

Imagine the chaos of a typical morning: the kids are arguing, breakfast is burning, and you're rushing to get out the door. In these moments, deep breathing can be a lifeline. Deep breathing activates the parasympathetic nervous system, which counteracts stress by calming the body. When you take deep, slow breaths, it stimulates the vagus nerve, a crucial part of this system. This nerve runs from your brain through your neck and chest to your abdomen, playing a key role in calming your heart rate and lowering blood pressure. By engaging in deep breathing, you can reduce the physical symptoms of stress, helping you stay composed even in the most hectic situations.

One effective technique is box breathing. Start by sitting comfortably and closing your eyes. Inhale deeply through your nose for a count of four, feeling your lungs fill with air. Hold your breath for another count of four, then exhale slowly through your mouth for a count of four. Finally, hold your breath again for a count of four before repeating the cycle. This method helps regulate your breathing and brings a sense of calm. Another technique is the 4-7-8 breathing method. Inhale through your nose for four seconds, hold your breath for seven seconds, and then exhale slowly through your mouth for eight seconds. This technique can quickly reduce anxiety and prepare your mind for a more balanced response.

Integrating these exercises into your daily routine can make a significant difference. Try setting reminders on your phone to take breathing breaks throughout the day. You might start with a session in the morning to set a calm tone for the day. Practice deep breathing during transitions, such as before meals or bedtime. These moments are perfect opportunities to center yourself and prepare for the next task. By making deep breathing a regular part of your day, you'll find it easier to access this tool when stress levels rise unexpectedly.

Consider how these techniques can be applied in real-life parenting scenarios. Before responding to a child's tantrum, take a few deep breaths to calm your mind and body. This can help you approach the situation with patience rather than frustration. Similarly, take a few breaths before starting a challenging task, like helping with homework or managing bedtime routines. This small pause can make a big difference in how you handle the situation. One mother shared that she uses deep breathing whenever her toddler starts to throw a fit. By taking a moment to breathe, she finds that she can respond more calmly, which often helps to de-escalate the tantrum more quickly.

Another father mentioned that he practices deep breathing before entering the house after a long day at work. This helps him transition from the stress of his job to the responsibilities of home life in a calmer state. These simple, yet effective, techniques can transform how you handle everyday stressors, leading to a more peaceful and supportive family environment.

Quick Meditation Techniques for Busy Parents

In the whirlwind of daily life, finding even a few moments of peace can feel impossible. Yet, even short meditation sessions can significantly impact your stress levels and emotional regulation. Research has shown that brief meditative practices can lower stress hormones and improve your ability to handle emotional challenges. Imagine taking just a few minutes out of your hectic day to reset your mind and body. This small investment of time can yield substantial benefits, helping you navigate the ups and downs of parenting with greater ease.

Let's start with a one-minute mindfulness meditation. Find a quiet spot, sit comfortably, and close your eyes. Focus on your breath, feeling the air as it enters and leaves your body. If your mind wanders, gently bring your attention back to your breath. Just one minute of mindful breathing can calm your mind and center your thoughts. For those moments when you need a bit more grounding, try the three-minute breathing space. Begin by acknowledging what you're experiencing right now—thoughts, feelings, and bodily sensations. Next, focus on your breath for a full minute, noticing its natural rhythm. Finally, expand your awareness to your entire body, feeling the breath as it moves through you. This exercise can help you shift from a state of stress to one of calm.

A body scan for relaxation is another effective quick meditation technique. Lie down or sit comfortably and close your eyes. Slowly bring your attention to different parts of your body, starting with your toes and moving up to your head. Notice any sensations, tension, or discomfort without trying to change anything. This practice helps you tune into your body and release built-up tension. Even a short body scan can leave you feeling more relaxed and grounded.

Incorporating meditation into your daily life doesn't have to be complicated. Look for small windows of time when you can practice. Meditating during your children's nap time can be a perfect opportunity. Those few quiet moments can help you recharge and prepare for the rest of the day. If you find it challenging to meditate on your own, consider using meditation apps for guided sessions. There are many options available with short, guided meditations designed specifically for busy parents. These apps can provide structure and support, making it easier to establish a regular meditation practice.

Parents who have integrated quick meditation techniques into their lives often report significant improvements in their emotional responses. One mother shared that she began practicing one-minute meditations while waiting in the carpool line. Over time, she noticed that she felt less frazzled and more patient with her children. Another father found that taking a few minutes to meditate before bedtime helped him sleep better and wake up feeling more refreshed. These small practices can make a big difference in how you handle the daily stresses of parenting.

Real-Life Application: One parent mentioned using a three-minute breathing space technique during particularly stressful mornings. As soon as she felt her stress levels rising, she would take a moment to step away, focusing on her breath and grounding herself. This small practice helped her approach the rest of the morning with more patience and clarity.

For those moments when your children are playing quietly or watching a show, consider taking a minute or two to meditate. Even short sessions can help you maintain a sense of calm and balance throughout the day. The key is to find what works best for you and to make it a regular part of your routine. Whether it's a one-minute mindfulness meditation, a three-minute breathing space, or a short body scan, these quick techniques can help you manage stress and enhance your emotional well-being.

Developing a Mindfulness Routine

Imagine trying to manage a household without any sort of routine or structure. The chaos would be overwhelming. The same principle applies to mindfulness. Consistency is key. Practicing mindfulness sporadically is like trying to get in shape by going to the gym once a month. Regular practice, even in small doses, accumulates over time and offers long-term benefits. Consistent mindfulness practice enhances emotional regulation and reduces stress, making it easier to handle everyday parenting challenges. When you practice mindfulness regularly, it becomes a part of your life, helping you respond more calmly and thoughtfully in stressful situations.

Creating a mindfulness routine that fits your lifestyle is essential. Start by setting realistic goals. If you're new to mindfulness, begin with just a few minutes each day. You might start with a five-minute meditation in the morning or a short body scan before bed. As you become more comfortable, gradually increase the time. Combining different mindfulness techniques can keep your practice engaging. For instance, mix meditation with mindful walking or mindful eating. This variety ensures that your routine remains enjoyable and sustainable. The key is to find a balance that works for you and incorporate mindfulness into your daily routine.

Maintaining a mindful routine requires commitment and some practical strategies. Using habit trackers can be incredibly helpful. These tools allow you to monitor your progress and stay motivated.

You can use a simple journal or a dedicated habit-tracking app. Another effective strategy is finding a mindfulness buddy. This could be a friend, partner, or fellow parent. Having someone to share your progress with and hold you accountable can make a significant difference. You can check in with each other regularly, share tips, and even practice mindfulness together. This social aspect can make the practice more enjoyable and less isolating.

Parents often face challenges when trying to maintain a mindful routine. Time constraints and distractions are common obstacles. It's easy to feel that there is no time for mindfulness amidst the demands of parenting. However, integrating mindfulness into your daily activities can help overcome this hurdle. Practice mindful breathing while washing dishes or take a mindful walk with your child. Staying motivated during busy periods can also be challenging. Remind yourself of the benefits you're experiencing, even if they seem subtle at first. Keeping a journal of your mindfulness journey can help you see your progress and stay motivated.

Distractions are another common challenge. Finding a quiet space might seem impossible in a bustling household. Consider setting boundaries with your family. Let them know that you need a few minutes of uninterrupted time for your mindfulness practice. Use this time to focus solely on your breath or a specific meditation technique. Over time, your family will learn to respect this boundary, and you'll find it easier to carve out this important time for yourself. Creating a designated space for mindfulness can also help. This doesn't need to be elaborate—a comfortable chair or a quiet corner can be enough. Having a specific spot can signal to your brain that it's time to focus and unwind.

One parent shared how they managed to develop a mindfulness routine despite a hectic schedule. They began by waking up ten minutes earlier each day to meditate before the rest of the household awoke. Over time, this small change made a significant difference in how they handled daily stress. They felt more patient and less reactive. Another parent found success by incorporating mindfulness into their evening routine. After putting the kids to bed, they would spend a few minutes practicing mindful breathing and reflecting on the day. This helped them wind down and sleep better, leading to a more rested and calm start to the next day.

Developing a mindful routine is a journey that requires patience and persistence. By setting realistic goals, combining various techniques, and employing practical strategies to stay committed, you can make mindfulness a consistent part of your life. This consistency will yield long-term benefits, enhancing your ability to manage stress and respond to parenting challenges with greater calm and clarity.

Using Visualization to Reduce Stress

Picture this: it's the end of a long day, and you're finally getting a moment to yourself after putting the kids to bed. Your mind is still racing from the day's events, and your body feels tense. This is where visualization can be a lifesaver. Visualization, also known as mental rehearsal, involves creating vivid mental images to induce relaxation and reduce stress. It's like giving your mind a mini-vacation. By envisioning peaceful scenes or positive outcomes, you can shift your focus away from stressors and cultivate a sense of calm in your body and mind.

Visualization is a powerful tool for emotional well-being. When you visualize, your brain responds as if the imagined scenario is real. This can help reduce the production of stress hormones and increase feelings of relaxation. Studies have shown that visualization can lower anxiety levels and improve mood. By regularly practicing visualization, you can train your mind to respond more calmly to stressful situations, enhancing your overall emotional resilience. This technique is particularly useful for parents who frequently find themselves juggling multiple responsibilities and facing unexpected challenges.

One effective visualization exercise is guided imagery. Start by finding a quiet, comfortable place where you won't be disturbed. Close your eyes and take a few deep breaths to center yourself. Imagine a peaceful place, like a serene beach or a quiet forest. Picture the details vividly—the sound of the waves, the smell of the forest, the warmth of the sun on your skin. Allow yourself to fully immerse in this scene. Spend a few minutes here, letting the tranquility wash over you. Guided imagery can help your mind and body relax, providing a much-needed break from daily stress.

Another technique is visualizing a calm, peaceful place. This can be a real location you've visited before or a completely imaginary one. The key is to make the image as detailed and vivid as possible. Picture yourself in this place, feeling completely at ease and safe. Notice the sights, sounds, and sensations. This mental escape can help reduce stress and provide a sense of comfort and relaxation. Practicing this regularly can train your mind to access these calming images more readily, helping you stay centered during stressful moments.

Visualizing positive outcomes in stressful situations is another powerful exercise. Before a challenging event, take a few moments to visualize everything going smoothly. Picture yourself handling the situation with confidence and ease. For instance, if you're anxious about a difficult conversation with your child, imagine it going well. See yourself speaking calmly and listening empathetically, and visualize your child responding positively. This mental rehearsal can prepare you to handle the actual situation more effectively, reducing anxiety and boosting your confidence.

Incorporating visualization into your daily routine can make it a natural part of your life. Start your day by visualizing a successful morning routine before getting out of bed. Picture yourself moving through your morning tasks smoothly and calmly. This positive start can set the tone for the rest of the day. During breaks at work, take a few minutes to visualize a peaceful scene or a positive outcome for an upcoming task. This can help reduce stress and improve your focus and productivity.

Parents who practice visualization often report significant benefits. One mother shared that she visualizes a peaceful beach scene whenever she feels overwhelmed. This practice helps her calm down and approach her children with more patience. Another parent found that visualizing positive outcomes before family gatherings reduced her anxiety and improved her interactions with relatives. Research supports these experiences, showing that visualization can effectively reduce stress and improve emotional well-being. Studies have found that regular visualization practice can lower anxiety levels and enhance overall mood.

Visualization is a versatile and accessible tool that can help you manage stress and enhance your emotional resilience. By practicing guided imagery, visualizing peaceful places, and rehearsing positive outcomes, you can create a mental refuge from the challenges of parenting. Incorporating these exercises into your daily routine can make a significant difference, helping you stay calm and centered no matter what comes your way.

Incorporating Mindfulness into Family Activities

Practicing mindfulness as a family can transform your household dynamics. It enhances communication and understanding, reducing conflicts and stress. When everyone is more present and aware, interactions become more meaningful and less reactive. Imagine a family dinner where each member listens attentively, shares their day without interruptions, and enjoys the meal mindfully. This practice fosters strong bonds and cultivates a supportive environment where everyone feels valued and heard.

Family mindfulness activities can be simple and enjoyable. Mindful family walks are a great start. Choose a quiet path or park, and as you walk, encourage everyone to take a moment to notice their surroundings. Ask your children to describe what they see, hear, and feel. This practice not only grounds everyone in the present moment but also fosters curiosity and appreciation for nature. Cooking together mindfully is another wonderful activity. Involve your children in preparing a meal, focusing on each step. Notice the colors, textures, and smells of the ingredients. This shared experience can turn a routine task into a bonding moment.

Family meditation sessions can be short and sweet. Find a comfortable spot, sit together, and guide a simple breathing exercise. Start with just a few minutes and gradually increase the time as everyone becomes more comfortable. This practice can help each family member develop their own mindfulness skills while enjoying the calming presence of the group. Mindful storytelling or reading time is another excellent way to incorporate mindfulness. Choose a quiet time, perhaps before bed, and read a story together. Encourage everyone to listen attentively, noticing the details and emotions in the story. This practice not only fosters mindfulness but also enhances your children's listening and comprehension skills.

Making mindfulness fun for children is key to engaging them. Use games and creative activities to teach mindfulness. For example, play a game where everyone takes turns describing an object in detail without naming it. This activity sharpens observation skills and encourages present-moment awareness. Mindfulness exercises specifically designed for children can also be effective. Try a "mind jar" activity: fill a jar with water and glitter, and shake it up. As the glitter settles, encourage your child to take deep breaths and watch the glitter fall. This visual representation of calming down can help them understand and practice mindfulness.

Real-life examples can illustrate the benefits of family mindfulness. One family I know started incorporating mindful walks into their weekend routine. They noticed that their children became more curious and observant, and the walks provided a peaceful time for the family to connect. Another family found that cooking together mindfully reduced the usual chaos of meal prep. By focusing on the process and working together, they created a more harmonious kitchen environment. These shared experiences can make mindfulness a natural and enjoyable part of family life.

Families who practice mindfulness together often see significant improvements in their dynamics. Conflicts become less frequent and intense, communication improves, and everyone feels more connected. Children learn valuable skills in emotional regulation and empathy, which can benefit them in many areas of life. One family shared that their evening meditation sessions helped their children wind down before bed, leading to better sleep and more peaceful mornings. Another parent noticed that their child became more patient and less reactive after practicing mindfulness games.

Incorporating mindfulness into family activities can create a supportive and harmonious home environment. By practicing mindfulness together, you can strengthen your family bonds, improve communication, and reduce stress. These simple yet powerful practices can transform your daily interactions, making your home a place of peace and connection.

As we move forward, we'll explore practical anger management strategies in the next chapter, providing tools to help you and your family navigate challenging emotions with greater ease

.

Chapter 3:
Practical Anger Management
Strategies

"Tools That Work: Real-Life Techniques to Keep Your Cool"

O ne sunny afternoon, you're in the middle of preparing lunch when you hear a crash from the living room. You rush in to find your toddler has knocked over a vase, and your preschooler is crying because they got scared. In that split second, you feel your heart rate spike and your muscles tense. Your initial reaction might be to yell, but you catch yourself. Instead, you take a deep breath and remember the "Pause and Breathe" technique. This simple yet powerful method can transform how you handle these high-stress moments.

The "Pause and Breathe" Technique

The "Pause and Breathe" technique is an effective strategy for managing immediate anger responses. It involves pausing for a moment, taking a deep breath, and then responding thoughtfully. This technique works by interrupting the automatic reaction that anger often triggers, giving you a chance to regain control over your emotions. When you pause and breathe, you activate your parasympathetic nervous system, which helps calm your body's fight-or-flight response. This physiological shift can make a significant difference in how you handle the situation, allowing you to respond with more patience and clarity.

To implement the "Pause and Breathe" technique, start by recognizing the moment of anger. Awareness is the first step. Notice the signs: your heart beating faster, muscles tensing, or a sense of rising frustration. Once you recognize these signs, take a deep breath. Inhale deeply through your nose for a count of four, feeling your lungs fill with air. Hold the breath for a moment, then exhale slowly through your mouth for a count of six. This slow, deliberate breathing helps lower your heart rate and relax your muscles. If you still feel tense, repeat the process. The goal is to create a moment of calm before you respond, which can prevent an immediate, reactive outburst.

This technique can be particularly helpful during a child's tantrum. When your child is screaming and kicking, it's easy to feel overwhelmed. Instead of reacting with anger, pause and take a deep breath. This brief pause allows you to approach the situation with a clearer mind, helping you respond more calmly and effectively. Similarly, when you're feeling overwhelmed by multiple demands—like managing household chores while attending to your children—pausing to breathe can help you regain your composure. It creates a mental space where you can prioritize and tackle tasks one at a time without succumbing to frustration.

Another common scenario where the "Pause and Breathe" technique can be beneficial is during moments of frustration with a partner. Parenting can strain relationships, and disagreements are inevitable. When tensions rise, taking a moment to pause and breathe can prevent harsh words and foster more constructive communication. By calming yourself first, you're better equipped to discuss issues rationally and empathetically, reducing the likelihood of escalating the conflict.

Parents who have incorporated this technique into their daily lives often share success stories. One mother described how she used to lose her temper every time her children fought. After learning the "Pause and Breathe" method, she began to pause and take deep breaths whenever she felt anger rising.

She found that this simple act helped her stay calm and address her children's behavior more effectively. Another parent shared that during a particularly stressful morning, when everything seemed to go wrong, pausing to breathe helped her reset her mindset. Instead of lashing out, she managed to get through the morning with a sense of calm, which had a positive impact on the entire family's mood.

Reflection Exercise

Reflect on the last time you felt overwhelmed with anger. Write down the following:

1. What were the physical signs of your anger (e.g., increased heart rate, tense muscles)?

2. What thoughts were running through your mind?

3. How did you react in the moment?

4. How might pausing and breathing have altered your reaction?

1. How can you remind yourself to use this technique in future situations?

By practicing the "Pause and Breathe" technique, you can transform your immediate responses to anger, creating a more peaceful and controlled environment for yourself and your family. This method is a powerful tool in your anger management toolkit, helping you navigate the challenges of parenting with greater ease and patience.

Creating a Calm-Down Corner at Home

Imagine a space in your home dedicated solely to calming down—a sanctuary where both you and your children can retreat to manage overwhelming emotions. This is the concept of a calm-down corner. It's a designated area designed to help de-escalate anger and stress. For children, it offers a safe place to practice self-regulation and learn healthy coping skills. For parents, it provides a moment to step back and regain composure. The psychological benefits of having such a space are immense. It helps normalize the use of coping skills and teaches valuable emotional regulation techniques. Plus, it reinforces that taking a break to calm down is a healthy and acceptable response to feeling overwhelmed.

Setting up a calm-down corner doesn't require much space or money. Start by choosing a quiet and comfortable location away from the main activity areas of your home. This could be a corner of the living room, a spot in a bedroom, or even a small area in a hallway. The key is to find a space where you and your children can retreat without constant interruptions. Once you've chosen the location, add calming elements like soft pillows, blankets, and sensory toys. These items create a cozy and inviting atmosphere that encourages relaxation. Including mindfulness tools like coloring books or stress balls can also be beneficial. These tools provide a focus for calming activities, helping to shift attention away from stressors.

Establishing rules and guidelines for using the calm-down corner is crucial for its effectiveness. Set clear boundaries for when and how to use the space. Explain to your children that the calm-down corner is not a punishment but a place to go when they need to calm down. Encourage voluntary use without forcing it. This helps children feel more in control and more likely to use the space when needed. Discuss appropriate behaviors for the calm-down corner, such as quiet activities and respectful use of the items within it. It's essential to model this behavior yourself, showing that it's okay for parents to use the space, too.

Specific activities can enhance the calming effect of the corner. Breathing exercises are a great start. Teach your children simple techniques, like taking slow, deep breaths while counting to four on the inhale and six on the exhale. This can help them regulate their breathing and calm their nervous system. Listening to calming music or guided meditations can also be incredibly soothing. Create a playlist of gentle, relaxing music or find age-appropriate guided meditations that your children enjoy. Reading or drawing quietly provides a peaceful focus and can be very effective in helping both children and parents wind down. Keep a selection of favorite books or drawing supplies in the calm-down corner for easy access.

One mother shared that after setting up a calm-down corner in her home, she noticed a significant change in her children's ability to manage their emotions. Whenever a tantrum began, her toddler would head straight to the corner, grab a favorite stuffed animal, and start coloring. This simple routine helped the child calm down more quickly and reduced the frequency of full-blown meltdowns. Another parent found that using the calm-down corner themselves set a powerful example for their children. By taking a few minutes in the corner to breathe and relax, they showed that everyone in the family benefits from taking time to calm down.

Reflection Exercise

Take a moment to reflect on how you might set up a calm-down corner in your home. Write down the following:

2.	Which location in your home would be ideal for a calm-down corner?

3.	What calming elements (pillows, blankets, sensory toys) would you include?

4.	What mindfulness tools (coloring books, stress balls) would be helpful?

5.	What rules and guidelines will you establish for using the calm-down corner?

6.	Which calming activities (breathing exercises, listening to music, reading) will you incorporate?

Setting up a calm-down corner can transform how your family handles stress and anger. This dedicated space provides a refuge where everyone can take a moment to breathe, relax, and reset, fostering a more peaceful and supportive home environment.

Using the S.T.O.P. Method (Stop, Take a Breath, Observe, Proceed)

Picture a typical scenario: you're trying to get your child ready for school, but they're refusing to put on their shoes. You feel your frustration mounting. This is where the S.T.O.P. method can make a world of difference. The S.T.O.P. method, rooted in Dialectical Behavior Therapy (DBT), is a structured technique designed to manage anger and other strong emotions effectively. The acronym stands for Stop, Take a Breath, Observe, and Proceed, offering a clear, step-by-step approach to regain control over your reactions. Structured techniques like this are particularly effective because they provide a tangible framework to follow, reducing the likelihood of impulsive, emotion-driven actions.

The first step, Stop, is all about recognizing the need to pause. When you feel your anger rising, immediately halt whatever you're doing. This break is crucial for interrupting the automatic response that anger triggers. The next step, Take a Breath, involves centering yourself with deep breathing. This helps calm your nervous system and provides a moment to collect your thoughts. Following this, observe your surroundings and internal state.

Notice what's happening around you, how you're feeling, and what thoughts are running through your mind. This step involves gaining awareness and a deeper understanding of the situation. Finally, proceed with a mindful and constructive response. By this point, you've given yourself the space to choose a reaction that aligns with your values and goals, rather than reacting impulsively.

This method is handy during heated arguments with your child. Imagine a situation where your child is yelling and refusing to cooperate. Instead of escalating the argument, you can use the S.T.O.P. method. First, stop and resist the urge to respond immediately. Take a deep breath to calm your body. Observe your child's behavior and your thoughts and feelings. Then, proceed by addressing the situation with a calm and composed mindset. This approach not only diffuses tension but also models healthy conflict resolution for your child.

Another scenario where the S.T.O.P. method shines is when you're feeling rushed or overwhelmed. Perhaps you're trying to juggle multiple tasks, and everything seems to be going wrong. Instead of letting the stress take over, stop and take a breath. This small pause can help you regain control and prioritize effectively. Observing your tasks and emotions allows you to see the bigger picture and identify what needs immediate attention. Proceeding mindfully ensures that you handle each task with greater clarity and less stress.

Unexpected stress can also benefit from the S.T.O.P. method. Imagine you receive an urgent work email while trying to manage your child's homework. The immediate reaction might be panic or frustration. By stopping and taking a breath, you give yourself the space to assess the situation calmly. Observing the urgency of the email and your child's needs helps you decide the best course of action. Proceeding with a clear plan reduces the stress and ensures both tasks are handled efficiently.

Parents who have adopted the S.T.O.P. method often share positive outcomes. One father recalled a time when he and his teenage son were arguing about curfew. Instead of letting the argument escalate, he used the S.T.O.P. method. By pausing and observing his son's perspective, he realized the issue was about trust rather than the curfew itself. This insight allowed him to address the underlying concern and resolve the conflict peacefully. Another mother shared that during a particularly stressful day, using the

S.T.O.P. method helped her manage her frustration. She stopped, took a breath, observed her feelings of overwhelm, and proceeded by asking for help from her partner, resulting in a more balanced and calm evening.

Implementing Timeouts for Parents

Imagine you're in the kitchen, trying to prepare dinner while your kids are arguing in the next room. Your stress level is rising, and you're feeling your patience wearing thin. This is the perfect moment to consider a time-out for parents. A parental timeout is a strategy where you take a break to cool down, stepping away from a triggering situation to regain your composure. It's an effective way to prevent anger from escalating. By removing yourself from the immediate source of stress, you give your mind and body a chance to reset. This helps you return to the situation with a clearer, calmer mindset.

Recognizing the need for a timeout is the first step. Pay attention to the physical and emotional signals your body sends when you're becoming overwhelmed—such as a racing heart, tense muscles, or a feeling of impending outburst. When you notice these signs, communicate your need for a timeout to your family. Use simple language to explain that you need a few minutes to cool down. For instance, you might say, "I need a quick break to calm down. I'll be back in a few minutes." This sets a positive example for your children, showing them that it's okay to take a moment to manage emotions. Next, find a quiet space for your timeout. It could be your bedroom, the bathroom, or even a corner of the living room. The key is to choose a spot where you won't be disturbed.

The duration and frequency of timeouts can vary based on individual needs and situations. Short breaks of 5-10 minutes are often sufficient to calm down and regain control. During particularly stressful times, you might find the need for more frequent timeouts. The goal is to use these breaks proactively, rather than waiting until you're on the verge of an outburst. By taking regular, brief timeouts, you can maintain a more balanced emotional state throughout the day. One mother shared how she takes a five-minute timeout in her bedroom whenever she feels overwhelmed. She sets a timer, sits quietly, and focuses on her breathing. This simple practice helps her reset and approach her children with renewed patience.

A father recounted a specific scenario where timeouts were particularly beneficial. During a heated argument with his teenage daughter, he felt his anger rising. Instead of continuing the argument, he told her he needed a few minutes to cool down. He stepped into his home office, closed the door, and took several deep breaths. After a few minutes, he returned to the discussion with a calmer demeanor, which helped de-escalate the situation. By modeling this behavior, he taught his daughter the value of taking a break to manage emotions.

Reflection Exercise

Reflect on your recent experiences with stress and anger. Write down the following:

1.   What physical and emotional signals indicate that you need a timeout?

2.   How will you communicate your need for a timeout to your family?

3.   Identify a quiet space in your home where you can take a timeout.

4.   Plan how long your timeouts will be and how frequently you might need them.

5.   Reflect on a recent situation where a timeout could have been beneficial. How might it have changed the outcome?

Taking timeouts for yourself can be a powerful tool in managing anger and stress. By stepping away from triggering situations, you give yourself the space to cool down and approach challenges with a clearer mind. This simple yet effective strategy can make a significant difference in your emotional well-being and overall family dynamics.

The Power of Journaling for Emotional Regulation

Imagine returning home after a stressful day, your mind buzzing with thoughts and emotions. Journaling can be a powerful tool for emotional regulation and anger management. It provides an outlet for expressing emotions that might otherwise build up and explode. Writing down your thoughts and feelings allows you to release pent-up stress and gain clarity. By putting your emotions on paper, you can see them from a different perspective, which can help you understand and manage them better. Journaling can help identify patterns and triggers, making it easier to anticipate and handle potential anger-inducing situations.

Reflecting on daily emotional experiences is a great way to start your journaling practice. Each evening, take a few minutes to write about your day. Focus on moments that triggered strong emotions. What happened? How did you feel? What were your thoughts and physical reactions? This reflection can help you spot recurring themes and situations that tend to provoke your anger. Another useful exercise is writing about your triggers and responses. Describe specific incidents where you felt angry. What triggered the emotion? How did you react? By analyzing these moments, you can identify patterns and develop strategies to respond more calmly in the future. Setting intentions for mindful reactions is another valuable journaling exercise. Each morning or evening, write down how you intend to handle challenging situations. For example, "Today, I will take a deep breath before responding when I feel frustrated." These intentions can help guide your behavior and reinforce positive changes.

There are different types of journaling, each offering unique benefits. Gratitude journaling involves writing down things you're grateful for each day. This practice shifts your focus from what's going wrong to what's going right, fostering a more positive mindset. Reflective journaling, on the other hand, encourages deeper introspection. It involves reflecting on your thoughts, feelings, and actions, helping you gain insights into your behavior and emotions. Stream-of-consciousness writing is more free-form. It involves writing whatever comes to mind without censoring or editing. This type of journaling can help you uncover subconscious thoughts and feelings, providing a deeper understanding of your emotional landscape.

Parents who journal often share transformative experiences. One mother found that gratitude journaling helped her shift her focus from the daily struggles of parenting to the small, joyful moments. She wrote about her child's laughter, the beauty of a sunset, and the warmth of a hug. This practice brought a sense of peace and reduced her overall stress. Another parent used reflective journaling to understand her triggers better. By writing about specific incidents, she identified that her anger often stemmed from feeling unappreciated. This insight allowed her to communicate her needs more effectively, reducing her frustration.

Research supports the benefits of journaling for emotional regulation. Studies have shown that regular journaling can reduce stress, improve mood, and enhance overall well-being. One study found that individuals who journaled about their emotions experienced a significant decrease in anxiety and depressive symptoms. The act of writing helps organize thoughts, making emotional experiences feel more manageable. By consistently journaling, you can develop greater emotional awareness and resilience.

Journaling Prompts

Try these prompts to guide your journaling practice:

1. Describe a recent situation that triggered anger. What happened, and how did you feel?

2. Reflect on a time when you managed your anger well. What strategies did you use?

3. Write about a recurring trigger. How can you respond differently next time?

4. List three things you're grateful for today. How do they make you feel?

5. Set an intention for tomorrow. How will you handle challenging situations?

Journaling can be a powerful tool for emotional regulation and anger management. By providing an outlet for expressing emotions, helping identify patterns and triggers, and offering various journaling methods, you can gain greater control over your emotions. This practice not only benefits you but also creates a more positive and supportive environment for your family.

Quick Physical Exercises to Release Tension

Imagine you're in the middle of a chaotic afternoon. The kids are arguing, the phone is ringing, and you're trying to finish a work deadline. Your stress levels are through the roof, and you can feel anger bubbling up. This is where quick physical exercises can be a game-changer. Physical activity is a powerful tool for emotional regulation because it helps release built-up tension and manage anger effectively. When you exercise, your body produces endorphins, which are natural mood lifters. These endorphins help reduce stress and improve your overall mood. Additionally, physical activity reduces levels of the body's stress hormones, such as adrenaline and cortisol. This physiological shift can bring a sense of calm and clarity, making it easier to handle parenting challenges.

To get started, try incorporating deep stretching routines into your day. Stretching can relieve muscle tension and increase blood flow, helping you feel more relaxed. Simple stretches like reaching for your toes, neck rolls, or side stretches can be done almost anywhere and take just a few minutes. Another effective option is quick cardio bursts. Activities like jumping jacks or running in place for a minute or two can get your heart rate up and release pent-up energy. These short bursts of cardio can invigorate you and improve your focus, making it easier to deal with stressors. Yoga poses for relaxation, such as child's pose, downward-facing dog, or cat-cow stretches, can also help. These poses are designed to stretch and relax your muscles, providing a calming effect.

These exercises can be particularly helpful during breaks from stressful situations. For instance, if you're feeling overwhelmed by household chores, take a few minutes to do some jumping jacks or a quick stretch. This brief physical activity can help reset your mind and body, making it easier to tackle the tasks ahead. Starting your day with a morning routine that includes physical exercise can set a positive tone for the rest of the day. Whether it's a quick yoga session or a short jog, incorporating exercise into your morning routine can boost your mood and energy levels. Similarly, engaging in physical activity before bedtime can help release built-up tension from the day. Gentle stretches or a calming yoga routine can prepare your body and mind for a restful night's sleep.

Parents who have integrated quick physical exercises into their daily lives often report significant benefits. One mother shared that she began doing a short stretching routine every morning before her kids woke up. This simple practice helped her start the day with a sense of calm and readiness, improving her patience and mood throughout the day. Another parent found that taking a quick walk around the block during particularly stressful moments made a huge difference. The fresh air and physical activity helped clear their mind and reduce feelings of frustration.

One father found that engaging in quick cardio bursts, like running in place for a minute, helped him manage his anger. Whenever he felt his frustration rising, he would step outside and do a quick run. This brief exercise helped release his tension and allowed him to return to his family with a calmer, more composed mindset. Another parent shared that incorporating yoga into their evening routine helped them wind down after a long day. The gentle stretches and focused breathing helped release the day's stress, leading to better sleep and a more relaxed start to the next day.

By incorporating quick physical exercises into your daily routine, you can effectively manage stress and anger. These exercises not only provide immediate relief but also contribute to long-term emotional health. Whether it's a quick stretch, a burst of cardio, or a relaxing yoga pose, physical activity can be a powerful tool in your anger management toolkit. As you integrate these practices into your life, you'll find yourself better equipped to handle the challenges of parenting with greater ease and resilience.

Summary

In this chapter, we've explored practical strategies for managing anger, from the "Pause and Breathe" technique to creating a calm-down corner, using the S.T.O.P. method, implementing parental timeouts, journaling for emotional regulation, and incorporating quick physical exercises. Each of these tools offers a way to regain control and foster a more harmonious family environment. As we move forward, we will delve into effective communication techniques to further improve your family dynamics and strengthen your relationships.

Chapter 4:
Emotional Self-Reflection and Personal Growth

"From Reaction to Reflection: Growing Alongside Your Child"

One evening, after a particularly challenging day, I found myself sitting quietly in the living room, reflecting on the events that had unfolded. My mind wandered back to a moment when my child's tantrum triggered an outburst from me. As I sat there, I realized that understanding my emotions was crucial for managing them better. This was when I discovered the power of self-reflective journaling. This practice has since become an invaluable tool in my parenting journey, helping me gain insights into my emotions and behaviors, and fostering personal growth.

Journaling Prompts for Self-Reflection

Self-reflective journaling is a powerful practice that can help you gain deeper insights into your emotions and behaviors. By writing down your thoughts and feelings, you create a space for introspection and understanding. Journaling encourages you to pause and consider your reactions, promoting greater emotional awareness. This practice allows you to explore the underlying causes of your emotions, which can lead to more effective emotional regulation. Regular journaling can help you identify patterns in your behavior, recognize triggers, and develop strategies for managing your emotions more effectively.

The role of journaling in emotional awareness cannot be overstated. When you take the time to write about your experiences, you engage in a process of active reflection. This helps you become more attuned to your emotional responses and the factors that influence them. By documenting your thoughts and feelings, you create a record that you can revisit, allowing you to track your progress and growth over time. Journaling fosters a sense of mindfulness, as you become more present and aware of your emotional landscape. This increased awareness can lead to better emotional regulation and a greater sense of wellbeing.

The benefits of regular self-reflection for emotional health are numerous. Journaling can help reduce stress by providing an outlet for expressing and processing emotions. When you write about your experiences, you release pent-up feelings and gain clarity on your thoughts. This can alleviate the mental burden of carrying unresolved emotions. Journaling also enhances problem-solving skills and creative thinking, as it encourages you to explore different perspectives and solutions. By reflecting on your experiences, you can develop a deeper understanding of yourself and your emotional triggers, leading to more effective coping strategies.

To guide you through the process of self-reflective journaling, here are some detailed prompts that can help you gain insights into your emotional triggers and reactions. Start by describing a recent situation where you felt anger. What triggered it? This prompt encourages you to explore the specific circumstances that led to your emotional response. Next, reflect on how you responded to the situation. What were the immediate and long-term effects? This helps you consider the impact of your reaction on yourself and those around you. Another valuable prompt is to reflect on a time in your childhood when you felt similar emotions. What parallels can you draw? This exercise allows you to identify patterns from your past that may be influencing your current behavior.

Consistency is key to making self-reflection an effective practice. Set aside dedicated time for journaling each day, even if it's just for a few minutes. This regular practice helps you develop a habit of introspection and ensures that you consistently engage in self-reflection. To maintain consistency, consider using a journal tracker. This tool can help you monitor your journaling practice and keep you motivated. By tracking your progress, you can see the benefits of regular journaling and stay committed to the practice.

Parents who have embraced self-reflective journaling often share success stories and the insights they have gained. One mother shared that journaling helped her understand why she felt particularly frustrated during her child's bedtime routine. Through her reflections, she realized that her frustration stemmed from her own childhood experiences of feeling rushed to bed. This insight allowed her to approach bedtime with more patience and empathy, creating a calmer environment for both herself and her child. Another parent found that journaling helped them recognize a pattern of feeling overwhelmed during chaotic mornings. By identifying this trigger, they developed strategies to manage their morning routine more effectively, reducing stress for the entire family.

Reflection Exercise

Take a moment to reflect on a recent stressful parenting situation. Write down the following:

1. Describe the situation in detail.

2. What were your immediate thoughts and emotions?

3. How did your body react (e.g., tense muscles, increased heart rate)?

4. How did you respond to the situation?

5. How might you apply mindfulness techniques to respond differently next time?

This exercise can help you become more aware of your reactions and explore how mindfulness can make a difference. Practice this regularly to deepen your mindfulness practice and enhance your emotional regulation skills.

Understanding Your Emotional Triggers

Emotional triggers are stimuli that provoke immediate and intense emotional responses. These triggers can be anything that sets off an emotional reaction, often linked to past experiences or deeply ingrained beliefs. Understanding your triggers is crucial because it allows you to anticipate and manage your emotional responses more effectively. When you recognize what sets you off, you can develop strategies to handle these situations calmly, reducing the likelihood of reacting impulsively. This awareness can lead to better emotional regulation, which is essential for maintaining a peaceful family environment.

To identify your specific emotional triggers, practical methods can be very helpful. One effective approach is keeping a trigger journal. In this journal, document the situations that provoke strong emotional reactions, noting the context, your feelings, and your responses. Over time, you'll notice patterns that can help you understand what consistently triggers your anger or frustration. Reflecting on past experiences and common patterns is another valuable method. Think back to previous instances when you felt overwhelmed or angry. What were the common elements? This reflection can provide insights into recurring triggers. Using mindfulness to notice immediate reactions is also beneficial. Pay attention to your body's signals when you start to feel triggered. Are your muscles tensing? Is your heart rate increasing? Mindfulness can help you catch these early signs and take proactive steps to calm down.

Common parenting triggers can vary widely but often include situations like tantrums and disobedience. When your child throws a tantrum, it can feel like a direct challenge to your authority, triggering frustration. Lack of appreciation or respect is another common trigger. When you feel unappreciated for your efforts, anger can quickly follow. Overwhelm from multitasking is also a significant trigger. Juggling multiple responsibilities can leave you feeling stretched thin, making it easier for small irritations to set you off. Recognizing these common triggers can help you prepare and develop strategies to manage them more effectively.

Once you've identified your triggers, it's important to have tools for managing them. Deep-breathing exercises are a simple yet effective way to calm your nervous system and reduce immediate stress. When you feel triggered, take a few slow, deep breaths, focusing on the sensation of the air entering and leaving your body. This can help lower your heart rate and relax your muscles, making it easier to respond calmly. Cognitive reframing techniques can also be helpful. This involves changing the way you interpret a triggering situation. Instead of thinking, "My child is being defiant to upset me," reframe it as, "My child is struggling to express their needs." This shift in perspective can reduce the emotional intensity of the trigger.

Timeout strategies are beneficial for both parents and children. When you feel triggered, taking a timeout gives you a chance to step away from the situation and calm down. Find a quiet space where you can take a few minutes to breathe and collect your thoughts. This break can prevent an immediate, reactive outburst and allow you to return to the situation with a clearer, calmer mindset. Encouraging your child to take a timeout can also teach them valuable self-regulation skills. Explain that the timeout is a moment to calm down and think, not a punishment.

Interactive Exercise

Reflect on a recent situation that triggered an emotional reaction. Write down the following:

6. Describe the situation in detail.

7. What were the specific triggers?

8. How did you respond emotionally and physically?

9. What strategies could you use to manage this trigger more effectively next time?

This exercise can help you gain a deeper understanding of your emotional triggers and develop practical strategies for managing them. Regularly practicing this reflection can enhance your emotional regulation skills, leading to a more balanced and harmonious family life.

Breaking Negative Cycles from Your Own Upbringing

Our childhood experiences profoundly shape the way we parent. These experiences leave an indelible mark, influencing our emotional responses and parenting styles. In many cases, the behaviors and attitudes we observed in our parents are unconsciously passed down to our own children. This concept of inherited parenting behaviors means that the way we were parented can have a lasting impact on how we raise our children. For instance, if you grew up in a household where yelling was the norm, you might find yourself raising your voice more often than you'd like. These negative cycles can perpetuate stress and conflict within the family, making it crucial to recognize and break them.

To identify these negative cycles, start by reflecting on your childhood experiences and their impacts on your current behavior. Think about specific situations where you felt scared, unsupported, or misunderstood. How did your parents react? Did they use punishment or withdrawal of affection as a means of control? Recognizing these patterns can help you understand why you might react in similar ways with your own children. Identifying specific behaviors and attitudes is another critical step. Do you notice yourself becoming overly critical, impatient, or distant when stressed? These reactions may mirror how your parents dealt with stress and conflict.

Once you've identified these negative cycles, it's essential to take proactive steps to break them. Developing new parenting techniques is a practical way to start. For example, instead of resorting to yelling, practice using calm, assertive communication. Explain your expectations clearly and follow through with consistent consequences. This approach not only helps in managing your emotions but also sets a positive example for your children. Seeking therapy or counseling can be incredibly beneficial for addressing unresolved issues from your past. A therapist can provide valuable insights and strategies for breaking negative cycles and developing healthier behaviors. Practicing positive affirmations and selftalk can also help reframe your mindset. Replace negative self-criticisms with affirmations like, "I am a patient and understanding parent," to reinforce positive behaviors.

Parents who have successfully broken negative cycles from their upbringing often share inspiring stories. One mother realized that her tendency to withdraw emotionally when stressed mirrored her own mother's behavior. By seeking therapy, she learned to communicate her feelings more openly, fostering a closer relationship with her children. Another father recognized that his quick temper was a reflection of his father's impatience. Through counseling and practicing mindfulness techniques, he learned to manage his anger more effectively. These positive changes not only improved their relationships with their children but also created a more supportive and loving home environment.

One family experienced a significant transformation after the parents committed to breaking negative cycles. The parents, both raised in households where emotional unavailability was common, found themselves struggling to connect with their children. By attending therapy sessions together, they learned to express their emotions and be more present for their children. This shift led to a noticeable improvement in their children's behavior and overall family dynamics. Another parent shared that practicing positive affirmations helped her overcome the fear of not being a good enough parent. By focusing on her strengths and accomplishments, she built confidence and resilience, creating a more positive atmosphere for her family.

Breaking negative cycles from your own upbringing is a journey of self-discovery and growth. By reflecting on your past, identifying patterns, and adopting healthier parenting techniques, you can create a more nurturing and supportive environment for your children. This process not only benefits your family but also sets a positive example for future generations. Embracing change and seeking support when needed can lead to lasting positive changes, fostering a loving and harmonious family dynamic.

The Role of Self-Compassion in Anger Management

Self-compassion is the practice of treating yourself with the same kindness and understanding you would offer to a close friend. It involves acknowledging your struggles without harsh judgment and recognizing that imperfections and mistakes are part of being human. When you practice self-compassion, you give yourself permission to be imperfect and to experience difficult emotions without self-criticism. This approach is crucial for anger management because it helps you respond to your own emotional struggles with care and patience, rather than frustration and guilt.

The benefits of self-compassion for emotional health are well-documented. Research shows that individuals who practice self-compassion experience lower levels of stress and anxiety, and higher levels of emotional well-being. By treating yourself with kindness, you reduce the internal pressure to be perfect, which can alleviate feelings of frustration and anger. Self-compassion fosters a sense of inner peace, making it easier to handle the challenges of parenting with greater resilience. When you are kind to yourself, you create a supportive internal environment that allows you to navigate difficult emotions more effectively.

To cultivate self-compassion, start with self-compassionate journaling. This involves writing about your experiences with a focus on kindness and understanding. Instead of criticizing yourself for feeling angry or overwhelmed, acknowledge your emotions and remind yourself that it's okay to struggle. For example, write, "I had a tough day today, and that's okay. I'm doing my best, and it's natural to feel frustrated sometimes." This practice helps shift your mindset from self-criticism to self-acceptance. Another technique is mindful self-compassion meditation. Find a quiet space, sit comfortably, and close your eyes. Focus on your breath and bring to mind a recent experience where you felt inadequate or upset. As you reflect, place your hand over your heart and silently repeat phrases like, "May I be kind to myself," and "May I accept myself as I am." This meditation helps reinforce a compassionate attitude towards yourself.

Positive self-affirmations are another powerful tool for practicing self-compassion. These are statements that remind you of your worth and strengths. Create a list of affirmations that resonate with you, such as, "I am a loving and capable parent," or "I am worthy of compassion and understanding." Repeat these affirmations daily, especially during moments of self-doubt or frustration. Over time, these positive messages can help rewire your brain to respond to challenges with kindness rather than criticism.

Self-compassion can have a profound impact on your parenting. When you reduce self-criticism and guilt, you create a more positive and supportive environment for yourself and your children. This internal shift can improve your patience and empathy towards your children, as you are more likely to respond to their struggles with understanding rather than frustration. Research supports this connection. Studies have found that parents who practice self-compassion are more emotionally available and responsive to their children's needs, leading to better parent-child relationships.

Parents who have embraced self-compassion often share transformative stories. One mother recounted how practicing self-compassion helped her manage the guilt she felt after losing her temper with her child. By acknowledging her struggles and reminding herself that it's okay to make mistakes, she was able to approach her child with an open heart and repair the relationship. Another parent found that selfcompassion reduced their overall stress levels. By treating themselves with kindness, they felt more resilient and capable of handling the challenges of parenting.

A study conducted by Kristin Neff, a leading researcher in self-compassion, found that individuals who practiced self-compassion experienced lower levels of stress and greater emotional well-being. This research highlights the importance of being kind to yourself, especially in the demanding role of a parent. By integrating self-compassion into your daily life, you can create a more supportive internal environment that enhances your ability to manage anger and foster a positive family dynamic.

Visual Element: #### Reflection Exercise

Take a moment to reflect on how you practice self-compassion. Write down the following:

1. Describe a recent situation where you felt overwhelmed or frustrated.

2. How did you respond to your emotions? Were you kind to yourself?

3. Write a compassionate response to yourself for that situation.

4. List three positive affirmations that resonate with you.

Practicing these exercises regularly can help you cultivate self-compassion, leading to improved emotional regulation and a more positive approach to parenting.

Setting Personal Boundaries for Emotional Health

Setting personal boundaries is crucial for maintaining emotional well-being and effectively managing anger. Boundaries act as protective barriers that safeguard your emotional health, helping you maintain a sense of control and balance. When you establish clear boundaries, you define what is acceptable and what is not in your interactions with others, reducing the likelihood of feeling overwhelmed or taken advantage of. Boundaries play a significant role in reducing stress and anger by creating a buffer between you and potential stressors. They allow you to prioritize your needs and manage your time and energy more effectively, leading to a healthier, more balanced life.

Identifying necessary boundaries begins with reflecting on your current stressors and emotional triggers. Take a moment to consider the situations that leave you feeling drained or frustrated. Are there specific interactions or tasks that consistently cause stress? By pinpointing these stressors, you can identify areas where boundaries are lacking. For instance, you might realize that constantly responding to work emails during family time leaves you feeling overwhelmed. Recognizing this, you can set a boundary to check emails only during designated work hours. Identifying specific situations where boundaries are lacking helps you understand where changes are needed to protect your emotional health.

To set and maintain boundaries, start by communicating them clearly and assertively. Use "I" statements to express your needs without placing blame. For example, say, "I need some quiet time after dinner to unwind," instead of, "You always make so much noise in the evening." This approach focuses on your needs and feelings, making it easier for others to understand and respect your boundaries. Practicing consistency in enforcing boundaries is equally important. Once you've established a boundary, stick to it. If you've decided to limit work-related tasks to certain hours, avoid making exceptions unless absolutely necessary. Consistency reinforces the importance of the boundary and helps others respect it.

Parents who have successfully set boundaries often share how it has improved their emotional health. One parent, overwhelmed by constant interruptions while working from home, set a boundary by creating a designated workspace and communicating specific work hours to their family. This clear separation of work and family time reduced stress and improved their focus and productivity. Another parent, feeling frustrated by the lack of personal time, established a boundary for a weekly "me time" hour. During this time, they engaged in activities they enjoyed, such as reading or taking a walk. This simple boundary provided a much-needed break and helped them recharge, leading to a more positive and patient approach to parenting.

A mother shared her experience of setting boundaries around bedtime routines. She realized that the chaotic evenings were a major stressor, leaving her feeling frazzled and short-tempered. By establishing a consistent bedtime routine and setting clear expectations with her children, she created a calmer environment. The routine included quiet activities like reading and a set bedtime, which helped everyone wind down. This boundary not only improved her emotional well-being but also created a more peaceful and structured evening for the entire family.

Another father found success by setting boundaries around his availability for non-urgent tasks. Constantly feeling pulled in different directions, he decided to allocate specific times for tasks like checking emails or running errands. This clear structure allowed him to focus on one task at a time, reducing the overwhelming feeling of multitasking. By communicating these boundaries to his family and colleagues, he was able to manage his time more effectively and reduce stress.

Setting personal boundaries is a powerful tool for protecting your emotional health and managing anger. By reflecting on your stressors, identifying areas where boundaries are needed, and communicating them clearly, you can create a more balanced and fulfilling life. Practicing consistency in enforcing these boundaries reinforces their importance and helps maintain a sense of control. The positive impact on your emotional well-being and overall family dynamics can be profound, leading to a more harmonious and supportive environment.

Building Emotional Resilience as a Parent

Emotional resilience is the ability to adapt and recover from stress and adversity. It's about bouncing back from challenges and maintaining a sense of balance and well-being. For parents, emotional resilience is vital because it enables you to handle the inevitable ups and downs of parenting with greater ease.

When you are emotionally resilient, you can navigate stressful situations without feeling overwhelmed or defeated. This resilience not only benefits you but also creates a more stable and supportive environment for your children.

Developing emotional resilience involves engaging in specific activities and exercises that strengthen your ability to cope with stress. One effective approach is challenging negative thoughts. When you catch yourself thinking negatively, question the validity of those thoughts and reframe them in a more positive light. For instance, instead of thinking, "I can't handle this," try, "I'm doing my best, and I can find a way through this." Practicing gratitude and positive thinking can also enhance resilience. Take a moment each day to reflect on things you are grateful for. This practice shifts your focus from what's going wrong to what's going right, fostering a more positive outlook.

Building a strong support network is another key component of emotional resilience. Surround yourself with people who uplift and support you, whether they are family members, friends, or fellow parents. Having a network of supportive individuals can provide emotional and practical assistance during challenging times. They can offer a listening ear, share advice, or simply be there to lend a hand. Knowing that you have a support system can make a significant difference in how you handle stress and adversity.

Self-care plays a crucial role in maintaining emotional resilience. Regular self-care routines help you recharge and stay balanced. This can include activities like exercise, hobbies, or simply taking time to relax. Balancing personal needs with parenting responsibilities is essential. It's easy to put your needs on the back burner when you have a family to care for, but neglecting self-care can lead to burnout. Make it a priority to carve out time for yourself, even if it's just a few minutes each day. This practice helps you stay emotionally and physically healthy, enabling you to be a more effective and present parent.

Parents who have prioritized self-care often share the positive impact it has on their emotional resilience. One mother found that incorporating a daily walk into her routine provided a much-needed break and a chance to clear her mind. This simple act helped her return to her parenting duties with renewed energy and patience. Another parent discovered that setting aside time for a hobby, like painting, allowed them to express themselves creatively and reduce stress. These self-care practices not only improve your well-being but also set a positive example for your children, showing them the importance of taking care of oneself.

Research supports the benefits of emotional resilience for parenting. Studies have shown that parents who practice resilience-building activities experience lower levels of stress and greater overall wellbeing. One study found that parents who engaged in regular mindfulness practices, such as meditation or deep breathing, reported increased emotional resilience and better family dynamics. These practices help parents stay calm and composed, even in the face of challenges, leading to a more harmonious home environment.

Embracing emotional resilience can transform your parenting experience. By challenging negative thoughts, practicing gratitude, building a strong support network, and prioritizing self-care, you can enhance your ability to handle stress and adversity. These practices not only benefit you but also create a more stable and supportive environment for your children. As you develop greater emotional resilience, you'll find yourself better equipped to navigate the ups and downs of parenting with grace and confidence.

Summary

Emotional self-reflection and personal growth are ongoing processes that can significantly improve your parenting experience. By understanding your triggers, breaking negative cycles, and building resilience, you create a more supportive and nurturing environment for your family. In the next chapter, we will explore effective communication techniques to further strengthen your family relationships and foster a positive home atmosphere.

Chapter 5:
Effective Communication with Children

"Speak with Heart: Connecting Through Calm, Not Conflict"

On a rainy afternoon, you find yourself in a quiet moment with your child, who just returned from school looking visibly upset. You ask how their day went, but they mumble a vague response and retreat to their room. You want to help, but you're unsure how to get them to open up. This scenario is familiar to many parents. The key to navigating such moments lies in effective communication, and one powerful tool in your arsenal is reflective listening.

The Basics of Reflective Listening

Reflective listening is more than just hearing words; it's about truly understanding and empathizing with the speaker. This technique involves actively listening to what your child says, reflecting their feelings, and validating their experiences. It's a way to show empathy and understanding, making your child feel valued and heard. Reflective listening goes beyond mere acknowledgment; it involves engaging with your child's emotions and thoughts, fostering a deeper connection.

To practice reflective listening, give your child your full attention. Make eye contact, put away distractions, and focus entirely on them. This simple act of presence can make a significant difference. When your child speaks, paraphrase what they've said to confirm your understanding. For instance, if your child says, "I had a terrible day at school," you might respond with, "It sounds like your day was tough." This not only shows that you're listening but also helps clarify their feelings.

Responding with empathy is crucial. Validate their emotions by acknowledging their feelings without judgment. If your child is upset about a conflict with a friend, you might say, "I understand why you're feeling hurt. It's hard when friends argue." This validation makes your child feel supported and understood, reducing their emotional burden. Reflective listening isn't about offering solutions immediately; it's about creating a safe space for your child to express themselves.

The benefits of reflective listening for children are profound. When children feel heard and understood, their self-esteem and confidence grow. They learn that their feelings matter and that they can trust you with their emotions. This sense of validation can reduce behavioral issues, as children are less likely to act out when they feel emotionally secure. Reflective listening enables children to process their emotions, fostering improved self-regulation and problem-solving skills. By fostering a supportive environment, you encourage your child to express themselves openly, building a stronger parent-child relationship.

Consider practical examples where reflective listening can be applied. When your child talks about a bad day at school, listen actively and reflect their feelings. If they say, "I didn't do well on my test, and my teacher was disappointed," respond with, "It sounds like you're feeling disappointed and worried about your teacher's reaction." This shows empathy and understanding. During sibling conflicts, use reflective listening to mediate. If one child says, "She took my toy, and it's not fair," you might respond with, "I hear that you're feeling upset because your toy was taken without asking." This helps both children feel heard and promotes resolution.

Understanding a child's frustration during homework time is another opportunity for reflective listening. If your child says, "I can't do this math problem, it's too hard," respond with, "It seems like you're feeling frustrated because the math problem is challenging." This validation can help your child feel supported and less overwhelmed. Reflective listening fosters a collaborative approach, where you and your child work through challenges together.

Reflective listening is a powerful tool for effective communication with your child. By actively listening, paraphrasing, and validating their feelings, you create a supportive environment where your child feels heard and valued. This technique promotes emotional well-being, reduces behavioral issues, and strengthens the parent-child bond. Whether dealing with school struggles, sibling conflicts, or daily frustrations, reflective listening can transform how you connect with your child.

Validating Your Child's Emotions

Imagine your child coming home from school, visibly upset. They throw their backpack on the floor and say, "I hate school! No one likes me." Your first instinct might be to reassure them quickly, saying something like, "I'm sure that's not true," or "It'll be better tomorrow." However, this approach might make your child feel dismissed. Emotional validation means recognizing and accepting your child's feelings without judgment. It involves acknowledging their emotions, even if their behavior isn't ideal. Validation is crucial because it helps children understand that their feelings are legitimate and worthy of exploration.

By saying, "I understand you're feeling hurt because you think no one likes you at school," you acknowledge the emotion without dismissing it. This simple act can have a profound impact on their emotional development. Children who feel validated are more likely to develop a healthy sense of self-worth and emotional intelligence. They learn that it's okay to feel a range of emotions and that these feelings are a natural part of life. When you validate your child's emotions, you create a safe space for them to express themselves, which is essential for their emotional growth.

Practical techniques for validation include using phrases that demonstrate an understanding of their feelings. For instance, you might say, "I see that you're outraged right now because your toy broke." This not only acknowledges their emotion but also helps them articulate what they're feeling. Avoiding dismissive language is equally important. Phrases like "You're overreacting" or "It's not a big deal" can make your child feel misunderstood and unheard. Instead, try saying, "I get why you're upset; it's frustrating when things don't work out the way we want."

It's also crucial to acknowledge emotions, even when the behavior is unacceptable. If your child is throwing a tantrum, you can validate their feelings while addressing the behavior. For example, you might say, "I know you're angry because you can't have another cookie, but throwing things isn't okay." This approach separates the emotion from the behavior, teaching your child that while all feelings are valid, not all actions are. It helps them understand boundaries and self-regulation, which are vital skills for their emotional development.

The long-term benefits of emotional validation are significant. When children feel that their emotions are understood, they are more likely to trust you and communicate openly. This builds a strong foundation of trust and open communication, essential for a healthy parent-child relationship. Emotional validation also encourages emotional intelligence, helping children recognize and manage their own emotions. They learn to navigate their feelings instead of suppressing them, leading to better self-regulation and fewer behavioral issues.

Consider the story of a father who struggled with his son's frequent outbursts. Initially, he would tell his son to "calm down" or "stop crying," which only seemed to escalate the situation. After learning about emotional validation, he started acknowledging his son's feelings instead. One evening, when his son was upset about losing a game, the father said, "I see that you're really disappointed because you lost the game. It's okay to feel that way." To his surprise, his son calmed down more quickly and was willing to talk about his feelings. This shift in approach improved their communication and strengthened their bond.

Another mother shared how validation helped her daughter cope with anxiety. When her daughter expressed worry about an upcoming test, the mother used to say, "You always do fine, don't worry." While well-intentioned, this response didn't address the underlying anxiety. The mother then tried a different approach, saying, "I understand you're feeling anxious about the test. It's okay to feel nervous; let's talk about it." This validation made her daughter feel heard and supported, reducing her anxiety and improving her confidence.

Emotional validation is a powerful tool for fostering better emotional health and stronger parent-child relationships. By recognizing and accepting your child's feelings without judgment, you create a supportive environment where they feel valued and understood. This approach not only enhances their emotional development but also builds a foundation of trust and open communication, essential for a healthy, lasting bond.

Using "I" Statements to Express Feelings

Imagine you're walking into the living room and there are toys scattered all over the floor. You feel a surge of frustration because you've asked your children countless times to pick up after themselves. Instead of saying, "Why do you always make such a mess?" which can sound accusatory and provoke defensiveness, you can use an "I" statement. "I" statements are a way to express your feelings without blaming or criticizing others. They follow a simple structure: "I feel… when… because…"

The structure of an "I" statement involves three parts. First, you identify and express your own feelings. This requires you to pause and consider what you're feeling—whether it's frustration, sadness, or worry. Then, you describe the behavior that caused this feeling. Lastly, you explain the impact of the behavior without placing blame. For example, you might say, "I feel frustrated when toys are left on the floor because I'm worried someone might trip and get hurt." This statement communicates your feelings and the reason behind them, fostering understanding and reducing defensiveness.

Using "I" statements effectively requires practice. Start by identifying your feelings. Take a moment to reflect on what you're experiencing. Are you angry, disappointed, or anxious? Once you've pinpointed your emotion, describe the behavior that triggered it. Be specific and avoid generalizations. Instead of saying, "You never listen to me," try, "I feel ignored when I'm talking and you're watching TV." Finally, explain the impact of the behavior without blaming. For instance, "I feel upset when you don't come to the table because I've worked hard to prepare dinner for us."

The benefits of using "I" statements in parent-child communication are substantial. They help reduce misunderstandings and arguments by clearly articulating your feelings and the reasons behind them. This clarity can prevent conflicts from escalating and encourage more thoughtful responses. By modeling this way of speaking, you also encourage your children to express their own feelings in a constructive manner. They learn to communicate their emotions without resorting to blame or criticism, fostering a more respectful and supportive environment.

Consider practical examples where "I" statements can be particularly useful. Suppose your child is yelling during a disagreement. Instead of saying, "Stop yelling, you're being disrespectful," you might say, "I feel sad when you yell because I want us to talk calmly." This shifts the focus from blame to expressing your emotional needs. Another scenario could be when your child hasn't done their chores. Rather than accusing them of laziness, you could say, "I feel stressed when the chores aren't done because it makes me feel like I'm doing everything alone." This approach helps your child understand the impact of their actions on your feelings, promoting empathy and cooperation.

"I" statements can also be effective during more challenging conversations. If your child is struggling with schoolwork and feels overwhelmed, you might say, "I feel concerned when you're upset about your homework because I want to help you succeed." This not only expresses your concern but also opens the door for your child to share their feelings and seek support. By using "I" statements consistently, you create a safe space for open and honest communication, enhancing your relationship with your child.

One evening, a mother noticed her child was upset and not participating in family activities. Instead of reprimanding them, she used an "I" statement: "I feel worried when you stay in your room all evening because I miss spending time with you." Her child responded by opening up about a problem they were facing at school. This led to a constructive conversation and a deeper understanding between them. Such examples illustrate the transformative power of "I" statements in fostering effective communication and resolving conflicts within the family.

Role-Playing Scenarios to Improve Communication

Role-playing is a valuable tool for practicing communication skills. It allows you and your child to rehearse responses to various situations, making it easier to handle real-life interactions. Imagine your child is struggling with bedtime routines. Rather than simply instructing them on what to do, you can use role-playing to practice the scenario. This method helps both you and your child understand each other's perspectives, fostering better communication and empathy.

To set up a role-playing session, start by choosing realistic scenarios that your child encounters regularly. These could be anything from handling a disagreement about bedtime to responding to a refusal to do chores. Once you've selected a scenario, take turns playing different roles. For instance, one person can be the parent while the other acts as the child. This role reversal can be enlightening, as it allows each participant to see the situation from the other's viewpoint. After the role-playing session, take time to reflect on the experience and discuss what was learned. Ask questions like, "How did you feel when I said that?" or "What could we do differently next time?"

This reflection helps solidify the lessons learned and provides insights into improving future interactions.

Role-playing offers numerous benefits. It builds confidence by providing a safe space to practice responses without the pressure of real-life consequences. Your child learns to navigate challenging situations with greater ease, knowing they've practiced it before. Role-playing also enhances problem solving skills and emotional regulation. By exploring different scenarios, your child learns to think critically about their actions and responses. Moreover, seeing things from different perspectives develops empathy, a crucial component of effective communication.

Consider a scenario where you practice handling a disagreement about bedtime. You and your child take turns playing the parent and the child. As the child, you might say, "I don't want to go to bed yet!" Your child, playing the parent, responds with, "I understand you want to stay up, but it's important to get enough sleep." This practice helps your child understand the reasoning behind bedtime rules and feel heard, reducing resistance. Another scenario could involve responding to a child's refusal to do chores. In this case, role-playing allows your child to express their frustrations and practice negotiating solutions.

Practicing calm responses to sibling conflicts is another excellent use of role-playing. Sibling rivalry can be a significant source of stress, but by rehearsing responses, you can equip your children with the tools to handle these disputes constructively. For instance, if one child grabs a toy from the other, you can role-play how to ask for it back politely or how to share. This practice reduces the likelihood of conflict escalation and teaches valuable conflict-resolution skills.

Role-playing can also be integrated into everyday life. For example, you might practice a scenario during a car ride, turning a routine activity into an opportunity for learning. This approach makes roleplaying more natural and less formal, encouraging your child to engage without feeling pressured. The key is to make it fun and interactive, ensuring that your child feels comfortable and willing to participate.

Parents who have incorporated role-playing into their communication strategies often report significant improvements. One parent shared how role-playing bedtime routines transformed their evenings from a battleground to a peaceful transition. By practicing and understanding the expectations, their child became more cooperative. Another parent used role-playing to address homework struggles. They practiced different ways to ask for help and manage frustration, leading to smoother homework sessions. These examples illustrate the practical benefits of role-playing in enhancing communication and reducing stress within families.

Navigating Difficult Conversations with Empathy

Navigating difficult conversations with your child can be daunting. These talks often involve sensitive topics, making them emotionally intense and challenging. Whether it's discussing poor academic performance, addressing behavioral issues, or talking about significant family changes like divorce or relocation, the stakes are high. Without empathy, these conversations can quickly escalate into conflicts, leaving both you and your child feeling frustrated and misunderstood.

Approaching these conversations with empathy requires preparation. Start by mentally and emotionally preparing yourself. Take a few moments to calm your mind and center your thoughts. Reflect on your child's perspective and what they might be feeling. This mindset sets the stage for a more compassionate and understanding dialogue. Using techniques like reflective listening and "I" statements can help you navigate these conversations more effectively. Reflective listening shows your child that you genuinely care about their feelings, while "I" statements help you express your concerns without sounding accusatory.

Staying calm and composed, even when emotions run high, is crucial. If you find yourself getting upset, take a deep breath and remind yourself of the goal: to understand and support your child. Maintaining your composure helps create a safe space where your child feels comfortable sharing their thoughts and feelings. It can be helpful to practice deep breathing or mindfulness techniques before starting the conversation to ensure you're in the right frame of mind.

The timing and setting of these conversations also play a significant role in their effectiveness. Choose a quiet, private space where you can talk without interruptions. This environment helps both you and your child feel more at ease. Picking a time when both of you are calm and not rushed is equally important. Avoid bringing up difficult topics during stressful moments, like right before bedtime or during a busy morning. Instead, find a moment when you can both sit down and focus on the conversation.

Consider discussing a child's poor academic performance. Approach the topic with empathy by acknowledging your child's feelings. You might say, "I noticed your grades have slipped, and that must be really frustrating for you." This shows that you understand their emotions and are not just focused on the grades themselves. Then, use an "I" statement to express your concern: "I feel worried when your grades drop because I know how capable you are, and I want to help you succeed." This approach opens the door for a constructive conversation about how you can support them.

Addressing behavioral issues like lying or aggression can be particularly challenging. Start by acknowledging the behavior and expressing your concerns without judgment. For instance, you might say, "I noticed you've been getting into more arguments with your siblings, and I understand that you're feeling frustrated." This validation helps your child feel heard. Follow up with an "I" statement: "I feel concerned when you argue with your siblings because it affects our family's harmony." This approach helps your child understand the impact of their behavior and encourages them to reflect on their actions.

Talking about significant family changes, such as divorce or relocation, requires a great deal of empathy and sensitivity. Start by explaining the situation in simple terms that your child can understand. Acknowledge their feelings by saying something like, "I know this news might make you feel scared or confused, and that's completely normal." Use an "I" statement to express your own emotions: "I feel sad about this change too, but I want us to support each other through it." This approach fosters a sense of unity and reassures your child that they are not alone.

One parent shared how they navigated a difficult conversation about their child's poor academic performance. They began by acknowledging the child's efforts and frustrations, saying, "I see how hard you've been working, and it's tough when the results don't match your efforts." This empathetic approach helped the child feel understood and opened up a productive dialogue about finding solutions. Another parent faced the challenge of discussing their impending divorce with their child. They chose a quiet evening, sat down together, and started by acknowledging the child's potential feelings of fear and confusion. This empathy laid the foundation for a supportive and honest conversation.

Navigating difficult conversations with empathy can transform how you communicate with your child. By preparing mentally and emotionally, choosing the right timing and setting, and using empathetic techniques, you create a safe space for open and honest dialogue. This approach fosters understanding, reduces conflicts, and strengthens your relationship with your child.

The Importance of Consistent Communication

Imagine a typical weekday evening. You're trying to juggle dinner prep, homework help, and your own work emails. Amidst the chaos, your child starts telling you about their day, but you're only half-listening, responding with an occasional nod. While this scenario is all too common, it underscores the importance of maintaining consistent and open lines of communication. Consistent communication builds trust and reliability in the parent-child relationship. When your child knows they can count on you to listen and be present, it fosters a sense of security and trust. This reliability prevents misunderstandings and miscommunications, as it ensures that both you and your child are on the same page.

To ensure ongoing, open communication, it's helpful to set aside regular times for family discussions. This can be as simple as a daily check-in during dinner or a weekly family meeting. These dedicated times create a routine where everyone can share their thoughts and feelings without distractions. Daily check-ins can be brief but meaningful. Ask your child about the best and worst parts of their day, and share yours as well. This practice maintains open lines of communication and ensures that everyone's experiences are valued and matter. Encouraging open dialogue without judgment is also crucial. When your child shares something, listen without immediately offering solutions or judgments. This creates a safe space where they feel comfortable expressing themselves.

Consistent communication offers numerous benefits. It increases emotional security and trust, making your child feel valued and understood. This emotional security leads to better problem-solving and conflict resolution. When your child feels heard, they are more likely to approach conflicts with a willingness to find solutions rather than escalating the situation. Consistent communication also helps in addressing issues before they become significant problems. By regularly discussing concerns and feelings, you can identify and address potential issues early on, preventing them from escalating into more significant conflicts.

Consider the story of a family that implemented regular family meetings. Every Sunday evening, they would gather to discuss the past week and plan for the upcoming one. Initially, their children were hesitant, but over time, these meetings became a cherished routine. The children began to open up about their struggles and successes, knowing they had dedicated time to be heard. Another family found success with daily check-ins at bedtime. Each night, they spent a few minutes discussing their day, sharing both the highs and lows. This practice not only improved their communication but also strengthened their emotional bond.

One parent shared how consistent communication transformed their relationship with their teenage daughter. They started a routine of morning check-ins during breakfast. These brief moments of connection helped them stay attuned to each other's lives, reducing misunderstandings and fostering a deeper connection. Another parent used daily check-ins to address their child's anxiety about school. By talking about their worries each evening, they were able to develop strategies to manage anxiety, leading to a more confident and happier child.

Regular communication builds a foundation of trust and understanding within the family. When your child knows they can count on you to listen and be present, it fosters a sense of security that is invaluable. This trust makes it easier to navigate the ups and downs of family life, creating a more harmonious and supportive environment. As you continue to practice consistent communication, you'll likely notice improvements in your child's emotional and behavioral responses, leading to a more connected and resilient family.

Summary

In this chapter, we've explored various strategies for effective communication with your child, including reflective listening, validating emotions, using "I" statements, role-playing, and navigating difficult conversations with empathy. By mastering these techniques, you can foster a deeper connection and create a supportive environment where your child feels heard and valued. As we move forward, we will explore practical exercises and worksheets to further enhance your parenting skills, providing you with tangible tools to apply these strategies in your daily life.

Chapter 6:
Strategies for Reconnecting After Conflict

"Healing Together: Rebuilding Trust and Strengthening Bonds"

Imagine a late afternoon, the sun setting as you find yourself in the aftermath of a heated argument with your child. The tension lingers in the air, and both of you are left feeling hurt and disconnected. Moments like these are challenging, but they also present an opportunity to rebuild trust and strengthen the parent-child bond. Reconnecting after conflict is not just about smoothing things over; it's about restoring trust and creating a foundation for a healthier relationship.

Steps to Rebuild Trust After an Outburst

Trust is the cornerstone of any strong relationship, especially between a parent and a child. When trust is broken due to an outburst, it can leave emotional scars on your child. They may feel confused, hurt, or even fearful, wondering if they can rely on you to be their safe haven. The emotional impact of broken trust can manifest in various ways, such as increased anxiety, withdrawal, or defiance. If left unaddressed, these trust issues can have long-term effects on your child's emotional well-being and your relationship with them. Rebuilding trust requires intentional and consistent effort, demonstrating to your child that they can count on you even after moments of conflict.

To rebuild trust, start by acknowledging the outburst and its impact. This means openly admitting that you lost control and recognizing the emotional hurt it caused. For example, you might say, "I know I raised my voice earlier, and I can see that it upset you. I'm really sorry for that." This acknowledgment validates your child's feelings and shows them that you understand the gravity of the situation. Following this, consistently demonstrate trustworthy behavior. This involves showing empathy, keeping promises, and being emotionally available. When you commit to spending time with your child or attending their school event, make sure you follow through. These actions reinforce the message that you are reliable and that your words hold weight.

Consistency is key in rebuilding trust. It's not enough to apologize once and move on; your child needs to see a pattern of dependable behavior. Regular check-ins can help gauge their emotional well-being and show that you are invested in their feelings. These check-ins don't always have to be formal. A simple "How are you feeling today?" or "Is there anything on your mind?" can open the door for meaningful conversations. Being emotionally available means being present and attentive during these interactions, making your child feel heard and valued. Over time, this consistent emotional presence helps restore the sense of security that may have been shaken by the conflict.

Take the story of Sarah, a mother who often found herself losing her temper during stressful moments. After one particularly intense argument with her son, she decided to make a change. She began by acknowledging her outbursts and their impact, telling her son, "I know I haven't been handling things well, and I'm sorry for the times I've yelled. I want to do better." Sarah then made a conscious effort to demonstrate trustworthy behavior. She kept her promises, attended her son's soccer games, and regularly checked in on his feelings. Over time, her son started to feel more secure and less anxious, knowing that his mother was committed to being a stable presence in his life.

Another example is John, a father who struggled with maintaining his composure during his children's bedtime routine. After realizing the emotional toll his outbursts were taking on his kids, he decided to rebuild trust by showing empathy and understanding. He began by acknowledging the impact of his behavior, saying, "I know bedtime has been stressful, and I'm sorry for raising my voice. Let's work together to make it easier." John then implemented consistent bedtime routines, ensuring that he was calm and patient each night. He also made a point to check in with his children during storytime, asking about their day and listening to their concerns. These consistent actions helped restore trust, making bedtime a more peaceful and bonding experience.

Rebuilding trust after an outburst is a process that requires patience, empathy, and consistent effort. By acknowledging your mistakes, demonstrating trustworthy behavior, and being emotionally available, you can restore your child's sense of security and strengthen your relationship. Remember, it's the small, consistent actions that build a foundation of trust and create a lasting connection with your child.

The Art of Apologizing to Your Child

Apologizing to your child is a powerful tool for repairing relationships and teaching accountability. When you apologize, you model humility and responsibility, showing that everyone, including parents, can make mistakes and learn from them. This act of acknowledging wrongdoing can have a profound impact on emotional healing, helping to mend the hurt caused by the outburst. It also teaches your child the importance of taking responsibility for their actions, fostering a sense of accountability. This lesson is invaluable as it instills in them the understanding that admitting mistakes and making amends is a vital part of healthy relationships.

To apologize effectively, it's crucial to follow a few key steps. Start by acknowledging the specific behavior that caused the hurt. For example, you might say, "I apologize for raising my voice earlier." This acknowledgment shows that you are aware of your actions and their impact. Next, express genuine remorse. It's important that your apology comes from a place of sincerity. You could say, "I feel really sorry for making you feel upset." This helps your child see that you genuinely regret your actions. After that, make amends and ask for forgiveness. This involves taking steps to repair the damage and showing a commitment to change. You might say, "I will work on being more patient. Can you forgive me?" This not only helps heal the relationship but also reassures your child that you are actively working to improve your behavior.

A meaningful apology should include several essential components. Specificity in describing the behavior is crucial. Instead of a vague "I'm sorry," be clear about what you are apologizing for. This shows that you understand the specific actions that caused the hurt. Expressing understanding of your child's feelings is equally important. Acknowledge how your behavior affected them emotionally. You might say, "I understand that my yelling made you feel scared and sad." This validation helps your child feel seen and heard. Lastly, a commitment to change future behavior is vital. Clearly state what steps you will take to avoid repeating the mistake. For example, "I will practice taking deep breaths when I start to feel angry." This demonstrates your dedication to becoming a better parent.

Consider a scenario where you lose your temper during a stressful moment. An effective apology might sound like this: "I'm really sorry for yelling earlier when you spilled your juice. I know it scared you and made you upset. I feel really bad about it. I will work on staying calm next time. Can you forgive me?" This apology is specific, expresses genuine remorse, acknowledges the child's feelings, and includes a commitment to change. Another example could be dismissing your child's feelings when they try to share something important. A thoughtful apology might be, "I'm sorry for not listening to you earlier when you tried to tell me about your day. I understand that it hurt your feelings and made you feel unimportant. I promise to give you my full attention next time. Can you forgive me?"

When done sincerely, apologies can transform your relationship with your child, fostering a deeper connection and mutual respect.

Engaging in Shared Activities for Reconnection

Spending quality time together is one of the most effective ways to strengthen bonds and facilitate reconnection with your child. Shared activities create opportunities for meaningful interactions, allowing both of you to connect on a deeper level. These experiences help build a foundation of trust and understanding, essential for a healthy parent-child relationship. The emotional benefits are immense— both you and your child can experience increased happiness, reduced stress, and a greater sense of security. When you engage in an activity together, it signals to your child that they are valued and loved, fostering a sense of belonging and emotional well-being.

One effective way to reconnect is through cooking a meal together. Whether it's baking cookies, making pasta, or preparing a family favorite, the kitchen can be a great place for bonding. The process of cooking together involves teamwork, communication, and shared joy, making it an ideal activity for rebuilding connections. Engaging in a hobby or interest like painting or gardening is another excellent option. These activities not only provide a creative outlet but also offer a relaxed environment where you can talk and share thoughts without the pressure of structured conversation. Taking a nature walk or going on a picnic can also be incredibly rejuvenating. Being outdoors and exploring nature together can create lasting memories and provide a peaceful setting for meaningful conversations.

Being fully present during these activities is crucial. It's easy to get distracted by phones, work, or other responsibilities, but giving your undivided attention to your child during these moments is essential for building a strong connection. Minimizing distractions means putting away your phone, turning off the TV, and focusing solely on the activity and your child. Active participation and genuine interest in the activity show your child that you care about them and value your time together. This presence fosters a sense of security and trust, making your child feel important and loved.

Consider the experience of Lisa, a mother who reconnected with her daughter through gardening. They started a small vegetable garden in their backyard, spending time each week planting, watering, and tending to their plants. This shared hobby not only provided a peaceful setting for conversations but also taught her daughter responsibility and patience. Lisa noticed that her daughter became more open about her feelings during their gardening sessions, strengthening their bond. Another parent, Mark, found that cooking meals with his son helped rebuild their connection. They started a weekly tradition of making pizza together, from kneading the dough to choosing toppings. This activity became a time for them to talk, laugh, and enjoy each other's company, significantly improving their relationship.

One mother shared how taking nature walks with her son transformed their relationship. They would explore nearby trails, collect leaves and rocks, and talk about their day. These walks provided a calm and distraction-free environment where her son felt comfortable opening up about his thoughts and feelings. Another father mentioned how painting sessions with his daughter helped them reconnect. Every Saturday afternoon, they would set up a painting station in the living room and create art together. These sessions became a cherished time for both of them, fostering creativity and deepening their bond.

Engaging in shared activities offers a powerful way to reconnect with your child. By being fully present and actively participating in these moments, you can strengthen your relationship and create lasting memories. Whether it's cooking, gardening, painting, or taking a nature walk, these activities provide opportunities for meaningful interactions, helping to rebuild trust and foster a sense of security and love.

Using Reconciliation Rituals to Heal

Reconciliation rituals are powerful tools for healing conflicts and restoring harmony in your family. These rituals serve as symbolic acts of making amends, helping both parents and children move past disagreements and emotional hurt. They offer a structured way to address and mend the emotional rifts that occur during conflicts. Engaging in these rituals provides emotional benefits by creating a sense of closure and reinforcing positive behaviors. They signal a commitment to repairing the relationship and show that both parties are willing to work toward a better understanding.

One effective reconciliation ritual is creating a "peace corner" in your home. This designated space can be used for discussions and apologies. When a conflict arises, you and your child can retreat to this corner to talk things out calmly. The peace corner should be a comfortable and inviting area, perhaps with cushions, calming colors, and stress-relief items like fidget toys or coloring books. This space becomes a sanctuary where both of you can express feelings, apologize, and find common ground. Another meaningful ritual involves writing letters to each other. This allows both you and your child to articulate feelings and apologies in a thoughtful manner. Writing can sometimes be easier than speaking, especially for children who might struggle to express their emotions verbally. A heartfelt letter can be a keepsake that your child holds onto, serving as a reminder of the commitment to improved behavior and mutual respect.

Sharing a special meal or treat together after making up can also be a powerful ritual. Food has a way of bringing people together, and sharing a meal can symbolize unity and forgiveness. You might decide to bake cookies together or have a small picnic in the backyard. The act of preparing and enjoying food together can provide a relaxed setting for rebuilding trust and connection. These rituals create a tangible way to mark the resolution of conflict, making the process of reconciliation more memorable and impactful for both you and your child.

Rituals play a crucial role in providing emotional closure. The psychological impact of engaging in these structured behaviors helps reinforce the importance of making amends and moving forward. When a ritual is performed consistently after conflicts, it becomes a part of the family culture, teaching children the value of reconciliation and forgiveness. These rituals not only help in resolving the immediate conflict but also build a foundation for handling future disagreements in a healthy manner. They create a predictable and comforting pattern that your child can rely on, fostering a sense of security and emotional stability.

Consider the experience of Emily, a mother who introduced a peace corner in her home. After a heated argument with her daughter, they both retreated to the peace corner, where they took a few moments to calm down before discussing their feelings. Emily found that this ritual helped her daughter articulate her emotions more clearly, leading to a more constructive and empathetic conversation. Another family adopted the ritual of writing letters after conflicts. A father shared how writing letters to his son allowed them both to express their feelings without the pressure of immediate responses. This practice helped them understand each other's perspectives better and strengthened their bond over time.

One parent shared how their family adopted the ritual of sharing a special meal after conflicts. After a disagreement, they would come together to prepare and enjoy a favorite meal. This ritual provided a peaceful setting for apologies and heartfelt conversations. Another family found success in creating a peace corner, where they would go to resolve conflicts. The designated space helped the children feel safe and encouraged open communication. These examples highlight the effectiveness of reconciliation rituals in healing emotional wounds and fostering a supportive family environment.

Reconciliation rituals offer a structured and meaningful way to address and heal conflicts within your family. By creating rituals such as a peace corner, writing letters, or sharing a special meal, you can provide emotional closure and reinforce positive behaviors. These rituals not only help resolve immediate conflicts but also build a foundation for handling future disagreements with empathy and understanding. The consistent practice of these rituals fosters a sense of security, trust, and emotional stability, strengthening the parent-child bond and creating a harmonious family atmosphere.

Creating a Family Reconnection Plan

A structured reconnection plan can be a lifeline for families looking to systematically rebuild relationships after conflicts. This proactive approach ensures that efforts to reconnect are not haphazard but intentional and organized, giving every family member a clear path to follow. Having a plan in place allows everyone to see that rebuilding relationships is a shared priority, fostering a sense of unity and purpose. It also helps to involve all family members in the process, making sure that everyone feels included and valued. When each person contributes ideas and sees their input reflected in the plan, it strengthens their commitment to the family and the reconnection process.

To create an effective family reconnection plan, start by identifying areas of disconnection. This might involve reflecting on recent conflicts, noting patterns of miscommunication, or pinpointing moments where emotional distance was felt. Once these areas are identified, set specific and achievable goals to address them. For instance, if bedtime routines are a common source of stress, a goal might be to establish a calming pre-bedtime ritual. Next, schedule regular family meetings to discuss progress and make adjustments to the plan. These meetings provide a platform for open communication, allowing everyone to voice their thoughts and feelings in a supportive environment. They also serve as a reminder that reconnecting is an ongoing process, requiring consistent effort and attention.

Planning activities and rituals for reconnection is another crucial step. These activities should be enjoyable and meaningful, offering opportunities for positive interactions and shared experiences. Consider incorporating a mix of daily, weekly, and monthly activities to keep the momentum going. Daily activities might include shared meals or family walks, while weekly activities could involve game nights or movie nights. Monthly activities might be larger events like a family outing or a special project. The key is to choose activities that everyone can look forward to and participate in, fostering a sense of togetherness and joy.

Family involvement is paramount in the success of the reconnection plan. Encourage input and ideas from all family members, especially children, as this makes them feel heard and valued. Ask them what activities they enjoy and how they think the family can spend more quality time together. This collaborative approach not only enriches the plan with diverse ideas but also boosts everyone's enthusiasm and commitment. Ensure that each family member's voice is respected and considered in the decisionmaking process. This inclusivity helps build a culture of mutual respect and understanding, laying the groundwork for stronger family bonds.

Consider the story of the Johnson family, who successfully implemented a reconnection plan after a period of frequent conflicts and misunderstandings. They began by identifying their main areas of disconnection, which included rushed mornings and chaotic evenings. Together, they set goals to establish smoother routines and improve communication. They scheduled weekly family meetings to check in on their progress and discuss any challenges they faced. The Johnsons also planned various activities, such as cooking together on weekends and having themed movie nights. By involving everyone in the process and ensuring that each family member's preferences were considered, they were able to create a plan that worked for them. Over time, they noticed significant improvements in their family dynamics, with fewer conflicts and more positive interactions.

Another family, the Smiths, found success by incorporating regular outdoor activities into their reconnection plan. They identified that spending time in nature helped them relax and bond more effectively. They scheduled monthly hikes and picnics, which became cherished family traditions. These outings provided a break from the daily grind and allowed them to connect on a deeper level. The Smiths' commitment to their reconnection plan paid off, as they experienced increased harmony and a stronger sense of unity within the family.

Creating a family reconnection plan is a powerful way to systematically rebuild relationships and foster a supportive family environment. By identifying areas of disconnection, setting goals, and planning meaningful activities, families can take intentional steps towards reconnecting. Involving all family members in the process ensures that everyone feels heard and valued, strengthening their commitment to the plan. With consistent effort and collaboration, families can transform conflicts into opportunities for growth and deeper connection.

Power of Play in Strengthening Parent-Child Relationships

Play is a powerful tool for rebuilding bonds and fostering connection with your children. It goes beyond mere entertainment; it serves as a critical means of expressing and processing emotions. When you engage in play with your child, you create a safe space for them to explore their feelings and experiences in a non-threatening way. The emotional and psychological benefits of play are immense. It helps children develop resilience, problem-solving skills, and emotional intelligence. For parents, it offers a unique opportunity to connect with their children on their level, breaking down barriers and building trust.

Consider the emotional landscape of a child who has just experienced a conflict with you. They might be feeling a mix of confusion, sadness, and even anger. Play can serve as a bridge to help them navigate these complex emotions. For instance, playing a board game together can shift the focus from the conflict to a shared activity, allowing both of you to relax and enjoy each other's company. Card games can also be a fun and interactive way to spend time together, promoting communication and teamwork. Engaging in imaginative play or role-playing can be particularly effective. These activities allow children to act out scenarios and emotions, providing insight into their inner world and helping them process recent events.

Outdoor activities like sports or scavenger hunts offer a different kind of connection. They provide a physical outlet for pent-up energy and frustration, making it easier for children to calm down and refocus. Sports encourage cooperation and healthy competition, while scavenger hunts can turn a simple walk in the park into an exciting adventure. These activities not only strengthen physical health but also nurture emotional bonds. Being outdoors and active together helps create positive memories, reinforcing the idea that family time is enjoyable and rewarding.

The importance of active participation in play cannot be overstated. It's not enough to simply be present; you need to be engaged and enthusiastic. Children are incredibly perceptive and can sense when your mind is elsewhere. Being fully present during playtime shows them that you value this time together, fostering a sense of security and importance. Encourage creativity and cooperation by letting your child lead the play. Whether they want to build a fort, create a story, or invent a new game, your willingness to follow their lead enhances their self-esteem and strengthens your bond.

Take the story of Laura, a mother who used imaginative play to reconnect with her son after frequent arguments. They created a make-believe world where they were explorers on a treasure hunt. This roleplaying game allowed her son to express his feelings and frustrations in a safe environment. Over time, Laura noticed that her son was more open about his emotions and their relationship improved significantly. Another family found that playing board games together every weekend helped them reconnect. They chose games that required teamwork and strategy, which not only made the experience fun but also improved their communication and problem-solving skills.

One father shared how engaging in outdoor sports with his daughter transformed their relationship. They started playing soccer in the backyard, and these sessions became a cherished time for both of them. The physical activity helped release stress, and the shared goal of improving their skills fostered a sense of teamwork and mutual support. Another mother mentioned how scavenger hunts in the local park brought her closer to her children. They would create lists of items to find, turning their walks into exciting adventures. These activities provided a break from routine and allowed them to connect in a relaxed and joyful setting.

Play is not just a tool for passing the time; it is a powerful means of rebuilding bonds and fostering emotional connection. By engaging in playful activities, being fully present, and encouraging creativity and cooperation, you can create a nurturing environment that strengthens your relationship with your child. The joy and connection that come from play can help heal emotional wounds, making it a vital part of the reconnection process after conflict.

In our next chapter, we will explore the importance of building a supportive network, focusing on how to leverage your community and professional resources to create a nurturing environment for your family.

Chapter 7:
Building a Support System

"You're Not Alone: Finding the Support Every Parent Deserves"

Imagine a quiet evening after the kids are finally asleep. You sit down with a cup of tea, feeling the weight of the day lift slightly from your shoulders. The house is silent, but your mind is not. You think about the tantrums, the sibling squabbles, and the endless to-do list. You wonder how you can manage it all and realize that you don't have to do it alone. Building a support system can be a game-changer in your parenting journey, providing both emotional relief and practical help.

Identifying Potential Support Networks

Having a support network is crucial for your emotional well-being and effective anger management. When you have a group of people to lean on, you feel less isolated and more understood. This emotional support can be a lifesaver on tough days. According to research, parents with strong support networks report higher levels of happiness and lower levels of stress (Source 1). The emotional benefits are clear: having someone to talk to can help you process your feelings and gain new perspectives. Practical assistance from your support network can ease your daily load, allowing you to share responsibilities like childcare, errands, or even just having someone to talk to during a difficult moment.

First, let's identify the potential support systems you might already have. Start with your family members. Is there a sibling, cousin, or even a parent who is willing to help out? Many parents find that grandparents are eager to spend time with their grandchildren, providing both a break for you and quality time for them. Friends are another invaluable resource. Think about those friends who offer emotional support, the ones who listen without judgment and offer a shoulder to lean on. These friends can be a crucial part of your support network, helping you navigate the ups and downs of parenting.

If your existing network feels limited, there are several ways to expand it. Consider joining local parenting groups. These groups often provide a sense of community and shared understanding. You can find them through local community centers, libraries, or online platforms. Attending community events and activities can also help you meet other parents who are in the same stage of life. Networking through your children's school is another excellent way to build connections. Participate in school events, volunteer for activities, and engage with other parents. These interactions can lead to meaningful relationships that provide mutual support.

Your support network doesn't have to be confined to close family and friends. Diversifying your support sources can provide a broader range of assistance and perspectives. Professional services like counselors and therapists can offer invaluable emotional support and guidance. If you're dealing with specific challenges, such as managing anger or coping with stress, a therapist can provide strategies tailored to your needs. Online communities and forums are another excellent resource. Many parents find solace and advice in online parenting groups where they can share their experiences and get support from others who understand their struggles (Source 3). Religious or spiritual groups can also offer a sense of community and support. Many faith-based groups have programs for families and children, providing both emotional and practical help.

One mother shared how joining a local parenting group transformed her experience. She found a community of parents who understood her struggles and offered support without judgment. They exchanged advice, shared resources, and even organized playdates to give each other breaks. Another parent found that attending community events helped her build a network of friends who could help with childcare swaps, providing much-needed breaks and fostering a sense of camaraderie.

Building a diverse and robust support network can make a significant difference in your parenting journey. By identifying existing networks, expanding your connections, and embracing various sources of support, you create a web of relationships that can help you manage your emotions, share responsibilities, and feel less isolated. This support system not only benefits you but also creates a more stable and nurturing environment for your children.

Leveraging Online Communities for Support

In today's digital age, online communities offer a lifeline for parents seeking support, especially if local resources are limited. These virtual spaces provide valuable access to diverse perspectives and experiences, enabling you to connect with parents from different backgrounds and situations. One of the most significant benefits is the convenience. You can engage with these communities at any time, whether it's during a late-night feeding or a quiet moment after the kids are in bed. This flexibility ensures that support is just a click away, whenever you need it.

Finding the right online communities involves some research. Start by searching for reputable parenting forums. Websites like BabyCenter or The Bump have dedicated sections where parents discuss a wide range of topics, from sleep training to managing tantrums. These forums often have moderators who ensure that the discussions remain respectful and supportive. Joining social media groups focused on parenting and anger management can also be incredibly helpful. Facebook, for example, hosts numerous groups where parents share their experiences and offer advice. To find these groups, use specific keywords like "parenting support" or "anger management for parents" in the search bar. Participating in virtual support groups or webinars can provide real-time interaction and expert advice. Websites like Eventbrite or Meetup often list these events, allowing you to connect with others facing similar challenges.

Active participation is crucial to get the most out of online communities. Simply lurking in the background won't yield the emotional support and practical advice you need. Share your experiences and ask for advice. Opening up about your struggles can be therapeutic, and you'll likely find that many others have faced similar issues. Providing support to others in the community is equally important. Offering advice or even a sympathetic ear can build a sense of camaraderie and mutual support. This reciprocal relationship enriches the community and makes it a more valuable resource for everyone involved.

There are numerous supportive online platforms that parents have found helpful. One mother shared her positive experience with a Facebook group dedicated to parents of children with ADHD. She found the group to be a treasure trove of tips, from managing hyperactivity to dealing with school-related issues. Another parent praised a forum on Reddit, where they found comfort and practical advice during latenight scrolls. These platforms offer a sense of community and understanding that can be hard to find elsewhere. Websites like the Center for Parent Information and Resources (CPIR) even offer specialized resources and fact sheets on various disabilities, making it easier to find targeted support.

Visual Element: Online Community Checklist

1. Search for reputable forums (e.g., BabyCenter, The Bump)

2. Join social media groups (e.g., Facebook, Reddit)

3. Participate in virtual support groups or webinars (e.g., Eventbrite, Meetup)

4. Actively engage: share experiences, ask for advice, provide support

One father found solace in an online support group for parents dealing with postpartum depression. The group not only offered emotional support but also provided resources for professional help. Another parent discovered a virtual book club focused on parenting books. They found that discussing these books with other parents offered new insights and practical tips that they could immediately apply.

Digital communication tools, such as social media and apps, are widely used across demographic lines. Studies show that texting, mobile apps, and social media are effective ways to educate and support parents facing health issues (Source 3). Text messaging has shown high effectiveness in interacting with parents, with an 80% response rate. Traditional support groups have shifted to online platforms, reducing isolation and providing readily accessible support. One mother leveraged a parenting app that sent daily tips and reminders tailored to her child's age and developmental stage. This app became an invaluable resource, offering timely advice and a sense of community through its interactive features.

Leveraging online communities for support can make a significant difference in your parenting experience. By actively participating in these virtual spaces, you can gain emotional support, practical advice, and a sense of community that helps you navigate the challenges of parenting with greater ease and confidence. Whether through forums, social media groups, or virtual support groups, the digital world offers numerous opportunities to connect, share, and grow as a parent.

Building Supportive Relationships with Other Parents

Building relationships with other parents can be incredibly supportive. These connections provide a unique form of peer support that only other parents can truly understand. When you connect with someone who is also navigating the challenges of raising young children, you find a shared understanding that can be both comforting and empowering. These relationships offer not just emotional support but practical help as well. Imagine having a fellow parent who can pick up your child from school when you're stuck in traffic or someone who can offer a sympathetic ear after a particularly tough day.

To build these supportive relationships, start by initiating conversations at school events or activities. These settings naturally bring parents together, providing a perfect opportunity to connect. A simple, "Hi, I'm [Your Name], and my child is in [Child's Name]'s class," can open the door to deeper conversations. Volunteering for school events or joining the PTA can also create opportunities to meet other parents. Parenting classes or workshops are another excellent venue for forming connections. These settings often foster group activities or discussions, allowing you to bond with others who are experiencing similar challenges and learning new strategies together.

Reciprocity is key in maintaining these supportive relationships. It's not just about receiving help, but also offering it. When you provide support to other parents, whether it's through listening, sharing advice, or offering practical help, you build trust and strengthen the relationship. Consistent, supportive behavior shows that you are reliable and invested in the relationship. For instance, offering to watch a friend's child for a couple of hours can go a long way in building mutual trust and support. These acts of kindness create a cycle of giving and receiving that benefits everyone involved.

Parents who have successfully built supportive relationships often share inspiring stories. One mother, Sarah, talked about how she formed a close-knit group of friends through her child's preschool. They began by chatting during drop-off and pick-up times and eventually started organizing playdates and outings. This group became a lifeline, offering emotional support and practical help, like sharing babysitting duties. Another parent, John, shared how he found a supportive network through a local parenting workshop. The workshop participants formed a WhatsApp group to stay connected, share advice, and organize meetups. This group provided him with invaluable support, particularly during challenging times when he needed advice or just a listening ear.

These relationships can be incredibly beneficial. They provide a sense of community and belonging, reducing feelings of isolation. Emotional support from peers who truly understand your struggles can be immensely comforting. Practical support, like sharing childcare responsibilities, can ease your daily load and provide much-needed breaks. Moreover, these relationships offer a space for mutual learning and growth. By sharing experiences and strategies, you can learn new approaches to parenting challenges and gain fresh perspectives.

In my experience, building supportive relationships with other parents has been transformative. One evening, I found myself overwhelmed by the demands of parenting and work. I reached out to a fellow parent I had met at a school event. She listened, offered comforting words, and even suggested a few strategies that had worked for her. That simple conversation lifted my spirits and gave me the strength to keep going. It reminded me of the power of peer support and the importance of building and maintaining these relationships.

Connecting with other parents can provide invaluable support and friendship. Initiate conversations at school events, join parenting classes, and volunteer for activities. Remember, reciprocity is key. Offer help and support, and you'll find that these relationships become a cornerstone of your parenting journey. The shared experiences, understanding, and mutual support create a strong foundation for navigating the challenges of raising young children.

Utilizing Local Resources and Groups

Local resources offer a wealth of support for parents, providing both emotional relief and practical assistance. Community centers and organizations are often the first places to look. These centers typically offer a range of programs tailored to parents and families, including workshops, parenting classes, and support groups. These activities provide opportunities not only to learn new skills but also to connect with other parents who are facing similar challenges. Parenting support groups can be particularly beneficial, offering a safe space to share experiences, seek advice, and gain emotional support. Classes on topics ranging from anger management to practical communication skills can equip you with the tools you need to navigate the complexities of parenting.

Finding these local resources can feel daunting, but there are practical steps you can take to make the process easier. Start by checking community bulletin boards and websites. Many local community centers, libraries, and schools post information about upcoming events and available resources. Websites for local government or community organizations often have sections dedicated to family and parenting resources. Another practical approach is to ask for recommendations from healthcare providers or schools. Pediatricians, therapists, and school counselors are often well-connected within the community and can point you toward valuable resources. They may know of local support groups, workshops, or family activities that could be beneficial.

The benefits of local support groups extend beyond emotional relief. These groups often host regular meetings and events where parents can share their experiences and offer mutual support. Workshops and seminars on parenting and anger management provide practical strategies and tools that you can implement in your daily life. These sessions are not only informative but also offer a sense of community, making you feel less isolated in your struggles. Regular participation in these groups can lead to lasting friendships and a robust support network that you can rely on during challenging times. The combination of emotional and practical assistance makes these local groups invaluable for navigating the demands of parenting.

Consider the story of one parent who found solace in a local community organization. She attended weekly parenting classes that focused on stress management and effective communication. These classes provided her with practical tools and techniques, but more importantly, they connected her with other parents who shared similar experiences. The group became a source of emotional support, helping her feel understood and less alone. Another parent shared how a local support group for parents of children with special needs transformed her life. The group offered specialized workshops, resource sharing, and a safe space to discuss unique challenges.

This support network became a lifeline, offering both emotional relief and practical advice.

Community organizations often offer a wide range of services. For example, some organizations provide childcare during meetings, allowing parents to participate without worrying about their children. Others may offer one-on-one mentoring or counseling services, providing personalized support tailored to your specific needs. Local libraries frequently host storytime sessions, playgroups, and parenting workshops, making them a valuable resource for parents looking to connect and learn. Schools and educational institutions also offer resources, such as parent-teacher associations (PTAs), that organize events and provide a platform for parents to engage with each other and the school community.

Accessing local resources can significantly ease the burden of parenting. Whether it's through community centers, parenting support groups, or specialized workshops, these resources offer a blend of emotional support and practical assistance. By taking advantage of local resources, you can build a strong support network that helps you navigate the challenges of parenting with greater ease and confidence.

Reach out, connect, and discover the rich tapestry of support available in your community.

Communicating Your Needs to Your Support System

Clear communication is vital when it comes to utilizing your support system effectively. It ensures that the help you receive is relevant and genuinely beneficial. When you communicate your needs clearly, you avoid misunderstandings and ensure that your support network knows exactly how to assist you. This clarity not only makes the support more effective but also strengthens your relationships. When people understand your needs, they can respond more appropriately, fostering a deeper sense of trust and mutual respect.

Imagine you're feeling overwhelmed by the daily demands of parenting and need some time to yourself. Instead of vaguely mentioning that you're stressed, use "I" statements to express your needs and feelings. For example, say, "I feel overwhelmed with all the tasks I have to manage. I need some time this weekend to relax and recharge. Could you take the kids for a few hours?" This clear and assertive communication helps others understand exactly what you need and why. Being specific about the type of support required ensures that your needs are met effectively. Whether you need someone to watch the kids, help with household chores, or just lend an ear, being direct can make all the difference.

Listening is just as important as speaking when it comes to effective communication. Reciprocal communication means actively listening to others' perspectives and needs as well. This two-way communication fosters mutual understanding and support. When a friend expresses their need for support, listen attentively and respond thoughtfully. This practice not only strengthens your relationship but also ensures that the support is balanced and reciprocal. By listening, you demonstrate empathy and understanding, which are crucial for maintaining strong, supportive relationships.

Consider the story of a mother named Laura, who successfully communicated her needs to her support network. Feeling overwhelmed by her responsibilities, she reached out to her sister and used clear "I" statements to express her feelings. "I'm feeling really stressed with everything I have to manage at home. I need some help with the kids this weekend so I can take a break." Her sister appreciated the clarity and was more than willing to help. This open communication not only provided Laura with the support she needed but also strengthened her bond with her sister.

Another parent, Mark, found that being specific about his needs made a significant difference. He needed help with school pick-ups because his work schedule had changed. Instead of vaguely asking for help, he said, "I need someone to pick up the kids from school on Tuesdays and Thursdays. Could anyone help with this?" This clear request made it easy for his friends to understand his need and offer support. One of his friends volunteered, and the arrangement worked out smoothly, providing Mark with the help he needed without any confusion.

Reciprocity in communication is also illustrated in the story of Sarah, who found that actively listening to her friends' needs deepened their relationship. When her friend mentioned feeling isolated, Sarah made an effort to check in regularly and offer support. This mutual understanding and support strengthened their friendship and created a reliable support network for both of them.

Effective communication is essential for utilizing your support system to its fullest potential. By clearly expressing your needs with "I" statements, being specific about the type of support required, and actively listening to others, you can build stronger, more understanding relationships. These practices ensure that the support you receive is relevant and effective, making your parenting journey smoother and more manageable.

The Benefits of Professional Counseling and Therapy

Professional counseling and therapy can be transformative for managing anger and stress. These services offer emotional and psychological benefits that go beyond what friends and family can provide. A trained therapist can help you explore underlying issues that contribute to your anger, offering a safe space to unpack emotional baggage. By addressing these root causes, you can develop coping strategies tailored to your specific needs. The emotional relief of having a non-judgmental professional to talk to can be immense. Therapy provides tools for emotional regulation, helping you respond to stressors in healthier ways. This professional support can significantly improve your mental health and overall well-being.

Finding the right counselor or therapist involves several steps. Start by checking credentials and areas of expertise. Look for professionals who specialize in anger management, stress reduction, or family therapy. Websites like Psychology Today offer directories that allow you to filter therapists by specialty, location, and insurance acceptance. Seeking recommendations from trusted sources such as your primary care doctor, friends, or family members can also be valuable. Personal referrals often lead to more satisfactory experiences because they come from people who understand your needs and can vouch for the therapist's effectiveness. Additionally, many workplaces offer Employee Assistance Programs (EAPs) that provide initial counseling sessions and referrals.

Consistency is crucial for achieving the best results in therapy. Regular sessions help build a therapeutic relationship, enabling the therapist to gain a deeper understanding of your issues and provide more effective guidance. Set a consistent schedule for therapy sessions, whether weekly or bi-weekly, and stick to it. This regularity helps reinforce the coping strategies you learn and provides ongoing support as you navigate challenges. Committing to the therapeutic process involves more than just attending sessions. It means actively engaging in the exercises and strategies your therapist suggests, reflecting on your progress, and being open to change. This commitment can lead to significant improvements in managing your emotions and reducing stress.

Many parents have found therapy to be a lifeline. Take the example of Jessica, a mother of two, who struggled with frequent outbursts. She felt overwhelmed and disconnected from her children. After seeking therapy, she learned to identify her triggers and developed strategies to manage her anger. Jessica's therapist helped her explore past experiences that contributed to her emotional responses, providing her with a deeper understanding of herself. Over time, Jessica noticed a significant reduction in her anger episodes and felt more connected to her family. Her story is a testament to the transformative power of professional counseling.

Research supports the effectiveness of therapy for anger management. Studies have shown that Cognitive Behavioral Therapy (CBT), a common therapeutic approach, can significantly reduce anger and improve emotional regulation. CBT helps individuals identify negative thought patterns and replace them with healthier ones, leading to more constructive responses to stress. Another study found that parents who participated in therapy reported lower levels of stress and improved relationships with their children. These findings highlight the potential for therapy to bring about meaningful, long-lasting change.

Consider the case of Mark, a father who felt constantly stressed and irritable. He sought therapy after realizing that his anger was affecting his relationship with his children. Through regular sessions, Mark learned mindfulness techniques and practiced relaxation exercises. His therapist also helped him develop communication skills to express his needs more effectively. Over time, Mark noticed a significant improvement in his emotional well-being and a stronger bond with his family. These examples illustrate how therapy can provide essential tools and strategies for managing anger and stress, leading to a more harmonious family life.

Professional counseling and therapy offer invaluable support for managing anger and stress. By addressing underlying issues and developing coping strategies, therapy provides emotional relief and practical tools for better emotional regulation. Finding the right therapist involves checking credentials and seeking recommendations, while consistency and commitment are key to achieving the best results. Personal stories and research underscore the transformative potential of therapy, making it a vital resource for parents seeking to improve their mental health and family dynamics.

Chapter 8:
Consistency and Long-Term Success

"Staying the Course: Building Habits That Last a Lifetime"

One evening, after a particularly chaotic dinner with spaghetti flying and juice spilling, you finally get the kids to bed. You sit down on the couch, feeling drained and wondering if there's a better way to handle these everyday storms. That's when it hits you—having a plan might just make all the difference. A structured action plan can be your roadmap to maintaining calm and managing anger effectively over the long term.

Creating a Personal Action Plan for Anger Management

Creating a personal action plan is essential for maintaining long-term success in managing your anger. Think of it as your guide to navigating the emotional ups and downs of parenting. A well-structured plan provides clear direction and focus, helping you stay on track even during the most challenging times. It also serves as a valuable tool for tracking your progress and identifying areas where you might need to make adjustments. By having a concrete plan, you give yourself a framework to follow, reducing the chances of feeling overwhelmed or lost when emotions run high.

To develop your action plan, start by identifying your specific triggers and responses. Reflect on the situations that consistently provoke anger. Is it the morning rush, sibling fights, or bedtime battles? Once you've pinpointed your triggers, think about how you typically respond. Do you raise your voice, withdraw, or feel your heart racing? Understanding these patterns is the first step toward managing them more effectively. Next, set both short-term and long-term goals. Short-term goals might include practicing deep breathing during stressful moments or taking a timeout when you feel anger rising. Long-term goals could involve developing a more consistent daily routine or improving overall family communication.

Setting clear, achievable goals gives you something to work toward and helps measure your progress.

Your action plan should include various components to ensure comprehensive coverage of your needs. Daily mindfulness practices are a cornerstone of managing anger. These can be as simple as dedicating five minutes each morning to mindful breathing or practicing mindful walking during your lunch break. Regular self-reflection and journaling are also crucial. Set aside time each day to jot down your thoughts and emotions. Reflect on what went well, what triggered your anger, and how you responded. This practice not only helps you process your feelings but also provides valuable insights into your progress and areas for improvement. Scheduled timeouts and deep-breathing exercises are practical tools that can be incorporated into your plan. For instance, you might decide to take a five-minute timeout whenever you feel overwhelmed or practice deep breathing before responding to your child's tantrum.

Consider the success stories of other parents who have effectively used action plans for anger management. One mother, Sarah, identified her primary trigger as the chaos of getting her kids ready for school. She set a short-term goal to remain calm during the morning rush by practicing deep breathing. Over time, she noticed a significant reduction in her stress levels and found mornings more manageable. Another parent, John, struggled with bedtime routines. He created an action plan that included a nightly mindfulness practice and a consistent bedtime schedule. By sticking to his plan, John transformed bedtime from a battleground to a peaceful routine. These examples highlight how a structured action plan can make a tangible difference in managing anger.

Reflection Exercise: Create Your Personal Action Plan

- Identify Triggers: Reflect on the situations that trigger your anger.

- Set Goals: Outline both short-term and long-term goals for managing your anger.

- Daily Practices: Incorporate daily mindfulness practices, self-reflection, and journaling.

- Practical Tools: Include scheduled timeouts and deep-breathing exercises in your plan.

- Track Progress: Regularly review and adjust your plan as needed.

Creating a personal action plan is a proactive step toward long-term success in managing anger. By identifying your triggers, setting clear goals, and incorporating daily practices and practical tools, you equip yourself with the resources needed to navigate the emotional challenges of parenting. The journey may not always be easy, but with a well-structured plan, you can maintain focus and make meaningful progress toward a calmer, more harmonious family life.

Setting Realistic Goals and Tracking Progress

Setting realistic goals is crucial for maintaining motivation and ensuring steady improvement. When you set achievable goals, you prevent the discouragement and frustration that often come from aiming too high too soon. Realistic goals pave the way for consistent, sustainable progress, making the journey of managing anger feel more manageable and less overwhelming. They serve as stepping stones, each small victory adding to your confidence and reinforcing positive behaviors.

To set effective goals, consider using the SMART framework—Specific, Measurable, Achievable, Relevant, and Time-bound. Begin by clearly defining what you want to achieve. For instance, instead of vaguely aiming to "stay calm," specify that you want to "practice deep breathing for five minutes every morning." This specificity makes the goal tangible. Next, make your goal measurable. You could track the number of times you practice deep breathing each week. Ensure the goal is achievable within the constraints of your daily life. It's important that your goal is relevant to your overarching aim of managing anger effectively. Finally, set a clear timeframe, such as "within the next month."

Breaking down larger goals into smaller, manageable steps can make them less daunting. If your longterm goal is to maintain a calm demeanor throughout the day, start with short-term goals like practicing mindfulness for five minutes each morning or taking a timeout during particularly stressful moments. Use goal-setting worksheets and templates to organize your thoughts and outline your steps. These tools provide a structured approach to goal setting, helping you visualize your progress and stay on track.

Tracking your progress is just as important as setting your goals. Keeping a progress journal can be a valuable tool for monitoring your journey. Document your daily experiences, noting what worked well and where you faced challenges. This practice not only helps you stay accountable but also provides insights into patterns and triggers. Additionally, consider using apps or tools designed to track milestones. Many apps offer features like reminders, progress charts, and motivational quotes to keep you engaged.

Regularly review and adjust your goals based on your progress. Flexibility is key; if a particular approach isn't working, don't hesitate to tweak your plan.

Consider the story of Maria, a mother of two who struggled with staying calm during the chaotic morning routine. She set a SMART goal to "practice deep breathing for five minutes every morning for the next four weeks." Maria used a simple app to track her daily practice and reflected on her progress in a journal. Over time, she noticed a significant reduction in her morning stress levels. Another parent, David, aimed to improve communication with his teenage son. He set a goal to "have a ten-minute check-in conversation every evening for the next month," tracking their talks in a notebook. This consistent effort not only improved their relationship but also helped David manage his frustration more effectively.

Goal-Setting Worksheet

- Specific Goal: Clearly define your goal.

- Measurable Criteria: Determine how to measure progress.

- Achievable Steps: Ensure the goal is realistic.

- Relevant Purpose: Connect the goal to your broader aim.

- Time-bound Deadline: Set a clear timeframe.

Setting realistic goals and tracking your progress can transform the way you manage anger. By using the SMART framework, breaking down goals, and regularly monitoring your achievements, you create a structured approach that fosters steady improvement and sustained motivation. The stories of parents like Maria and David illustrate the power of setting and tracking goals, showing that even small, consistent steps can lead to meaningful change.

Dealing with Setbacks and Staying Motivated

Setbacks are an inevitable part of any meaningful endeavor, including managing anger. They're like unexpected detours on your journey, moments where things don't go as planned. It's easy to feel disheartened when these moments occur, but understanding that setbacks are opportunities for learning can change your perspective. Instead of seeing them as failures, view them as temporary challenges that offer valuable lessons. This mindset shift can help you navigate setbacks more constructively and maintain your motivation.

Reflecting on the cause of a setback is the first step in overcoming it. Take a moment to consider what led to the setback. Was it a particularly stressful day at work, a lack of sleep, or perhaps a miscommunication with your partner? Identifying the root cause helps you understand what went wrong and how to avoid similar situations in the future. Once you've pinpointed the cause, adjust your goals and action plans as needed. Flexibility is key; sometimes, you might need to tweak your strategies or set more achievable goals to stay on track. Seeking support from your network can also be incredibly beneficial. Whether it's talking to a friend, joining a support group, or consulting a therapist, leaning on others can provide the encouragement and guidance you need to move forward.

Self-compassion is crucial during challenging times. It's easy to be hard on yourself when things don't go as planned, but practicing self-forgiveness and positive self-talk can make a world of difference. Remind yourself that everyone experiences setbacks and that they don't define your worth or abilities. Engaging in self-care activities to recharge is another important aspect of dealing with setbacks. Whether it's taking a relaxing bath, going for a walk, or spending time on a hobby you love, self-care helps replenish your energy and restore your motivation.

Consider the story of Lisa, a mother of two who struggled with managing her anger during the morning rush. One particularly hectic morning, she lost her temper and yelled at her kids. Instead of dwelling on the setback, Lisa took time to reflect on what had gone wrong. She realized that a lack of preparation the night before had contributed to the chaos. Lisa adjusted her action plan, setting a new goal to prepare lunches and outfits before bedtime. She also reached out to a fellow parent for support and encouragement. With these adjustments, Lisa found her mornings becoming more manageable and her setbacks less frequent.

Another parent, Tom, faced a setback when his usual deep-breathing exercises didn't seem to help during a stressful family dinner. Feeling frustrated, Tom reflected on the situation and realized that he hadn't been consistent with his mindfulness practices. He adjusted his plan to include a short meditation session before dinner and sought advice from an online support group. This small change made a significant difference, helping Tom stay calm and composed during future meals.

Case Study: Parent Reflection on a Setback

- Situation: Reflect on a recent setback in managing anger.

- Cause: Identify the root cause of the setback.

- Adjustment: Adjust goals and action plans as needed.

- Support: Seek support from your network.

- Self-Compassion: Practice self-forgiveness and positive self-talk.

- Self-Care: Engage in activities to recharge.

Setbacks don't have to derail your progress. By viewing them as learning opportunities, reflecting on their causes, and making necessary adjustments, you can stay motivated and continue moving forward. Practicing self-compassion and engaging in self-care activities further supports your journey, helping you maintain resilience and perseverance. The experiences of parents like Lisa and Tom illustrate that setbacks are not the end but rather moments of growth and learning.

Integrating Anger Management Strategies into Daily Life

Integrating anger management strategies into your daily routine is crucial for long-term success. This approach reinforces positive habits, ensuring consistent practice and ongoing improvement. When you incorporate these techniques into your everyday life, they become second nature. This consistency helps you manage stress more effectively and maintain emotional balance. By embedding these strategies into your routine, you create a stable foundation for emotional well-being, which is essential for navigating the ups and downs of parenting.

One practical way to integrate anger management into your daily routine is through mindfulness during everyday activities. Mindful eating, for instance, involves focusing on the taste, texture, and aroma of your food, allowing you to savor each bite fully. This practice not only enhances your eating experience but also provides a moment of calm and reflection. Similarly, mindful walking encourages you to pay attention to the sensation of your feet hitting the ground, the rhythm of your breath, and the sights and sounds around you. These small, mindful practices can significantly reduce stress and promote a sense of peace.

Regular check-ins and self-reflection times are also vital. Schedule a few minutes each day to assess your emotional state. Ask yourself questions like, "How am I feeling right now?" and "What triggered my emotions today?" This practice helps you stay attuned to your feelings and recognize patterns over time. Additionally, practicing deep-breathing exercises during routine breaks can be incredibly beneficial. Whether you're taking a short break at work or pausing between household chores, take a few deep breaths to center yourself. This simple act can lower your heart rate and reduce muscle tension, helping you stay calm and focused.

Consistent daily practice of anger management strategies leads to lasting emotional regulation and well-being. Improved emotional resilience allows you to bounce back more quickly from stressful situations. Enhanced family dynamics result from your ability to remain calm and composed, setting a positive example for your children. Regular practice also fosters stronger relationships, as your family members feel more secure and supported in a stable emotional environment. As you consistently apply these techniques, you'll notice a significant improvement in your overall quality of life.

Consider the story of Amy, a mother who struggled with managing her anger during hectic mornings. She decided to integrate mindfulness into her daily routine by practicing mindful eating during breakfast and mindful walking during her commute. Over time, these practices helped her start the day with a sense of calm, significantly reducing her morning stress levels. Another parent, Mark, found that regular checkins and deep-breathing exercises during his work breaks made a substantial difference. By taking just a few minutes each day to reflect and breathe deeply, he noticed a marked improvement in his ability to handle stress and maintain emotional balance.

Success stories like these illustrate the power of consistent daily practice. Integrating anger management strategies into your daily routine might seem challenging at first, but with dedication and persistence, it becomes easier. These practices not only help you manage your emotions more effectively but also enhance your overall well-being and family dynamics. As you continue to incorporate these techniques into your life, you'll find yourself more equipped to handle the challenges of parenting with grace and resilience.

Encouraging Family-Wide Emotional Health

Fostering emotional health within your entire family is crucial for long-term success. When every family member feels emotionally supported and understood, it creates a nurturing environment where everyone can thrive. This supportive atmosphere reduces overall family stress and conflict, promoting a sense of security and well-being. Imagine a home where open communication is the norm, where each person feels heard and valued. Such an environment not only benefits the present but also sets the stage for emotionally healthy future generations.

One effective strategy for promoting family-wide emotional health is holding regular family meetings. These meetings provide a safe space for everyone to discuss their emotions and concerns. It's a way to check in with each other, share experiences, and address any issues before they escalate. During these meetings, encourage every family member to speak openly about their feelings. You can start by asking simple questions like, "How was your day?" or "Is there anything on your mind?" This practice fosters a habit of open communication and emotional expression. Another beneficial approach is practicing shared mindfulness and relaxation activities. Whether it's a family yoga session, a guided meditation, or simply taking a few deep breaths together before bedtime, these activities can help everyone unwind and connect on a deeper level. These moments of shared calm can strengthen family bonds and create a collective sense of peace.

Encouraging open communication and emotional expression is vital. Make it clear that all emotions are valid and that it's okay to feel angry, sad, or frustrated. Teach your children to articulate their feelings instead of bottling them up. You can model this behavior by expressing your own emotions in a healthy way. For instance, instead of saying, "I'm fine," when you're not, try, "I'm feeling a bit overwhelmed right now, and I need a moment to myself." This honesty sets a powerful example for your children, showing them that it's okay to be vulnerable and that emotions are a natural part of life.

Parental modeling plays a significant role in shaping a child's emotional health. Children learn by observing their parents, so demonstrating effective anger management techniques is crucial. Show your children how to take deep breaths when feeling upset or how to step away from a heated situation to cool down. Displaying empathy, patience, and understanding in your interactions with them will teach them to do the same. When you handle your emotions constructively, your children are more likely to adopt similar behaviors. For example, a father named Mark noticed his frustration levels rising during his children's constant bickering. Instead of reacting with anger, he calmly told them he needed a moment to breathe. His children, seeing his approach, began to mimic this behavior, leading to a more peaceful home environment.

Consider the success stories of families who have successfully promoted emotional health within their household. One mother, Jessica, started holding weekly family meetings where everyone shared their highs and lows of the week. This practice not only improved communication but also helped her children feel more connected and supported. Another family, the Johnsons, incorporated a nightly mindfulness routine. Each evening, they spent ten minutes practicing deep breathing and gratitude exercises together. This simple routine significantly reduced their overall stress levels and brought them closer as a family.

Their children began looking forward to these moments of calm and reflection, reinforcing the importance of emotional well-being.

Promoting family-wide emotional health requires consistent effort and commitment, but the benefits are profound. By creating a supportive environment, practicing shared relaxation activities, encouraging open communication, and modeling healthy emotional behaviors, you lay the groundwork for a harmonious and resilient family. The experiences of families like Jessica's and the Johnsons illustrate the transformative power of prioritizing emotional health within the household.

Celebrating Success and Continued Growth

Celebrating success is more than just a moment of joy; it's a vital part of maintaining motivation and morale. When you recognize and celebrate achievements, no matter how small, you reinforce positive behaviors and progress. This sense of accomplishment not only boosts your confidence but also encourages you to keep moving forward. Imagine the satisfaction of seeing your efforts pay off, knowing that each step you take makes a difference in your family's emotional well-being.

Practical ways to celebrate success can make these moments even more meaningful. Holding family celebrations or special outings is an excellent way to acknowledge milestones. Whether it's a picnic in the park, a movie night, or a favorite meal, these activities provide a tangible reward and create lasting memories. Another idea is to create a "success wall" at home with notes and achievements. Each time someone in the family reaches a goal or demonstrates positive behavior, add a note to the wall. This visual reminder serves as a constant source of encouragement and pride. Sharing successes with your support network, such as friends or online communities, can also amplify the joy. Celebrating together fosters a sense of community and shared achievement.

Continued growth is just as crucial as celebrating success. It's essential to set new goals and challenges to maintain momentum. Learning and improving anger management techniques should be an ongoing process. As you grow, you'll find new areas to explore and refine. This commitment to personal and family growth ensures that you're always moving forward, even when you encounter setbacks. For instance, after mastering deep-breathing exercises, you may explore more advanced mindfulness practices or engage in family therapy sessions to further strengthen your emotional bonds.

Consider the story of Emily, a mother who celebrated each small victory in her journey toward anger management. When she successfully practiced deep breathing during a stressful situation, she treated herself to a relaxing bath. For more significant milestones, like maintaining a calm demeanor for an entire week, she organized a family outing to their favorite nature trail. These celebrations kept her motivated and provided her family with positive reinforcement. Another parent, Mike, used a "success wall" to track his progress. Each note represented a moment of triumph, from handling a tantrum calmly to resolving a conflict with his partner. Seeing the wall fill up with achievements gave him a profound sense of accomplishment and encouraged him to keep striving for more.

Emily and Mike's experiences illustrate the power of celebrating success and committing to continued growth. These practices not only enhance your motivation but also create a positive and supportive environment for your family. As you celebrate your achievements and set new goals, you foster a culture of growth and resilience. This ongoing journey of learning and improvement not only benefits you but also sets a powerful example for your children, teaching them the importance of perseverance and selfimprovement.

Celebrating success and committing to continued growth are vital components of long-term success in managing anger. Recognizing achievements reinforces positive behaviors, while setting new goals ensures ongoing progress. By creating meaningful celebrations and maintaining a focus on growth, you build a foundation for a resilient and emotionally healthy family. Emily and Mike's stories show that with dedication and the right mindset, you can achieve lasting positive change. As we move forward, we will explore how to apply these principles in practical ways to further enhance your family's emotional wellbeing and strengthen your relationships.

Chapter 9:
Practical Exercises and Worksheets

"Your Personal Parenting Toolkit: Hands-On Support for Daily Growth"

Imagine this: after a long day filled with the usual chaos of parenting young children, you finally have a moment to yourself. The house is quiet, and you find a few minutes to sit down with your thoughts. It's in these moments of solitude that you can reflect on the day's events, your reactions, and what you might want to do differently tomorrow. Daily reflections can be a powerful tool for improving emotional regulation and gaining insights into your behavior. This chapter will guide you through the concept of daily reflections and provide practical exercises to help you integrate this practice into your routine.

Daily Reflection Worksheets

Daily reflections are more than just a recap of your day; they are an opportunity to gain deeper insights into your emotions and behaviors. Reflecting on your daily experiences is crucial for improving emotional awareness. When you take the time to look back on your day, you begin to notice patterns in your behavior and identify what triggers your emotional responses. This self-awareness is the first step toward making intentional changes that can lead to a more harmonious family life.

Self-reflection helps you gain a deeper understanding of your emotional landscape. It allows you to pinpoint specific moments that triggered anger or frustration and examine the underlying causes. For example, you might notice that your patience wears thin during the evening rush when everyone is tired and hungry. By recognizing this pattern, you can take proactive steps to manage your emotions and create a calmer environment. Reflecting on your day also helps you appreciate the joyous moments, which can boost your overall well-being and shift your focus from the negative to the positive.

To make the most of your daily reflections, it's helpful to use a structured worksheet. This worksheet can guide you through the reflection process, ensuring that you cover all the essential aspects of your day. Here's a template you can use:

1. **Significant Events**: Note the key events that stood out to you today. This could be anything from a joyful moment with your child to a stressful incident that triggered anger.

2. **Emotional Reactions and Triggers:** Describe your emotional reactions to these events. What emotions did you feel? What specific situations or behaviors triggered these emotions?

3. **Reflective Prompts:** Use guided prompts to delve deeper into your experiences. Questions like "What went well today?" can help you focus on the positive aspects of your day. "What situations triggered anger, and how did I respond?" encourages you to examine your emotional responses critically. "What can I do differently tomorrow?" helps you set intentions for improvement.

By using this template, you can systematically analyze your day and gain valuable insights into your emotions and behaviors. It's essential to approach this exercise with an open mind and a willingness to learn. The goal is not to judge yourself but to understand your reactions better and find ways to improve.

When analyzing your reflections, look for recurring triggers and patterns. Are there specific times of day or situations that consistently trigger anger? For example, you might notice that mornings are particularly stressful because everyone is rushing to get ready. Identifying these patterns allows you to anticipate and mitigate your triggers. You can then set specific goals for improvement. For instance, if mornings are a trigger, you might decide to wake up 15 minutes earlier to give yourself extra time to prepare.

Daily reflections also provide an opportunity to celebrate small victories. Acknowledge the moments when you effectively managed your emotions and responded calmly to challenging situations. These positive reinforcements can boost your confidence and motivate you to continue practicing emotional regulation.

Reflection Exercise

Take a few minutes each evening to fill out your daily reflection worksheet. Start by noting the significant events of the day, then describe your emotional reactions and triggers. Use the guided prompts to reflect on what went well, what triggered your anger, and what you can do differently tomorrow. Over time, this practice will help you gain deeper insights into your emotions and behaviors, enabling you to make intentional changes that lead to a more balanced and harmonious family life.

Incorporating daily reflections into your routine can be a transformative practice. It helps you understand your emotional triggers, recognize patterns in your behavior, and set goals for personal growth and improvement. By taking the time to reflect on your day, you can cultivate greater self-awareness and emotional regulation, ultimately fostering a more positive and supportive family environment.

Anger Trigger Identification Worksheets

Understanding what triggers your anger is crucial for effective management of your anger. Identifying these triggers helps you anticipate and mitigate your responses, allowing you to handle situations more calmly. The purpose of trigger identification is to bring awareness to the specific events or behaviors that provoke your anger. When you understand what triggers your reactions, you can develop strategies to manage them more effectively. This awareness reduces the frequency and intensity of anger outbursts, creating a more peaceful home environment.

Think about moments when your anger flares up unexpectedly. Maybe it's when your child refuses to listen, or perhaps it's the chaos of the morning rush. By identifying these triggers, you can prepare yourself for these situations and respond in a way that aligns with your values and parenting goals. Awareness of your triggers is the first step in breaking the cycle of reactive behavior. As you become more attuned to what provokes your anger, you can take proactive steps to manage your emotions and respond more constructively.

To help you systematically identify your triggers, a detailed worksheet can be handy. This worksheet will guide you through documenting specific events that trigger your anger and help you analyze your emotional and physical reactions. Here is a structured template you can use:

Identifying Your Anger Triggers Worksheet

1. Start by describing the situation that led to your anger. Be specific about what happened, where it occurred, and who was involved. For example, "My child refused to put on their shoes when we were already running late for school."

2. Emotional Reactions: Note your emotional response to the triggering event. What emotions did you feel? Anger, frustration, and irritation are common, but you might also experience feelings of helplessness or disappointment.

3. Physical Reactions: Describe how your body reacted to the situation. Did you feel your heart rate increase? Did your muscles tense up? Physical reactions can provide valuable insights into your emotional state.

4. Thoughts: Reflect on the thoughts that went through your mind during the triggering event. Were you thinking, "Why does this always happen?" or "I can't handle this right now"? Identifying these thoughts can help you understand the mental patterns that accompany your anger.

By using this template, you can create a comprehensive record of your anger triggers. This record will help you recognize patterns and understand the underlying causes of your anger. For example, you might notice that your anger is often triggered by situations where you feel a lack of control, such as when your children refuse to follow instructions.

To make the most of your trigger identification worksheet, it's essential to use it regularly. Set aside a few minutes each day to document any triggering events and your reactions. Over time, you'll start to see patterns that can inform your anger management strategies. For instance, if you notice that your anger is frequently triggered by the morning rush, you might decide to implement a more organized morning routine to reduce stress.

Review your worksheet weekly to identify recurring patterns and triggers. This regular review allows you to track your progress and make adjustments to your strategies as needed. It also helps you stay accountable and committed to your anger management goals. As you review your worksheet, look for common themes and consider how you can address them proactively.

Developing personalized coping strategies is another crucial aspect of using the trigger identification worksheet effectively. Once you've identified your triggers, think about specific actions you can take to manage your reactions. For example, if you know that your anger is triggered by your child's refusal to listen, you might decide to practice deep-breathing exercises before responding. Alternatively, you could use a calm-down corner to give yourself a few moments to regain composure.

Incorporating these strategies into your daily routine can significantly improve your ability to manage anger. For instance, if mornings are a common trigger, consider waking up a bit earlier to give yourself extra time to prepare. This small change can reduce the sense of urgency and create a calmer start to the day. Similarly, if sibling fights trigger your anger, establish clear rules and consequences for conflicts, and practice staying calm when enforcing them.

As you continue to use the trigger identification worksheet, you'll find that your awareness of your triggers increases. This heightened awareness allows you to anticipate challenging situations and respond more effectively. Over time, you'll develop a deeper understanding of your emotional landscape and gain greater control over your reactions.

Identifying your anger triggers is a powerful step towards effective anger management. By using a structured worksheet to document and analyze your triggers, you can gain valuable insights into your emotional responses and develop personalized strategies to manage them. This practice not only helps you reduce the frequency and intensity of anger outbursts but also fosters a more positive and supportive family environment.

Family Meeting Agendas and Worksheets

Family meetings can be transformative in fostering open communication and resolving conflicts. These meetings provide a structured platform where everyone, from the youngest to the oldest, can voice their thoughts, concerns, and ideas. When done regularly, family meetings can become a cornerstone of your household, promoting cooperation and reinforcing family rules. They create a safe space for each family member to express themselves, ensuring that everyone's voice is heard and valued. This practice helps reduce misunderstandings and fosters stronger relationships. Regular family meetings can also set the stage for problem-solving and collective decision-making, making everyone feel more involved and invested in the family's well-being.

One of the key benefits of family meetings is that they foster open communication and cooperation. In the hustle and bustle of daily life, it's easy for meaningful conversations to get lost. Family meetings carve out dedicated time to discuss issues, share updates, and plan. By setting it aside this time, you signal to your children that their opinions are valued and matter. This can be incredibly empowering for them, fostering a sense of responsibility and ownership. When children feel heard, they are more likely to cooperate and contribute positively to family dynamics. It's an opportunity to address any potential conflicts before they escalate, ensuring that everyone is aligned.

Family meetings also play a crucial role in setting and reinforcing family rules. Clear and consistent rules are essential for a harmonious household, but they must be communicated effectively to be followed. During these meetings, you can discuss the importance of each rule, its benefits to the family, and the consequences that will result if it is not followed. This transparency helps children understand the reasoning behind the rules, making them more likely to adhere to them. Additionally, involving children in the rule-setting process gives them a sense of agency, making them feel like active participants in the family unit rather than passive recipients of directives.

To make family meetings effective, it's helpful to use a structured agenda. This ensures that the meeting stays on track and covers all necessary topics. Here's a template you can use:

1. Welcome and Check-In: Begin with a warm welcome and a brief check-in to gauge everyone's current mood and well-being. This sets a positive tone for the meeting and allows you to gauge the mood of each family member.

2. Review of Previous Meeting: Go over the points discussed in the last meeting and check on the progress of any action items. This helps in maintaining continuity and accountability.

3. Discussion Points: List the main topics that need to be discussed. This could include anything from planning a family outing to addressing a recurring issue, like screen time or chores.

4. Open Floor: Allow each family member to bring up any concerns or ideas they have. This ensures that everyone gets a chance to speak and contributes to the meeting's agenda.

5. Decision Making: Summarize the key points discussed and make collective decisions. Ensure that everyone agrees on the action items and understands their responsibilities.

6. Wrap-Up and Positive Note: End the meeting on a positive note by sharing something uplifting or planning a fun family activity. This leaves everyone with a good feeling and reinforces the value of coming together.

Effective family meetings require some guidelines to ensure they are productive and respectful. First, set ground rules for respectful communication. Encourage everyone to listen actively, speak one at a time, and avoid interrupting. This creates an atmosphere of mutual respect and understanding. Make sure that everyone has an opportunity to speak. Use a talking stick or another object to designate the speaker, ensuring that each person gets their turn. This is especially important for younger children who might feel overshadowed by older siblings or adults.

Using family meeting worksheets can help track meeting outcomes and follow-up actions. These worksheets provide a written record of what was discussed, the decisions made, and the responsibilities assigned. This not only keeps everyone accountable but also serves as a reference for future meetings. For instance, you can include sections for summarizing the meeting's outcomes and noting action items. This way, you can easily review what was agreed upon and ensure that everyone follows through on their commitments. Over time, these records can also help you track your family's progress and celebrate milestones together.

Family Meeting Worksheet Template

1.   Date:

2.   Welcome and Check-In:

3.   Review of Previous Meeting:

4.   Discussion Points:

5.   Open Floor:

6.   Decisions Made:

7.   Action Items and Responsibilities:

8.   Wrap-Up and Positive Note:

By incorporating family meetings into your routine, you can create a structured environment where open communication and cooperation thrive. These meetings provide an invaluable opportunity to set and reinforce family rules, ensuring that everyone understands their role and responsibilities. Using a structured agenda and worksheets helps keep the meetings focused and productive, fostering a sense of unity and shared purpose. Over time, this practice can significantly improve your family dynamics, making your household a more harmonious and supportive place for everyone.

Progress Tracking Tools for Long-Term Success

Understanding the importance of tracking your progress in anger management and communication improvement cannot be overstated. Tracking progress helps maintain motivation and accountability. When you see tangible evidence of your growth, whether it's fewer angry outbursts or improved communication with your children, it fuels your determination to keep going. It also holds you accountable by providing a clear picture of where you stand and what areas require further improvement. Additionally, tracking helps identify trends and areas for continued growth. By reviewing your progress over time, you can identify patterns that may not be apparent in the moment. This awareness allows you to make informed adjustments to your strategies, ensuring that you're always moving forward.

To effectively track your progress, it's helpful to have a variety of tools at your disposal. Each tool can focus on a different aspect of your journey, providing a comprehensive view of your development. For anger management, an anger management progress tracker can be invaluable. This tracker can help you document each instance of anger, noting the frequency and intensity of your outbursts. By keeping a detailed log, you can identify specific triggers and observe how your responses change over time. This ongoing record provides a clear picture of your progress and identifies areas that require further attention.

Improving communication skills is another crucial aspect of creating a harmonious family environment. A communication skills improvement log can help you track your interactions with your children and other family members. This log can include entries about conversations where you successfully used reflective listening or "I" statements. It can also document instances where communication broke down, providing insights into what went wrong and how to improve. By regularly reviewing this log, you can track your growth in communication and identify areas that require further practice.

Emotional regulation is at the heart of managing anger and improving communication. A journal for emotional regulation practice can help you track your progress in this area. This journal can include entries about your daily mindfulness practices, deep-breathing exercises, and other techniques you use to stay calm. By documenting your practices and their effects, you can identify which methods work best for you and ensure that you're consistently incorporating them into your routine.

To make your tracking efforts more effective, it's important to use specific metrics and criteria. For instance, when tracking anger management, you can note the frequency and intensity of your outbursts. Were there fewer outbursts this week compared to last? Did you feel less intense anger in similar situations? These metrics provide a clear measure of your progress. For communication skills, you can track improvements in behaviors such as using reflective listening, "I" statements, and maintaining eye contact. Did you successfully use these techniques more often? Did they lead to better outcomes in your conversations?

Consistency in practicing emotional regulation techniques is another key metric. How often did you practice mindfulness or deep-breathing exercises? Did you notice a difference in your emotional state when you practiced regularly? By setting specific goals and milestones, you can give your efforts direction and purpose. For example, you might set a goal to practice deep-breathing exercises three times a day or to use reflective listening in every conversation with your child for a week.

Regularly reviewing your progress is essential for staying on track and making necessary adjustments. Set aside time each week to go over your trackers and journals. Look for patterns and trends that can inform your next steps. Are there specific times of day when you're more prone to anger? Are there particular situations where your communication skills shine or falter? Use these insights to adjust your strategies and set new goals. Maybe you need to focus more on morning routines or find new techniques for handling bedtime conflicts.

Incorporating these tracking tools into your routine might feel like an extra task at first, but the benefits far outweigh the effort. By keeping detailed records, you gain a clearer understanding of your progress and can celebrate your successes. You also create a roadmap for continued growth, ensuring that you're always moving towards a more harmonious family life.

Tracking your progress is not just about keeping tabs on your actions; it's about understanding your journey and making informed decisions to improve. With the right tools and a commitment to regular review, you can transform your efforts into lasting positive change. As you continue to use these tools, you'll find that your ability to manage anger and communicate effectively improves, creating a more peaceful and supportive environment for your family.

Conclusion

Our journey together through this book has been about providing you, a busy parent, with practical and easy-to-implement strategies for managing your emotions, improving communication, and creating lasting connections within your family. The vision was to offer straightforward, compassionate, and nonjudgmental advice, giving you the tools to navigate the emotional rollercoaster of parenting with more confidence and calm.

Throughout the chapters, we have explored various aspects of anger management and emotional regulation, always keeping in mind the unique challenges you face daily.

In Chapter 1, Understanding Parental Anger, we discussed the emotional highs and lows of parenting. We identified common anger triggers and explored how our childhood experiences shape our current parenting styles. Understanding what happens in our brains when we're angry and recognizing early warning signs are critical steps in learning to manage our emotions better.

Chapter 2, "Mindfulness and Stress Reduction Techniques," introduces mindfulness as a tool to help you stay calm amidst chaos. We covered deep-breathing exercises, quick meditation techniques, and visualization practices. By incorporating these into your daily routine, you can reduce stress and respond to parenting challenges with greater ease.

In Chapter 3, Practical Anger Management Strategies, we delved into techniques like the "Pause and Breathe" method, creating a calm-down corner, and using the S.T.O.P. method. We also discussed the importance of parental timeouts and the power of journaling for emotional regulation. These strategies provide immediate and long-term benefits in managing anger.

Chapter 4, Emotional Self-Reflection and Personal Growth, emphasized the value of self-reflective journaling, understanding your emotional triggers, and breaking negative cycles from your upbringing. We explored how self-compassion and setting personal boundaries can enhance your emotional health, fostering personal growth and resilience.

In Chapter 5, Effective Communication with Children, we focused on reflective listening, validating your child's emotions, and using "I" statements to express your feelings. Role-playing scenarios and navigating difficult conversations with empathy were also covered, highlighting the importance of consistent communication in building stronger relationships.

Chapter 6, Strategies for Reconnecting After Conflict, provided steps to rebuild trust after an outburst and the art of apologizing to your child. We discussed engaging in shared activities, using reconciliation rituals, and creating a family reconnection plan. The role of play in rebuilding bonds was also emphasized.

In Chapter 7, Building a Support System, we explored the importance of identifying potential support networks, leveraging online communities, and building supportive relationships with other parents. Utilizing local resources and groups, communicating your needs to your support system, and the benefits of professional counseling and therapy were key points covered.

Chapter 8, Consistency and Long-Term Success, highlighted the importance of creating a personal action plan for anger management, setting realistic goals, and tracking progress. We discussed dealing with setbacks, integrating anger management strategies into daily life, and encouraging family-wide emotional health. Celebrating success and continued growth were also emphasized.

Finally, Chapter 9, Practical Exercises and Worksheets, provided tools for daily reflection, anger trigger identification, family meeting agendas, and progress tracking. These exercises and worksheets are designed to help you internalize the strategies discussed and make lasting positive changes in your family dynamics.

Key Takeaways from this book include understanding and managing your anger, the power of mindfulness, the importance of effective communication, reconnecting after conflict, building a support system, and maintaining consistency for long-term success. By incorporating these strategies into your daily life, you can create a more harmonious and supportive family environment.

Now, it's time to take action. Implement the strategies discussed in this book. Start small, be consistent, and make adjustments as needed. Remember, change doesn't happen overnight, but with patience and persistence, you will see progress.

In closing, I want to remind you that parenting is a journey filled with challenges and rewards. It's okay to feel overwhelmed at times. What matters is how you respond and grow from those experiences. You have the tools and knowledge to make positive changes. Embrace them with confidence and compassion.

Thank you for allowing me to be a part of your journey. I'm here to support you, just as you strive to support and nurture your family. You've got this. Keep moving forward, and remember, every small step counts. Wishing you and your family a future filled with understanding, connection, and joy.

References

1. Kalil, A., Ryff, C. D., & Seeman, T. E. (2019). Maternal stress, sleep, and parenting.

   Psychoneuroendocrinology, 110, 104451. https://doi.org/10.1016/j.psyneuen.2019.104451

2. Palacios, N., Sharma, S., & Flynn, R. (2021). Daily stress and use of aggressive discipline by parents: A longitudinal study. Journal of Family Psychology, 35(8), 1042–1050. https://doi.org/10.1037/fam0000785

3. Davidson, R. J., & McEwen, B. S. (2011). Emotion regulation and brain plasticity: Implications for the treatment of affective disorders. Biological Psychiatry, 70(11), 958-964. https://doi.org/10.1016/j.biopsych.2011.05.032

4. Mindful Little Minds. (n.d.). Parenting triggers: 3 important things you should know. https://www.mindfullittleminds.com/managing-parenting-triggers/

5. Cherry, K. (2023). Mindful parenting: Benefits and strategies for raising kids. Verywell Mind. https://www.verywellmind.com/benefits-of-mindful-parenting-7254332

6. American Psychological Association. (n.d.). Mindfulness meditation: A research-proven way to reduce stress. https://www.apa.org/topics/mindfulness/meditation

7. WebMD. (n.d.). Breathing techniques for stress relief. https://www.webmd.com/balance/stressmanagement/stress-relief-breathing-techniques

8. Workman Publishing. (2021). 5-minute meditation for busy moms and dads. https://blog.workman.com/5-minute-meditation-busy-moms-dads

9. Raypole, C. (2020). Anger management exercises to help you stay calm. Healthline. https://www.healthline.com/health/anger-management-exercises

10. Strong4Life. (n.d.). Creating a calming corner at home for kids. https://www.strong4life.com/en/emotional-wellness/coping/creating-a-calming-corner-at-homefor-kids

11. Dialectical Behavior Therapy Tools. (n.d.). STOP skill - DBT tools. https://dbt.tools/emotional_regulation/stop.php

12. Centers for Disease Control and Prevention. (n.d.). Tips for using time-out | Essentials for parenting toddlers. https://www.cdc.gov/parenting-toddlers/time-out/index.html

13. University of Liverpool. (n.d.). Journaling to increase self-awareness. https://prosper.liverpool.ac.uk/postdoc-resources/reflect/journaling-to-increase-self-awareness/

14. Styles, C. (n.d.). Common parenting triggers and how to solve them. Camille Styles. https://camillestyles.com/wellness/parenting-triggers/

15. Psyched Mommy. (n.d.). 7 ways to break generational parenting cycles. https://www.psychedmommy.com/blog/7-ways-to-break-generational-parenting-cycles

16. Neff, K. (2019). Self-compassion for parents. Self-Compassion. https://self-compassion.org/wpcontent/uploads/2019/03/Self-Compassion-for-Parents-Greater-Good.pdf

17. West, H. (n.d.). Reflective listening for parents. https://www.harperwest.co/reflective-listeningfor-parents/

18. CHOC Children's. (n.d.). How to validate your child's feelings: Six steps for parents. https://health.choc.org/how-to-validate-your-childs-feelings-six-steps-for-parents-andcaregivers/

19. Boston University Medical Campus. (n.d.). Messages or "I" statements. https://www.bumc.bu.edu/facdev-medicine/files/2011/08/I-messages-handout.pdf

20. Christian Counseling & Educational Foundation. (n.d.). Role-playing: A creative parenting tool. https://www.ccef.org/role-playing-creative-parenting-tool/

21. First 5 California. (n.d.). Ideas for rebuilding trust with your child after a conflict. https://www.first5california.com/en-us/articles/ideas-for-rebuilding-trust-with-your-child-aftera-conflict/

22. Greater Good Science Center. (n.d.). Making an effective apology | Practice. Greater Good in Action. https://ggia.berkeley.edu/practice/making_an_effective_apology

23. The Stay-at-Home Mom Survival Guide. (n.d.). 55+ activities to strengthen the parent-child relationship. https://thestay-at-home-momsurvivalguide.com/activities-for-kids-parent-childrelationship/

24. Gobledale, T. (n.d.). Ritual of reconciliation for a distressed couple or family group. Worship Words. https://worshipwords.co.uk/ritual-of-reconciliation-for-a-distressed-couple-or-familygroup-tod-gobledale-uk/

25. Child Psych. (n.d.). The importance of a support network for parents. https://www.childpsych.co.za/the-importance-of-a-support-network-for-parents/

26. Center for Parent Information and Resources. (n.d.). Parent groups. https://www.parentcenterhub.org/parentgroups/

27. Wilksch, S. M., et al. (2017). The role of online social support in supporting and protecting mental health. Internet Interventions, 9, 51-58. https://doi.org/10.1016/j.invent.2017.06.003

28. Beverly Hills Psychology. (n.d.). Tips on how to effectively communicate your needs in a relationship. https://www.psychologybeverlyhills.com/blog/tips-on-how-to-effectivelycommunicate-your-needs-in-a-relationship

29. Mastering Anger. (n.d.). How to create an anger control plan. https://masteringanger.com/blog/anger-control-plan/

30. Verywell Mind. (n.d.). How to set and use SMART goals. https://www.verywellmind.com/smartgoals-for-lifestyle-change-2224097

31. Raising Children Network. (n.d.). Managing anger: Ideas for parents. https://raisingchildren.net.au/guides/first-1000-days/looking-after-yourself/anger-managementfor-parents

32. Abundance Therapy Center. (n.d.). Why everyone should learn anger management skills. https://www.abundancetherapycenter.com/blog/why-everyone-should-learn-anger-managementskills

33. Huckleberry. (n.d.). What is positive parenting self-reflection? https://huckleberrycare.com/blog/what-is-positive-parenting-self-reflection

34. Understood.org. (n.d.). Identifying your child's behavior triggers. https://www.understood.org/en/podcasts/parenting-behavior/identify-child-behavior-triggers

35. Fellow. (n.d.). Family meetings: What are they? 12 tips to make them successful. https://fellow.app/blog/meetings/tips-for-running-successful-and-fun-family-meetings/

36. Military OneSource. (n.d.). AIMS for anger management mobile app. https://www.militaryonesource.mil/resources/mobile-apps/aims-for-anger-management/

Appendix:

Use Prompts to Simplify: Each day, answer these three quick prompts:

- What went well today?

- What challenged me today?

- What's one thing I'm grateful for?

Focus on Small Wins: Keep entries short—one or two sentences are enough. This makes it easier to commit daily and still reflect on important aspects of your day.

Set a Timer: Dedicate just 5 minutes before bed or in the morning for journaling. Having a time limit reduces the pressure to write long entries.

Use Your Phone: For ultimate convenience, use a note-taking app or a dedicated journaling app, so you can jot down thoughts while on the go—during kids' naps, while waiting in the car, or between tasks.

Be Flexible: If daily journaling feels too much, start with 2-3 times a week. The key is consistency rather than frequency.

We'd Love Your Feedback!

Your voice matters—and so does your experience.

This book was written with care, compassion, and deep research to support real parents facing real challenges. If Anger Management Solutions for Parents helped you find clarity, calm, or even just a few moments of peace in the chaos, we'd be truly grateful if you could share your thoughts.

Your review not only helps others discover this resource—it also supports our mission of creating stronger, more connected families.

Please take a moment to leave a review on Amazon or wherever you purchased the book. Just a few words can make a big difference.

Thank you for being a part of this journey

PART -II

Anger Management for Teens Mad to Calm

Holistic approaches, Practical exercises, and Valuable Insights to help Overcome Challenges, Manage

Anger, and Build Emotional Resilience

By
Agnes Blake

Introduction

Why Your Emotions Matter and How This Book Can Help

Have you ever felt like your anger gets the best of you? Maybe it's when your blood starts boiling because your friend didn't text back or a sibling borrowed something without asking. It's as if a storm suddenly erupts inside, and you're left wondering how to calm it down. If that sounds familiar, you're not alone.

I remember being a teen and feeling like my emotions were a rollercoaster I couldn't control. One day, I was on top of the world, and the next, I was angry at everything—from schoolwork to friends. There was one time when I lost my cool at a soccer game. I was so frustrated with my performance that I yelled at my teammates. Looking back, I wish I had known then what I know now about managing anger and emotions.

This book is here to help you navigate those stormy emotions with practical tools and techniques. It's designed to give you the skills to manage anger, improve emotional intelligence, and build healthier relationships. We'll explore ways to turn anger into something positive, using it as a stepping stone for growth rather than a stumbling block.

The book is structured to guide you step-by-step. We'll start by understanding what anger is and why we feel it. Then, we'll explore techniques to calm down at the moment and dig deeper into the roots of our frustrations. From there, we'll tackle the pressures teens face today, like social media stress and peer relationships. Each chapter builds on the latter, creating a roadmap to emotional balance and self-awareness.

This journey will benefit you as a teen and be a valuable resource for parents. Parents will gain insights into supporting their child's emotional growth and learn strategies to strengthen family bonds.

Together, families can work towards creating an environment where everyone feels understood and respected.

Let's face it—being a teen today isn't easy. There are academic pressures, the constant buzz of social media, and the challenge of fitting in with peers. These stresses can build up, and sometimes anger is the only way to express them. Acknowledging these challenges is the first step in managing them.

By the end of this book, you can expect to feel more in control of your emotions. You'll gain self-awareness, learn how to communicate effectively and find a greater sense of emotional balance. These skills will not only help you now but will also set a strong foundation for the future.

I invite you to embark on this journey of transformation. The exercises, reflections, and stories you'll find here are not just words on a page. They're tools for change, meant to be engaged with and reflected upon. This book is more than a guide—it's a partner in your journey toward personal growth and family harmony.

So, let's get started. Together, we'll turn anger from a force that divides into a force that unites and empowers. Grab your pen and journal for an unforgettable journey!

Chapter 10:
Understanding Anger and Its Roots

Discover the "Why" Behind Your Reactions and What Fuels the Fire

Have you ever wondered why a seemingly minor comment from a friend could send you into a spiral of irritation or why a minor mishap can feel like the end of the world? Anger can be puzzling, especially when it seems to erupt out of nowhere. It's like having an unpredictable storm brewing inside, catching you off guard. As a teen, I often felt like I was constantly battling these unexpected tempests, unsure of why they happened or how to calm them. Understanding the roots of anger is the first step toward managing it, and that journey begins in the brain, where tiny, unseen processes significantly impact how we feel and respond.

The Science of Anger: What Happens in Your Brain

When you experience anger, your brain is complicated at work, processing emotions in complex ways. At the heart of this process is the amygdala, a small, almond-shaped cluster of nuclei deep within the brain. The amygdala acts like an emotional alarm system. It's quick to react to perceived threats or stressors, signaling something is wrong, which can trigger an immediate emotional response. This is what often leads to intense feelings of anger. But the amygdala doesn't work alone. The prefrontal cortex, located at the front of the brain, plays a crucial role in regulating these emotions. It helps you analyze situations, consider consequences, and make rational decisions. However, the amygdala can override the prefrontal cortex during intense anger, leading to impulsive reactions without much thought. This is particularly true during adolescence when the brain is still developing, and the prefrontal cortex is not yet fully matured (SOURCE 1).

Hormones like adrenaline and cortisol also affect how you experience anger. Adrenaline, often called the "fight or flight" hormone, prepares your body to react to threats by increasing your heart rate and energy levels. Cortisol, the stress hormone, helps your body manage long-term stress. Together, these hormones can heighten emotional states, making anger more intense and immediate. Adolescents are susceptible to these hormonal changes, exacerbating emotional responses (SOURCE 1).

Beyond these immediate reactions, the concept of neuroplasticity offers hope. Neuroplasticity is the brain's ability to reorganize itself by forming new neural connections. Your brain can change and adapt based on your experiences and practices. By consistently applying anger management techniques, you can train your brain to respond differently, enhancing emotional control over time. This adaptability is key in transforming how you perceive and react to frustrating situations, allowing you to respond more calmly and thoughtfully.

Understanding these biological processes can empower you to manage your emotions more effectively. Knowing why your body reacts in a certain way makes it easier to take control. You can start recognizing the signs of an emotional response before it spirals, allowing you to engage your prefrontal cortex and make conscious choices about reacting. This knowledge turns anger from a mysterious and overpowering force into something you can manage and use to your advantage. Recognizing these brain mechanisms helps demystify anger, allowing you to approach it with curiosity and understanding rather than fear or frustration.

Source 1

Dynamic mapping of human cortical development

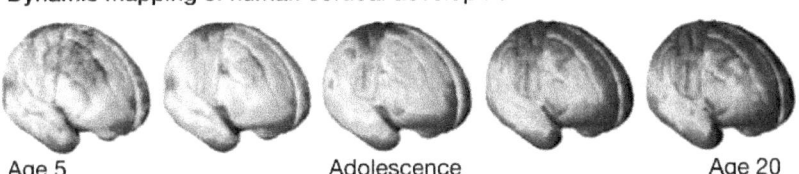

Age 5   Adolescence   Age 20

Source: "Dynamic mapping of human cortical development during childhood through early adulthood." Nitin Gogtay et al., Proceedings of the National Academy of Sciences, May 25, 2004; California Institute of Technology.

Interactive Element: Stress and Anger Checklist

Take a moment to reflect on situations that typically trigger your anger. Grab a notebook and write down these triggers. Next to each, note how your body and mind respond. Do you feel your heart racing?

Does your mind start racing with thoughts? This exercise helps you recognize patterns in your emotional responses, providing insight into your brain's workings. Understanding these patterns is the first step in changing them, giving you more control over your reactions and helping you to approach situations with a calmer mindset.

Stress and Anger Checklist

Take a moment to reflect on your emotions and responses. Use the prompts below to guide your journaling. Write your answers directly on the lines provided.

Step 1: Identify Your Triggers

What situations or events typically make you feel angry or stressed?

Example: Being stuck in traffic, feeling misunderstood, or being criticized.

Write your triggers below:

_____

_____

_____

_____

Step 2: Observe Your Physical Reactions

How does your body respond in these moments? *Example: Heart racing, muscle tension, or stomach discomfort.* Write your physical reactions below:

_____

_____

_____

_____

Step 3: Track Your Mental Reactions

What happens in your mind when you feel angry or stressed? *Example: Racing thoughts, jumping to conclusions, or feeling overwhelmed.* Write your mental reactions below:

_____

_____

_____

_____

Step 4: Reflect on the Patterns

Look at your responses above. Do you notice any patterns in how you react?

Example: I often clench my fists when angry or assume the worst in stressful situations.

Write your observations below:

_____

_____

_____

_____

Step 5: Commit to Change

How can you use this awareness to respond differently in the future? *Example: Practice deep breathing, count to ten, or take a moment to step away.* Write your action plan below:

_____

_____

_____

_____

This journaling exercise helps you become more mindful of your emotional patterns, paving the way for positive change!

Hormonal Hurricanes: Navigating Teenage Changes

The teenage years are a whirlwind of change, and much of it is driven by hormones. Puberty is like a storm that sweeps through, changing not just your body but also your emotions and how you see the world. It's no wonder that anger can sometimes feel like a constant companion during this time. Hormones like testosterone and estrogen take the stage during these years, each uniquely shaping emotional experiences. For many boys, increased levels of testosterone can lead to heightened aggression and irritability. While essential for growth and development, this hormone often amplifies feelings of competitiveness and frustration.

FEELINGS AND EMOTIONS

Identifying feelings and emotions is crucial because it helps understand ourselves, communicate effectively with others, and build strong, empathetic relationships.

CHEERFUL — EXCITED — SATISFIED
HAPPY — PROUD — LOVED
PLAYFUL — CALM — SICK
EMBARRASSED — SURPRISED — SHY
SLEEPY — SAD — ANGRY
TIRED — WORRIED — HURT
DISAPPOINTED — CONFUSED — SCARED

Meanwhile, girls experience fluctuations in estrogen, which can lead to mood swings that sometimes feel out of control. These hormonal changes aren't biological but deeply intertwined with how we perceive and react to the world.

These hormonal shifts impact boys and girls differently. Boys might feel a surge of energy and impatience, leading to outbursts over things that seem trivial later. On the other hand, girls might find themselves riding an emotional rollercoaster, where one moment, they're elated, and the next, they're in tears. Understanding these differences can be enlightening, not just for teens but for parents, too. It highlights the need for empathy and patience, as these changes are part of growing up. The way these hormones influence emotions can sometimes make it feel like they're running the show, but there are ways to regain control.

Managing these hormonal impacts involves a combination of healthy habits and open communication. Diet plays a crucial role in stabilizing mood. Eating balanced meals with whole grains, lean proteins, and plenty of fruits and vegetables can help maintain energy levels and emotional stability. Regular exercise is another powerful tool. Physical activity releases endorphins, the body's natural mood lifters, which can counteract feelings of anger and frustration. Sleep, often overlooked, is vital. A good night's rest can significantly influence how you handle stress and emotions the next day. When well-rested, you're more likely to think clearly and react calmly.

Open dialogue about these changes is key. Talking about what you're going through with someone you trust—a parent, teacher, or friend—can be incredibly freeing. It's important to remember that you're not alone in this. Everyone goes through it, and having a support system can make a difference. Expressing how these hormonal changes affect you can help those around you understand your behavior better. It can also lead to finding solutions together, whether adjusting your routine or finding new ways to cope with overwhelming feelings.

Interactive Element: Hormonal Journal Prompts

Find hormones confusing? To help you navigate these changes, try keeping a journal. Here are a few prompts to get you started:

"Describe a day when you felt overly angry or emotional. What triggered those feelings?" "Reflect on the times you felt calm and in control. What were you doing differently?" Writing about your experiences can help you identify patterns and find strategies that work for you. This practice enables you to understand yourself better and provides a space to vent and process your emotions safely. Use the worksheet below:

Worksheet: Hormonal Journal Prompts

Understanding and Managing Your Emotions

Keeping a journal is a great way to explore your emotions, identify triggers, and discover what works for you in managing your feelings. Use the following prompts to reflect on your experiences and better understand your emotional responses.

Part 1: Reflecting on Emotional Responses

1. **Describe a day when you felt overly angry or emotional.**

   o What happened that day?

   o What triggered your feelings?

   o How did you react to those emotions?

   (Write your response here.)

   _____

   _____

   _____

2. **Reflect on the times you felt calm and in control.**

   o What was different about those moments?

   o What were you doing to stay calm and balanced?

o   How did it feel to have control over your emotions?

(Write your response here.)

_____

_____

_____

Part 2: Identifying Patterns

After completing the above reflections, review your answers and consider the following questions:

- Do you notice any common triggers for your intense emotions?

- Are there activities, environments, or people that help you feel calm and in control?

- What changes can you make to your daily routine to effectively manage your emotions?

(Write your response here.)

_____

_____

_____

Part 3: Setting Goals and Strategies

Based on your reflections:

1. **What is one thing you can do differently next time you feel overwhelmed?** *(Write your goal here.)*

_____

2. **What can you do to create more calm moments?**

(Write your strategy here.)

_____

_____

Tips for Successful Journaling

- Write honestly and without judgment—this journal is for you.

- Try to journal regularly, even if it's just for a few minutes a day.

- Use this space to vent, brainstorm, and explore solutions to help you grow.

By taking the time to write and reflect, you're investing in your personal growth and well-being. Keep practicing, and you'll find strategies that work best over time!

Family Dynamics: The Role of Home Environment

Family can be a source of comfort and support and a pressure cooker of emotions and expectations. How a family interacts can significantly influence a teen's emotional state, often tipping the scales toward either peace or turmoil. For instance, parents' guidance and discipline can make a big difference. An authoritative style, which balances firm guidance with warmth and open communication, can help teens feel secure and understood. In contrast, an authoritarian approach—strict, with little room for dialogue—may leave teens feeling trapped and rebellious, leading to more frequent outbursts of anger. It's like being in a classroom where the teacher only shouts orders without explaining why; eventually, frustration bubbles over.

HAVING FAMILY
* TIME IS *
IMPORTANT

Spending time with your family can increase happiness and satisfaction

WHY DO WE NEED TO SPEND TIME WITH OUR FAMILY?

Spending quality time with your family can encourage open communication and help establish loving relationships

OTHER BENEFITS OF SPENDING TIME WITH FAMILY

• Strengthen family bonds
• Promotes adaptability and resilience
• Fulfills emotional needs
• Boosts Self-Confidence

Sibling rivalry adds another layer of complexity to family dynamics. Competition for attention or resources can stoke the fires of resentment and anger. Imagine constantly feeling like you're in a race with your sibling, vying for the limited spotlight in a busy household. This competitive environment can significantly exacerbate feelings of inadequacy and frustration if one sibling consistently outshines the other. These dynamics can create a cycle of rivalry and anger, making home life more like a battlefield than a haven.

External stressors also play a significant role in shaping the emotional climate at home. Financial stress can be a silent yet powerful force, casting a long shadow over family interactions. When money is tight, tensions can rise, and everyone feels the ripple effects. Teens might pick up on the stress, leading to feelings of anxiety and anger that aren't always easy to articulate. Similarly, parental conflict—

frequent arguments or a tense silence—can leave a teen feeling caught in the middle, unsure how to navigate the emotional minefield. These stressors can amplify emotional responses, making it harder for teens to regulate anger.

Creating a supportive home environment starts with open communication. It's about building a space where everyone feels heard and valued. This means having regular family check-ins, where members can express what's on their minds without fear of judgment. It's like opening a window in a stuffy room, letting fresh air and light in. This practice helps identify and address issues before they escalate and strengthens family bonds. Parents and teens can work together to create family rules or agreements, fostering a sense of shared responsibility and respect.

Encouraging honest conversations about feelings and challenges can transform a household. It's essential to approach these talks with empathy and patience, understanding that everyone is working through their struggles. For example, a teen might not always know how to articulate their anger, but with gentle guidance, they can learn to communicate more effectively. This might involve using "I" statements, such as "I feel upset when..." instead of placing blame. Parents can model this behavior, showing teens how to express emotions constructively and calmly, turning potential conflicts into opportunities for growth.

Like in any group, family dynamics can shift and change over time. Acknowledging this fluidity and being willing to adapt is key. By fostering a nurturing and communicative environment, families can create a foundation where teens feel supported in navigating their emotions. This support can act as a buffer against adolescence's external pressures and internal changes, offering teens a stable base to face the world.

Past Experiences: Unpacking Childhood Influences

The past has a funny way of sticking with us, sometimes in ways we don't even realize. Early experiences linger beneath the surface for many teenagers, quietly shaping reactions and feelings. It's like when a song from childhood suddenly plays, and you're flooded with memories—some good, some not so much. Past traumas or significant events can leave marks on our emotional skin, influencing how we respond to the world around us. Whether it's a memory of being bullied in elementary school or the ache of a parent's divorce, these experiences can affect the way you handle anger today. Childhood trauma, in particular, can be like carrying a heavy backpack you forgot you were wearing. It affects your posture, your movements, and sometimes, your mood. The weight of those early experiences can manifest as quick tempers or unexplained sadness, even years later.

Beyond specific events, early attachment styles play a critical role in how emotions unfold during the teenage years. Attachment theory suggests that how you bond with caregivers as a child influences your relationships and emotional responses as you grow. For instance, a secure attachment tends to foster confidence and resilience. However, if the attachment is anxious or avoidant, it might lead to feelings of insecurity or difficulty trusting others. Imagine building a house on shaky ground; it might stand for a while, but the foundation could give way under stress. Recognizing these influences can be the first step toward understanding why certain situations trigger intense emotions.

Recognizing signs of unresolved past issues isn't always straightforward. It might be as simple as noticing patterns—like reacting disproportionately to criticism or feeling overwhelmed in specific situations. For a teen, this could mean realizing that every time a teacher raises their voice, it reminds them of past scoldings, triggering a defensive response. Parents, too, might notice that their

teen withdraws after family arguments, a sign that echoes past experiences. These behaviors can be clues pointing to the past, asking for attention and understanding.

Addressing these lingering effects involves more than just acknowledgment. It requires actively working through them, often with help. Therapy and counseling are potent tools for unpacking these emotions and learning new coping methods. A therapist can offer a safe space to explore these feelings, providing strategies to heal and move forward. They act as guides, helping you navigate the complex landscape of your emotions. Journaling can also be incredibly therapeutic. You create a dialogue with yourself by writing down thoughts and feelings, uncovering hidden emotions and patterns. It's like holding up a mirror to your mind, reflecting on what you see without judgment.

Resilience and growth aren't just buzzwords but tangible outcomes from facing past challenges. There are countless stories of individuals who have overcome difficult childhoods to build fulfilling lives. These stories inspire and remind us that the past doesn't have to define the future. Take, for example, someone who grew up in a tumultuous household yet learned to channel their experiences into a passion for helping others. Their past became a source of strength and empathy rather than a chain holding them back. This transformation is possible for anyone willing to face their history with courage and openness.

Building resilience means embracing the lessons of the past while forging a new path forward. It's about accepting that while you can't change what happened, you can change how it affects you. This process takes time, patience, and, often, a bit of help. But it's a journey worth taking, leading to a deeper understanding of yourself and a more peaceful relationship with your emotions. Embracing this growth can help turn past challenges into stepping stones, rather than stumbling blocks, on the path to emotional health.

Peer Pressure: Fitting In vs. Standing Out

Peer pressure is an invisible force that can feel overwhelming, especially during the teenage years when fitting in seems vital. Imagine being in a school cafeteria where everyone's wearing the latest sneakers, and you're stuck in last year's kicks. It's not just about shoes; it's about wanting to belong. This pressure to conform can lead to frustration and anger, particularly when it clashes with personal values. It's as if you're wearing a mask to fit in, suppressing your true self to avoid standing out for fear of exclusion. This fear can become a powerful motivator, pushing teens to act against their nature to remain in the group.

The constant need to compare oneself with others adds another layer to this struggle. Social comparison is like a double-edged sword. On one hand, it's natural to look around and see what others are doing. On the other hand, it can exacerbate feelings of inadequacy and anger. When everyone else seems to have it all together or looks perfect, it's easy to feel like you don't measure up. This can lead to anger directed inward, as you berate yourself for not being enough, or outward, as you lash out at others for seemingly having it more manageable. It's a cycle that can be hard to break, feeding on insecurity and self-doubt.

So, how do you resist the negative pull of peer pressure while staying true to yourself? It begins with assertiveness, a skill that allows you to stand firm in your beliefs without alienating others. Think of assertiveness as saying, "This is who I am, and I'm okay with it." It's about setting boundaries and expressing your needs clearly, even when it feels intimidating. Building a supportive network of friends who respect and encourage your individuality can make a significant difference. These friends celebrate your quirks and support your choices, providing a safe space to be yourself without fear of judgment.

Authenticity is your most incredible tool. Embracing what makes you unique is not just empowering; it's liberating. When you stop trying to fit into a mold that doesn't suit you, you can channel your energy into pursuits that genuinely bring you joy and fulfillment. Whether it's a passion for painting, a love for science fiction, or an interest in environmental activism, these are the things that define you. They are the colors that paint your canvas, making you stand out in the best possible way.

The value of being authentic cannot be overstated. It builds self-confidence and creates a ripple effect, inspiring others to do the same. It's like being a beacon in the fog, showing others that it's okay to be different. When you embrace your true self, you attract the right people into your life—the ones who appreciate you for who you are, not who you're pretending to be. This authenticity creates genuine connections and deepens existing relationships, allowing you to form bonds based on mutual respect and understanding.

Navigating peer pressure is challenging but also an opportunity to learn more about who you are and what you stand for. Each time you choose to be yourself, you strengthen your character and resilience despite the pressure to conform. It's a step toward self-discovery and personal growth, replacing anger and frustration with confidence and peace.

Digital Distress: The Impact of Social Media

Picture this: you wake up, and the first thing you do is grab your phone. Notifications flood the screen, drawing you into a world of endless scrolling. Social media is everywhere, and while it connects us, it also brings a unique set of challenges. Imagine the constant connectivity like a buzzing background noise that never lets you relax. It's no wonder that this digital world can lead to increased anxiety and anger. The pressure to stay connected and the fear of missing out can create a cycle of stress that's hard to break. Social media platforms, while offering a sense of community, often become arenas for comparison and competition. Every post, like, or comment adds pressure to maintain a perfect online persona. It's like curating an art gallery where each piece must be flawless, leaving no room for vulnerability or imperfection. This pressure can lead to feelings of inadequacy and frustration, as the desire to project a particular image overshadows the reality of who you are.

Cyberbullying is another dark side of this digital space. It's an issue that can't be ignored. The internet's anonymity can embolden individuals to say things they'd never dare to utter face-to-face. Hurtful comments and messages can have a profound emotional toll, leaving scars that aren't visible but are deeply felt. It's the modern-day equivalent of whispers behind your back, but they can only reach you anytime, anywhere. This can lead to feelings of isolation and anger as victims struggle with the constant barrage of negativity.

The effects of digital interactions on self-esteem are significant. Social media often sets an unrealistic standard for beauty, success, and happiness. It's easy to fall into the trap of measuring your worth by the number of likes or comments. This digital validation becomes a double-edged sword, providing temporary gratification and fueling a more profound sense of inadequacy when the likes don't match expectations. It's like chasing a moving target, always out of reach, leaving a trail of frustration and self-doubt.

To combat this digital distress, adopting healthy digital habits is crucial. Think of it like setting boundaries in any other relationship. Scheduled digital detox periods can provide much-needed breaks from the constant influx of information. Unplugging for a few hours each day or dedicating a day a week to being offline allows your mind and emotions to rest and reset, much like a mini-vacation for your brain. Mindful social media usage is another powerful tool. This means being intentional about how and when you engage online. Consider curating your feed to include content that inspires and uplifts rather than comparing or critiquing.

Promoting a positive digital presence is about using social media as a platform for good. Focus on sharing content that reflects your true self, interests, and passions. Whether posting about a hobby, sharing a personal achievement, or simply connecting with others over shared interests, use your online presence to express who you are authentically. It's about shifting from a place of performance to a genuine connection. By doing this, you improve your experience and contribute to a more supportiveand positive online community.

In this hyper-connected world, finding a balance between online and offline life is key. It's not about cutting out social media entirely but using it to enhance rather than detract from your life. By setting boundaries and focusing on authentic connections, you can navigate the digital landscape with confidence and calm. This approach reduces digital stress and strengthens your mental and emotional well-being, allowing you to engage with the world—both online and offline—in a healthier, more balanced way.

Chapter 11: Developing Emotional Intelligence

Know Yourself, Name Your Emotions, and Take Back Control

I magine being in a heated argument, where your heart races and your mind is a whirlwind of thoughts. We've all been there, feeling that rush of emotions and not knowing how to handle it. Emotional intelligence is about understanding these feelings and learning to manage them effectively. It's like having a toolbox for your emotions, where each tool helps you handle different situations more skillfully. Developing this intelligence is not just about feeling better but thriving in your relationships and personal life.

Recognizing emotional triggers is crucial and often the first step toward emotional control. Triggers are those little things that trigger an emotional reaction, sometimes so quickly that you barely notice them until you're upset. It could be unfair treatment in a group project at school, where one person doesn't pull their weight, leaving you to pick up the slack. Or perhaps it's the pressure of an upcoming exam, with expectations bearing down on you like a heavyweight. These situations can provoke anger, and understanding why they affect you so deeply is key to managing your reactions.

To identify these triggers, start by reflecting on your past experiences. Keep an emotional diary—it's a simple yet powerful tool. Write down moments when you felt angry, noting what happened, who was involved, and how it made you think. Over time, patterns will emerge. You may notice that certain situations consistently provoke a strong response. Maybe it's when you're in crowded places or when plans change unexpectedly. These insights are invaluable because they help you predict and prepare for similar situations in the future.

Once you've identified your triggers, the next step is to anticipate them. This doesn't mean avoiding life but equipping yourself with strategies to handle challenging scenarios. Visualization is a practical technique. Picture a situation that might provoke you, like a competitive sports match or a group discussion.

Imagine how you might feel and visualize yourself handling it calmly and confidently. This mental rehearsal prepares your mind, making you more likely to respond with poise when the situation arises.

Developing proactive responses is about planning constructive ways to deal with known triggers. Think of it as creating a personal action plan. For example, if public speaking makes you anxious, you should practice deep breathing before and during the event. Or if you know a particular friend's teasing tends to upset you, decide in advance to address it directly and calmly. Having these strategies ready is like having a map in unfamiliar territory—it guides you and helps prevent emotional outbursts.

Interactive Element: Trigger Reflection Exercise

Take a moment to jot down a few situations that often spark anger. Next to each, write how you typically react and consider how you might respond differently. This exercise isn't about judging your past reactions but exploring new possibilities and preparing for future encounters.

Building emotional intelligence is an ongoing process. It's about learning to navigate life's ups and downs with greater ease and understanding. Recognizing triggers and preparing for them, you develop resilience and self-awareness, paving the way for healthier relationships and a more balanced life. Whether you're a teen facing the daily challenges of school or a parent navigating family dynamics, these skills are invaluable. They empower you to take control of your emotional landscape and respond to life's challenges confidently and calmly.

Anger Reflection Journal

Date: [Insert Date] _____

Part1: Identifying Situations That Spark Anger

Take a moment to reflect on

recent situations that have triggered anger.

Write down a few examples describing

the context and the emotions you felt.

1.   **Situation:** [Brief description of the event]

_____
_____

_____
_____

_____
_____

- o **How I Typically React:** [Describe your usual response]

_____

_____

_____

_____

- o **How I Could Respond Differently:**
  [Write a potential new approach]

_____

_____

_____

_____

_____

_____

2. **Situation:** [Brief description of the event]

_____

_____

_____

_____

- o **How I Typically React:** [Describe your usual response]

_____

_____

_____

_____

o   **How I Could Respond Differently:**
[Write a potential new approach]

_____

_____

_____

_____

3.   **Situation:** [Brief description of the event}

_____

_____

_____

_____

o   **How I Typically React:** [Describe your usual response]

_____

_____

_____

_____

o   **How I Could Respond Differently:** [Write a potential new approach]

_____

_____

_____

_____

Part 2: Reflecting on Patterns and Possibilities

Answer the following questions to deepen your understanding:

1. **What common themes or triggers do I notice in these situations?** [Write your response here]

   _____

   _____

   _____

   _____

2. **How do my typical reactions affect my relationships and personal well-being?** [Write your response here]

   _____

   _____

   _____

   _____

3. **What tools or strategies could help me respond more calmly and constructively?** [Write your response here]

   _____

   _____

   _____

   _____

4. **How can I remind myself to use these new approaches in the moment?** [Write your response here]

   _____

   _____

_____

_____

Part 3: Building Emotional Intelligence Reflect on the
importance of emotional growth and resilience in managing anger.

1. **What have I learned about myself through this
   exercise?**
   [Write your response here]

_____

_____

_____

_____

2. **How can recognizing and preparing for triggers help
   me navigate challenges more effectively?** [Write your
   response here]

_____

_____

_____

_____

3. **What steps can I take to continue developing
   emotional intelligence?** [Write your response here]

_____

_____

_____

_____

Part 4: Moving Forward Summarize your insights and identify one specific action you can take to practice a healthier response to anger.

- **Summary:** [Write your summary here]

_____

_____

_____

_____

- **Actionable Step:** [Write one small, specific step you'll take]

_____

_____

_____

_____

This journal is a space for self-exploration and growth. Revisiting it regularly can help you stay attuned to your progress and remain committed to building resilience, self-awareness, and healthier relationships.

Self-Awareness Exercises: Know Thyself

Have you ever wondered why certain events stir up strong emotions while others barely make a ripple? Self-awareness is like a spotlight that illuminates these hidden corners of your mind, offering clarity and understanding. Developing this awareness starts with self-reflection, a practice that invites you to look

closely at your thoughts and feelings. Each day, set aside a few moments to ask yourself questions like, "What emotions did I experience today?" or "How did I react to challenges?" This daily reflection helps you connect the dots between your experiences and emotions, revealing patterns you might not have noticed before. It's like piecing together a puzzle, where each answer brings a new level of understanding.

Another powerful tool for self-discovery is personality assessments, like the Myers-Briggs Type Indicator (MBTI). This assessment helps you explore your emotional tendencies, highlighting your natural preferences and how they shape your interactions with the world. For instance, you might discover that you're more introverted, finding energy in solitude, or perhaps you're an extrovert, thriving in social settings. Understanding these traits can clarify why you react differently in different situations. Analyzing your personality profile is like looking at a map; it shows where you are now and offers insight into how you navigate life. While the MBTI is not the definitive word on who you are, it provides a framework for exploring your strengths and areas for growth.

Once you have a clearer picture of your personality, you can move on to identifying your core values—those guiding principles that influence your decisions and emotional responses. Imagine these values as the compass that directs your actions and choices. They might include honesty, compassion, or creativity. Spend some time reflecting on what matters most to you and why. This could be a

values identification workshop, where you list things that resonate deeply with you. Knowing your values is like having a personal guidebook; it helps you understand why certain situations evoke strong emotions and ensures your actions align with your beliefs.

Promoting self-compassion is equally crucial, especially when emotions are running high. Being kind to yourself means recognizing that everyone struggles and makes mistakes—including you. Instead of harsh self-criticism, practice speaking to yourself as you would to a friend, with understanding and patience. When you catch yourself in a critical thought loop, pause and ask, "Would I say this to someone I care about?" This shift in perspective can transform your inner dialogue, fostering a nurturing environment where growth and healing can occur. It's about permitting yourself to be human, to experience a range of emotions without judgment.

Interactive Element: Personal Values Reflection

To explore your core values, try this exercise. Write down ten qualities or principles that feel important to you. Then, narrow the list to five, focusing on the most resonating. Reflect on how these values influence your daily life and decisions. This practice clarifies what drives you and strengthens your sense of self, providing a solid foundation for emotional intelligence.

These self-awareness exercises are more than just activities; they're pathways to understanding yourself better. By engaging in self-reflection, personality assessments, and values exploration, you create a rich tapestry of insights that guide you through life's emotional landscape. Coupled with self-compassion, these practices empower you to embrace your unique identity and navigate challenges gracefully and confidently. As you deepen your self-awareness, you unlock new potential for emotional growth, transforming how you relate to yourself and others.

Personal Values Reflection Journal

Date: _____

Part 1: Identifying My Core Values

Take a moment to brainstorm and list ten qualities or principles you hold dear. These could be traits, beliefs, or ideas that define who you are or guide your actions.

1. _____
   _____

2. _____
   _____

3. _____
   _____

4. _____
   _____

5. _____
   _____

6. _____
   _____

7. _____
   _____

8. _____
   _____

9. _____
   _____

10. _____
    _____

Part 2: Narrowing Down to My Top Five Values

Review the list above and reflect on which values resonate with you most deeply. Select the five values most essential to your identity and life decisions.

1._____

_____

2._____

_____

3._____

_____

4._____

_____

5._____

_____

Part 3: Reflecting on My Values

Answer the following questions to deepen your understanding of how these values influence your life:

1. Why do these five values stand out to me?
[Write your response here]

_____

_____

2. How do these values influence my daily choices and actions?
[Write your response here]

_____

_____

3. How do these values guide me during challenging times?
[Write your response here]

_____

_____

4. What can I do to further embody these values in my life?
[Write your response here]

_____

_____

Part 4: Moving Forward

Summarize your reflections and identify one actionable step to strengthen your alignment with your core values.

- **Summary:**

- **Actionable Step:**
[Write one specific step you'll take]

Emotional Vocabulary: Naming Your Feelings

Imagine trying to describe a painting using only a handful of colors. You might capture the basic outlines, but the nuances, depth, and emotion would be lost. Emotions are a lot like that. When we limit ourselves to basic terms like "happy" or "angry," we miss the richness of our emotional experiences. There's a whole spectrum of feelings, each with its subtle shade. Expanding your emotional vocabulary can help you articulate what you're genuinely feeling. Instead of just "angry," you might feel "frustrated" when things don't go your way or "disappointed" when someone lets you down. Words like "overwhelmed" capture the sense of everything being too much, while "content" describes a quiet satisfaction. Having the right words is like having the right tools—they make it easier to express yourself accurately and understand others.

Practicing emotion identification in various contexts is a great way to get familiar with these words. Consider a recent social scenario: maybe you were at lunch with friends, and someone made a joke that rubbed you the wrong way. What did you feel? Was it "irritation" or "embarrassment"? By role-playing different situations, you can practice identifying and naming these emotions as they arise. It could be as simple as acting out a family disagreement or a classroom debate. The goal is to pause and label each feeling, noticing how it shifts as the situation unfolds. This practice enhances your emotional vocabulary and boosts your emotional intelligence, making it easier to navigate the ups and downs of daily life.

Precise language is crucial for emotional regulation and communication. When you can accurately name your feelings,l you take ownership of those emotions. It turns a vague, unsettling sense of unease into something tangible you can address. For instance, telling someone, "I'm feeling overlooked," is much more effective than simply expressing anger. It opens the door for constructive dialogue and solutions. Precise language also helps in self-reflection, allowing you to pinpoint the cause of your feelings and address

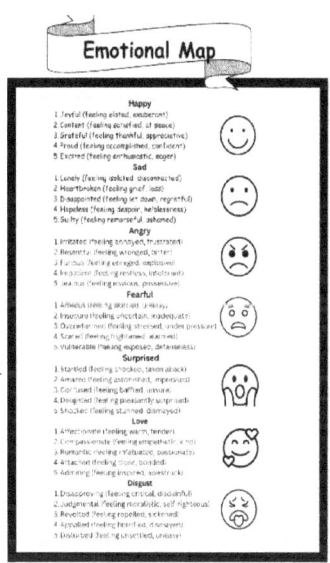

them head- on. It's like having a map for your emotions, guiding you through the maze of your inner world with clarity and purpose.

Creating emotion charts or maps can be a helpful visual tool in this process. Picture a chart divided into sections labeled with different emotions and their variations. You might have a section for "anger," branching into "frustration," "rage," and "annoyance." Another for "sadness" could include "melancholy," "grief," and "disappointment." Having this visual reference can aid in quickly identifying your emotional state, especially when words seem elusive. It can also serve as a reminder of the complexity of emotions, validating that it's okay to feel multiple things at once. This chart becomes a personal resource, a go-to guide for understanding and managing emotions in real time.

Interactive Element: Create Your Emotion Map

Grab some paper or use a digital tool to create your emotion map. Start with broad categories like "happy," "sad," and "angry," then branch out into more specific emotions like "joyful," "lonely," and "irritated." As you go through your day, refer to this map, marking the emotions you experience. Reflect on how accurately you can name your feelings and how this awareness impacts your interactions. This exercise deepens your understanding of emotions and encourages

empathy as you become more attuned to the emotional experiences of others around you.

Building a rich emotional vocabulary is like adding more colors to your palette. It allows you to paint a fuller picture of your experiences for yourself and others. Practicing this skill enhances your ability to communicate effectively and connect with others. Emotional vocabulary is a powerful tool in your emotional intelligence arsenal, fostering more profound understanding and healthier relationships.

Daily Emotion Tracker Form (use the Emotional Map above)

Date: _____

---

1. **Track Your Emotions**

- **Emotion**   **Experienced:**

- **Time:**

- **Recurring?** [ ] Yes [ ] No (Use additional rows if needed)

- **Emotion**   **Experienced:**

- **Time:**

- **Recurring?** [ ] Yes [ ] No

---

2. Reflect on Your Emotions

For each emotion you tracked, reflect on the following:

- **Emotion:** _____

  o What triggered this emotion?

  _____

  o How did I react?

  _____

  o Could I have reacted differently?

  _____

(Repeat for additional emotions as needed)

_____

3. End-of-Day Review

- Did naming my emotions help me regulate them better?
  [ ] Yes   [ ] No Notes:

_____

- How did my awareness of emotions affect my interactions with others?

  Notes:

_____

_____

Journaling for Clarity: Writing Your Emotions

Imagine your mind as a cluttered desk. Thoughts and feelings are scattered everywhere, and it's hard to find what you need when everything's in a jumble. Journaling is like organizing that desk, putting each piece of paper in its place so you can think clearly. There are countless ways to journal, and finding the right style can make all the difference. Stream-of-consciousness journaling might be your go-to if you prefer to let your thoughts flow freely. This involves writing whatever comes to mind without worrying about grammar or structure. It's like conversing with yourself, where you can vent, ponder, and explore without judgment. On the other hand, bullet journaling offers a more structured approach, using concise bullet points to capture key thoughts and events. It's a practical way to keep track of emotions and patterns over time. Some prefer prompt-based journaling, where specific questions guide their reflections. Prompts like "What emotion did I feel most strongly today and why?" can open doors to deeper insights, helping you explore emotions you might not even realize you have.

Regular journaling has a host of benefits. It's about recording your day and gaining clarity and understanding. Writing about your emotions helps you process them, breaking down complex feelings into manageable parts. It's like untangling a knot, slowly working through each twist and turn until you can see the whole picture. This practice can also highlight triggers and patterns in your responses, allowing you to approach future situations more clearly. Over time, you'll notice how journaling offers relief as if you're unloading a heavy weight from your shoulders. It provides a safe space to express thoughts and feelings that might be difficult to share with others.

To make journaling a regular habit, having a few prompts ready is helpful. These can serve as starting points, sparking introspection and guiding your writing. Consider questions like "What made me smile today?" or "How did I handle a challenging situation?" These prompts encourage you to reflect on positive and negative experiences, providing a balanced perspective. Another powerful practice is keeping a gratitude journal. In it, jot down things you're thankful for each day. They don't have to be big—sometimes, small moments bring the most joy, like a kind word from a friend or a beautiful sunset. This can shift your focus from what's wrong to what's right, fostering a more positive outlook.

Interactive Element: Daily Gratitude Prompt

Set aside time each evening to write down three things you're grateful for. Reflect on why these moments stood out and how they made you feel. Over time, this practice can help you see the good in your daily life, even when things seem harsh.

Journaling is a profoundly personal journey, and there's no right or wrong way to do it. The key is to find a style that resonates with you and make it part of your routine. Whether you journal every day or a few times a week, putting pen to paper (or fingers to keyboard) can be transformative. It offers a window into your inner world, helping you better understand yourself and navigate life's challenges more confidently and calmly. As you continue to explore your emotions through journaling, you'll uncover layers of insight and self-awareness that enrich your life unexpectedly.

How to Use This Worksheet

1. **Set Aside Time:** Choose a consistent time each evening for journaling practice.

2. **Create a Calm Environment:** Find a quiet space without distractions.

3. **Be Honest:** Write from the heart. There's no right or wrong way to journal.

4. **Reflect:** Consider why each moment stood out and how it made you feel.

Daily Gratitude Prompts Day 1:

1. What are three things you're grateful for today?

_____

_____

2. Why did these moments stand out?

_____

3. How did these moments make you feel?

_____

Day 2:

1. Think about someone who made your day better. What did they do?

_____

_____

2. What simple pleasure brought you joy today?

_____

_____

3. Describe a moment of peace or calm you experienced.

_____

_____

_____

_____

Day 3:

1. Reflect on a personal accomplishment, no matter how small.

_____

_____

2. What natural beauty did you notice today?

_____

3. Who or what inspired you today?

_____

Repeat similar prompts for 30 days to build a consistent gratitude habit.

Reflect and Grow Weekly Reflection:

1. Looking back over the week, what patterns do you notice in your gratitude entries?

_____

_____

2.   How has your perspective shifted?

_____

_____

3.   What moments of gratitude surprised you?

_____

_____

Monthly Reflection:

1. How has your emotional well-being changed since you started this practice?

_____

_____

2. What new insights have you gained about yourself?

_____

_____

3. How can you continue to incorporate gratitude into your daily life?

_____

_____

Section 5: Tips for Long-Term Success

- **Be Consistent:** Even on tough days, find one small thing to be grateful for.

- **Mix It Up:** Use different prompts to keep your practice fresh.

- **Celebrate Progress:** Acknowledge the effort you've put into your journaling.

- **Share Your Gratitude:** Expressing your appreciation to others deepens your practice.

Conclusion

Journaling is a profoundly personal journey that offers insight and self-awareness. As you continue this practice, remember to be kind to yourself and embrace the transformative power of gratitude. Over time, you'll uncover the beauty and joy even in life's smallest moments.

Mindfulness and Meditation: Finding Your Center

In the hustle and bustle of everyday life, finding a sense of calm can feel like chasing a mirage. Mindfulness offers a way to see through the chaos and find clarity. It's about tuning into the present moment and noticing what's happening around you without getting swept away. One of the simplest ways to start practicing mindfulness is through guided breathing exercises. By focusing on the rhythm of your breath, you anchor yourself in the present, quieting the noise of the mind. Imagine sitting comfortably, eyes closed, taking slow, deep breaths. Inhale, feel the air fill your lungs, then exhale, releasing tension with each breath. This practice is like hitting the reset button, giving you space to pause and regroup.

Another technique to ground yourself is the body scan meditation. During this practice, you bring awareness to different body parts, starting from your toes and working your way up to the top of your head. It's about noticing sensations, whether the tension in your shoulders or the warmth in your hands, without judgment. As you focus on each area, you release any tightness or stress, feeling your body relax with each exhale. This meditation enhances body awareness and fosters a sense of connection and presence. It's a gentle reminder that you're here now, and that's enough.

Exploring meditation techniques can further deepen your emotional well-being. Loving-kindness meditation, for example, is a practice that cultivates compassion and empathy. It involves silently repeating phrases that express good wishes for yourself and others. You might think, "May I be happy, may I be healthy, may I live with ease," then extend these wishes to friends, family, and even those you find challenging. This practice nurtures feelings of warmth and kindness, softening the edges of anger and frustration. It's like planting seeds of positivity, which grow into a garden of understanding and acceptance.

Regular mindfulness and meditation practice offers numerous benefits, from reducing stress to improving emotional regulation. When you consistently engage in these practices, you develop a greater capacity to handle life's ups and downs calmly and clearly. It's like strengthening a muscle; the more you practice, the more resilient you become. Over time, you'll notice a shift in how you respond to challenges. Instead of reacting impulsively, you pause, assess, and choose a thoughtful response. This change doesn't happen overnight, but with patience and commitment, it becomes a natural part of your life.

Creating a personal meditation space can enhance your practice. This doesn't have to be elaborate—a cozy corner with a cushion, a soft blanket, a candle, or plants. The key is to create an environment that feels inviting and peaceful, a place where you can retreat and recharge. Having a dedicated space signals to your mind that it's time to slow down and focus inward. It's a sanctuary from the world's busyness, a space to connect with yourself and find your center.

Emotional Intelligence in Action: Real-Life Scenarios

Emotional intelligence often comes to life in the stories of everyday people who learn to navigate their emotions with skill and empathy. Take, for instance, the story of Jake. Jake was a typical teen juggling schoolwork, extracurriculars, and a social life. But there was one area where he struggled—peer conflict. In his friend group, disagreements often escalated into full-blown arguments, hurting and misunderstanding everyone. One day, after another argument over a group project, Jake decided to try something different. Instead of reacting defensively, he paused and listened. He asked his friends how they felt and shared his own feelings calmly. This shift in approach transformed the conversation. Instead of pointing fingers, they worked together to find a solution that satisfied everyone. Jake's ability to manage his emotions and communicate effectively strengthened his friendships, showing how emotional intelligence can turn conflict into collaboration.

Practicing emotional intelligence doesn't have to be limited to real-life situations. Role-playing scenarios can be an invaluable tool for honing these skills. Imagine a simulated family disagreement, where each person plays a role, much like actors in a play. In this safe setting, you can experiment with different responses, trying out strategies that might feel risky in real life. Maybe you practice expressing your feelings clearly or work on listening without interruption. Each role-play is a rehearsal for real-life interactions, where you can test out emotional intelligence techniques and see what works best for you. It's a chance to learn and grow without the pressure of real-world consequences.

The impact of emotional intelligence on relationships is profound. When you approach interactions with empathy and understanding, you create a space where true connection can flourish. Think about how much easier it is to open up to someone who listens without judgment or supports you without trying to fix your problems. This is the essence of emotional intelligence—building bridges of trust and communication that strengthen bonds. In families, this might mean parents and teens working together to navigate the challenges of adolescence with mutual respect. It might involve offering support during tough times or celebrating successes without jealousy among friends. These skills enhance relationships, making them more resilient and fulfilling.

After practicing these scenarios, it's crucial to reflect on the experience. Take a moment to evaluate your performance, identifying what went well and where there might be room for improvement. Ask yourself questions like, "How did I handle my emotions?" or "What could I have done differently?" This reflection helps solidify your learning, making each practice a stepping stone for future growth.

Consider seeking feedback from others in the role-play, as their perspectives can offer valuable insights. This continuous cycle of practice, feedback, and reflection is how emotional intelligence becomes second nature, evolving from a set of skills into an integral part of who you are.

Interactive Element: Reflection and Feedback Session

Gather a group of friends or family members and choose a scenario to role-play. Afterward, discuss what you noticed about your reactions and communication. Share feedback, focusing on strengths and areas for growth. This exercise builds emotional intelligence and strengthens your support network, creating a community where everyone is committed to growth and understanding.

As you apply emotional intelligence in everyday life, you begin to see its transformative power. It's about managing emotions and using them to connect, empathize, and communicate more effectively. These skills are the foundation for more prosperous, meaningful relationships with friends, family, or yourself. With each practice, you build a toolkit that equips you to handle life's challenges with grace and confidence. Emotional intelligence is a journey without a final destination, constantly evolving and expanding as you learn.

Reflection and Feedback Session Worksheet

Interactive Element: Role-Playing for Emotional
Intelligence Date of Session:

Facilitator (if applicable):

Scenario Chosen for Role-Play:

Participant Reflection

1.   What emotions did you experience during the role-play?

---

2.   How did you express these emotions? (e.g., tone,
body language, words)

---

3. Did you notice any moments where your emotions
influenced your communication style? If so, how?

---

4. What were the biggest challenges for you during the scenario?

_____

_____

5. What strengths did you demonstrate in your reactions or communication?

_____

_____

6. What areas for improvement did you notice in your reactions or communication?

_____

_____

Group Feedback

1. What did the group observe about your emotional and communication strengths?

_____

_____

2. What constructive feedback or suggestions did the group offer for improvement?

_____

_____

3. Did you notice any recurring themes across feedback given to multiple participants? (e.g., empathy, listening, tone)

_____

_____

_____

Takeaways for Growth

1. What specific skills or strategies would you like to practice or develop further?

_____

_____

2. How can your support network help you strengthen these skills?

_____

_____

3. What steps will you take to apply emotional intelligence in everyday life?

_____

_____

_____

Participant Signatures

(Optional, to signify commitment to growth and mutual support)

Name: _____

Signature: _____

Name: _____

Signature: _____

Name:_ _____

Signature: _____

Chapter 12: Practical Strategies for Managing Anger

Tools and Techniques to Stay Cool When Life Heats Up

Imagine you're in the middle of a heated argument. Words are flying, emotions are high, and you can feel your heart pounding like a drum in your chest. It's a familiar scene for many, but wouldn't it be incredible to have a tool that helps you find calm amid the chaos? That's where breathing techniques come in. They might seem simple, but these exercises are powerful. They can quickly transform a tense moment into one of clarity and control. It's like having a reset button for your emotions, allowing you to pause and choose how to respond.

Breathing Techniques: Instant Calm for Intense Moments

The science of deep breathing is fascinating because it directly taps into your body's natural systems to create calm. When you take controlled, deep breaths, you activate the parasympathetic nervous system. This part of your nervous system is responsible for rest and digestion, counteracting the fight-or-flight response that kicks in during stressful moments. By calming the body, you also calm the mind, making it easier to think clearly and make thoughtful decisions. One particular method, diaphragmatic breathing, focuses on breathing deeply into your belly rather than shallowly into your chest. This technique allows more oxygen to enter your bloodstream, lowering heart rate and decreasing stress.

Let's dive into some specific breathing exercises you can use. Box breathing is a simple yet effective method. Picture a square as you breathe. Inhale through your nose for a count of four, hold your breath for another four, exhale slowly through your mouth for four, and pause for four counts before starting again. It's like drawing a box with your breath; each side brings you closer to calmness. Another popular technique is the 4-7-8 method. Start by inhaling quietly through your nose for four seconds. Hold the breath for a count of seven and then exhale completely through your mouth for eight seconds. This extended exhale helps release tension and stress, leaving you feeling more relaxed and grounded.

The benefits of breath control are immediate and profound. These techniques can instantly reduce stress and anger in a heated moment. Imagine a stormy sea suddenly calming to a gentle ripple; that's what controlled breathing can do for your emotions. Focusing on your breath creates a mental space to step back from the chaos, allowing you to assess the situation with a clearer mind. It's like having an internal anchor keeping you steady when everything else feels overwhelming.

Regular practice of these exercises can build a habit of calmness over time. Incorporating them into your daily routine can enhance their effectiveness, like regular exercise strengthens muscles. Start small—maybe with a few minutes each morning or evening—and gradually increase as you become more comfortable. You might find it helpful to pair these exercises with a routine activity, like brushing your teeth or waiting for the bus. Over time, you'll notice that your ability to manage stress and anger improves, leading to a more balanced and peaceful life.

Interactive Element: Daily Breathing Practice Checklist

Use the checklist below to track your breathing practice. Make time for morning and evening sessions, with space to note how you felt before and after each practice. Reflect on any changes in your stress levels or emotional responses throughout the day. This checklist can help reinforce the habit and make it easier to see the benefits of regular practice.

Breathing techniques offer a simple yet powerful way to manage anger and stress. By understanding and practicing these methods, you equip yourself with tools to navigate emotional challenges more effectively. They provide a pathway to calmness and clarity, transforming how you experience and respond to the world.

Techniques used for breathing.

Diaphragmatic Breathing

Also known as belly breathing, this technique focuses on deep, slow breaths that engage the diaphragm rather than shallow chest breathing.

How to practice:

1. Sit or lie down in a comfortable position.

2. Place one hand on your chest and the other on your stomach.

3. Inhale deeply through your nose, ensuring your stomach rises while your chest stays still.

4. Exhale slowly through your mouth, feeling your stomach fall.

5. Repeat for a few minutes, focusing on the rhythmic movement of your breath.

Box Breathing

This structured breathing technique involves inhaling, holding, exhaling, and holding your breath for equal counts, forming a "box" pattern.

How to practice:

1. Inhale through your nose for a count of 4.

2. Hold your breath for a count of 4.

3. Exhale slowly through your mouth for a count of 4.

4. Hold your breath again for a count of 4.

5. Repeat the cycle for a few minutes.

Alternate Nostril Breathing

In yoga, this technique is known as Nadi Shodhana. It involves breathing alternately through each nostril to balance energy and calm the mind.

How to practice:

1. Sit in a comfortable position with a straight spine.

2. Use your thumb to close your right nostril and inhale deeply through your left nostril.

3. Close your left nostril with your ring finger and release your thumb to exhale through your right nostril.

4. Inhale through the right nostril, close it with your thumb and exhale through the left nostril.

5. Repeat this cycle for several minutes, focusing on smooth and even breaths

Daily Breathing Practice Checklist Morning Session

1.   **Date:** _____

2.   **Start Time:** _____

3.   **Duration (minutes):** _____

4.   **Technique Used:**

o   ☐ Diaphragmatic Breathing

o   ☐ Box Breathing

o   ☐ Alternate Nostril Breathing

o   ☐ Other: _____

5.   How I Felt Before Practice:

o   ☐ Calm

o   ☐ Stressed

o   ☐ Angry

o   ☐ Anxious

o   ☐ Other: _____

6.   How I Felt After Practice:

o   ☐ Calm

o   ☐ Relaxed

o   ☐ Focused

- o   ☐ Still Stressed (but less intense)

- o   ☐ Other: _____

Evening Session

1. **Date:** _____

2. **Start Time:** _____

3. **Duration (minutes):** _____

4. **Technique Used:**

- o   ☐ Diaphragmatic Breathing

- o   ☐ Box Breathing

- o   ☐ Alternate Nostril Breathing

- o   ☐ Other: _____

5. How I Felt Before Practice:

- o   ☐ Calm

- o   ☐ Stressed

- o   ☐ Angry

- o   ☐ Anxious

- o   ☐ Other: _____

6. How I Felt After Practice:

- o ☐ Calm

- o ☐ Relaxed

- o ☐ Focused

- o ☐ Still Stressed (but less intense)

- o ☐ Other: _____

Reflection Section

1. **Notable Changes in Stress/Emotional Levels Throughout the Day:**

---

2. **Did Breathing Practice Help Me Navigate Emotional Challenges Today?**

- o ☐ Yes, definitely

- o ☐ Somewhat

- o ☐ Not really (Why?): _____

3. **Insights or Thoughts for Improvement:**

By reviewing this checklist regularly, you can track patterns in your emotional well-being and observe how consistent breathing practice transforms your ability to handle stress and anger.

Physical Outlets: Channeling Anger into Activity

There's something almost magical about how physical activity can transform a bad mood. When you're angry or stressed, your body is flooded with adrenaline, urging you to fight or flee. Exercise taps into this natural response, channeling that energy into something productive. It's like turning a raging river into a powerhouse that generates strength and calmness. Endorphins, the body's natural feel-good chemicals, are released during physical activity. These little wonders help reduce stress hormones, making you feel more relaxed and positive. Moving your body can be a powerful antidote to anger, whether it's a brisk run around the park or an intense martial arts session.

Running or jogging is one of the most accessible forms of exercise, requiring nothing more than a pair of good shoes and a little motivation. The rhythmic nature of running provides a meditative experience, allowing your mind to untangle thoughts while your feet pound the pavement. Each step can feel like shedding a layer of frustration, replaced by a sense of accomplishment. Similarly, martial arts offer a structured way to channel aggression. The discipline and focus required in martial arts improve physical fitness and teach valuable lessons in patience and self-control. It's a space where you can release pent-up energy in a supportive environment, leaving you feeling centered and empowered. Dance or movement classes are another fantastic outlet. Expressing emotions through movement can be liberating, turning negative energy into a creative force. Whether hip-hop, ballet, or contemporary dance, moving to music can be a joyful way to let go of anger.

Consistent exercise is key to reaping long-term emotional benefits. Making physical activity a regular part of your life builds resilience against stress and anger. It's like strengthening a muscle—the more you use it, the stronger it becomes. Regular exercise enhances physical health and sharpens mental clarity, making it easier to handle life's challenges. The discipline of sticking to an exercise routine can spill over into other areas of life, fostering a sense of accomplishment and control. Encouraging teens to explore different physical activities can open up new avenues for self-expression and well-being. Trying various sports or exercises allows you to find what resonates best with your interests and needs. It might be team sports like soccer or basketball, which offer camaraderie and a shared goal, or solo activities like yoga or swimming, which provide a more introspective experience. The important thing is to enjoy the discovery process, knowing that each new activity is a chance to learn about yourself.

Interactive Element: Physical Activity Exploration Chart

The chart below lists various physical activities you might want to try or add your own. It includes columns for your initial impressions, any challenges you face, and how you felt afterward. This chart is a personal record of your exploration, helping you identify which activities best help you manage anger and stress.

Finding the right physical outlets is not just about staying fit; it's about creating a toolkit for emotional well-being. Each activity adds a layer of resilience, helping you navigate life's ups and downs more easily. As you experiment with different forms of exercise, you'll improve your physical health and discover new aspects of yourself, fostering a deeper connection to your body and emotions. This self-discovery is rewarding, offering a sense of empowerment and confidence beyond the gym or playing field.

Samples of Activities to try:

1.   Pilates

2.   Tennis

3.   Rowing

4.   Trail Running

5.   CrossFit

6. Archery

7. Paddleboarding

8. Ice Skating

9. Soccer

10. Surfing

11. Add your own

Physical Activities	Initial Impressions	Challenges	How You Felt After

Creative Expressions: Art as an Emotional Outlet

Sometimes, words just aren't enough to express what you're feeling. That's where art comes in. Artistic expression offers a unique way to process and release emotions that might be too tangled or intense to articulate. Picture this: you're sitting with a blank canvas, a palette of colors before you, and a world of emotions inside. As you dip your brush and paint, each stroke becomes a pathway for your feelings to travel. Whether angry, sad, or joyful, painting or drawing can help you externalize those feelings, turning chaos into something tangible and beautiful. Creating can be meditative, allowing you to lose yourself in the moment and find clarity and calm. It's about translating those inner storms into something outside of yourself so they don't feel overwhelmed.

The beauty of creative expression lies in its diversity. If painting isn't your thing, perhaps writing poetry or stories is. Words have a rhythm and flow that can capture emotions in a powerful and healing way. You might find solace in crafting a poem that captures the essence of your feelings or in writing a story where you can control the narrative and outcomes. It's a way to reclaim your voice and assert control over unwanted emotions. Playing a musical instrument offers another avenue for expression. Music has an incredible ability to convey feelings without saying a word. Whether you're strumming a guitar, playing the piano, or beating a drum, each note can echo the emotions you're experiencing, providing a release that words sometimes cannot achieve. These forms of self-expression allow you to explore different facets of your emotional world, offering insight and release.

Starting a creative project might seem daunting, especially if you don't consider yourself an "artist." But remember, art isn't about perfection; it's about expression. Begin with simple steps, like doodling in the margins of your notebook or writing a few lines of verse. Gradually, as you become more comfortable, you can expand your skills and explore new mediums. Take a class, join a club, or set aside weekly time to create. The key is to allow yourself the freedom to experiment and make mistakes. Art is a personal journey, and each piece you create is a step toward understanding yourself better.

Inspiration can be found in countless stories of individuals who have creatively transformed their emotions. Take, for example, a young woman who turned to painting during a tumultuous period. Each canvas became a diary of her journey, capturing moments of pain, reflection, and healing. Over time, her artwork helped her process her emotions and became a source of inspiration for others going through similar experiences. Or consider the story of a teenager who found solace in writing music. What began as a way to cope with feelings of isolation grew into a passion that connected him with others and gave him a sense of purpose. These examples show how art can be a powerful tool for healing and connection, turning personal struggles into shared experiences that resonate with others.

Creating art is like opening a window to your soul. It allows you to explore the depths of your emotions and express them in a free and fulfilling way. Whether painting, writing, or making music, these creative outlets offer a refuge from the world's noise, where you can be yourself without judgment or expectation. As you explore these artistic paths, you'll find that the act of creation itself is a journey of discovery, revealing the beauty in the world around you and within.

Digital Detox: Balancing Online and Offline Worlds

It's no secret that screens have become a staple in our daily lives. From smartphones to laptops, we're constantly connected, and while technology has its perks, it can also be a source of stress and anger. Think about it— how often have you found yourself scrolling through social media only to feel a pang of jealousy or frustration? This phenomenon, often referred to as social media comparison stress, can take a toll on your mental health. When you're bombarded with highlight reels of others' seemingly perfect lives, it's easy to feel inadequate. These emotions can simmer beneath the surface, leading to an increase in stress and even anger. The pressure to keep up with trends and maintain an online persona can be exhausting, leaving little room for genuine self- reflection or relaxation.

To combat the negative effects of constant connectivity, it's important to establish boundaries with technology. One effective strategy is scheduling screen-free times. Consider designating certain day hours, like during meals or before bed, as tech-free zones. This helps reduce screen time and encourages more meaningful interactions with those around you. It's about creating moments of presence where you can fully engage with the world offline. Think of it as allowing your mind to breathe, free from the digital noise. Another practical tip is to turn off non-essential notifications. This simple action can prevent the constant barrage of alerts that pull your attention away from the present moment. By setting clear boundaries, you reclaim control over your time and focus, allowing space for calm and introspection.

Developing offline hobbies is another crucial aspect of achieving balance. Engaging in activities that don't involve screens can provide a refreshing change of pace and help reset your mental state. Imagine going for a hike or a nature walk, where the only notifications you receive are the rustling leaves and chirping birds. The physical act of moving through nature offers a grounding experience, helping you reconnect with yourself and the world around you. Or perhaps you enjoy gardening, cooking, or crafting—activities that require your full attention and offer a sense of accomplishment. These hobbies not only serve as a break from screens but also foster creativity and mindfulness. They remind you of the simple pleasures in life, often overshadowed by the digital hustle.

Mindful technology use is about being intentional with your online interactions. It's not about cutting out technology entirely but rather using it in a way that serves you rather than controls you. Start by curating your social media feeds to include content that inspires and uplifts you. Follow accounts that align with your values and interests, and don't hesitate to unfollow those that trigger negative emotions. It's your digital space, and you have the power to shape it. Another approach is to set specific goals for your online time. Whether it's researching a new hobby, connecting with friends, or learning something new, having a purpose can prevent aimless scrolling and help you make the most of your digital interactions. By practicing mindful technology use, you transform your relationship with screens, making it a tool for empowerment rather than a source of stress.

Finding a balance between the online and offline worlds is an ongoing process. It requires self-awareness and a willingness to make changes that support your well-being. As you experiment with digital detox strategies, you'll discover what works best for you, creating a lifestyle that promotes both mental clarity and emotional resilience. This balance not only enhances your mood but also enriches your daily experiences, allowing you to engage with life more fully and authentically.

Conflict Resolution: Turning Arguments into Discussions

Conflict is a part of life, but how we handle it makes all the difference. When disagreements arise, it's tempting to raise your voice and dig in your heels. But imagine a different outcome, where conflicts become opportunities for understanding rather than battles to win. Key principles of conflict resolution can transform arguments into meaningful discussions. It starts with active listening, which means genuinely hearing what the other person is saying without interrupting or planning your following rebuttal. Listening actively shows that you value the other person's perspective, laying the groundwork for mutual respect. Empathy plays a crucial role, too. Putting yourself in the other person's shoes creates a bridge of understanding that can turn adversaries into allies. And let's not forget compromise; it's about finding a middle ground where both parties feel heard and respected, even if it means giving a little to gain a lot.

A structured approach can help navigate conflict effectively. Begin with "I" statements to express your feelings without casting blame. Instead of saying, "You never listen to me," try, "I feel unheard when I'm interrupted." This subtle shift focuses on your experience rather than accusing the other person, reducing defensiveness. Next, engage in finding common ground exercises. Start by identifying shared goals or values. Maybe you both want a harmonious home environment or a successful group project. Highlighting these commonalities shifts

the focus from what divides you to what unites you. It's like focusing on the whole picture rather than getting lost in the details. As you progress, keep the conversation open and honest. It's important to acknowledge each other's points without dismissing them. This validates the person's feelings and opens the door to constructive dialogue.

Respect is the cornerstone of any successful conflict resolution. Maintaining respect during disagreements can prevent escalation and keep the conversation productive. Remember that the person you're arguing with has their own experiences and emotions influencing their perspective. Respect doesn't mean you have to agree, but it does mean acknowledging the other person's right to their view. This approach helps de-escalate tension and fosters an environment where solutions can flourish. If voices start to rise, pause and take a breath. Sometimes, a moment of silence can reset the tone and remind everyone of the ultimate goal: resolution, not victory.

Conflict resolution skills can be applied in various scenarios, from family disagreements to school debates. Imagine a situation at home where chores are a constant source of tension. Instead of letting frustration simmer, gather everyone involved for a discussion. Use active listening to understand each person's viewpoint and work together to find a fair solution. Maybe you establish a rotating schedule or agree on a reward system for completed tasks. In a school setting, when a group project leads to differing opinions, use these skills to facilitate a productive meeting. Encourage each team member to express their ideas, acknowledge strengths and weaknesses, and collaborate to create a plan that leverages everyone's talents. These scenarios illustrate how turning arguments into discussions resolves the immediate issue, strengthens relationships, and builds trust.

Interactive Element: Conflict Resolution Role-Play

Gather friends or family members and choose a common conflict scenario. Assign roles and practice a structured conflict resolution approach, focusing on active listening and empathy. Afterward, discuss what strategies worked well and where there might be room for improvement. This role-playing exercise provides a safe space to experiment with new skills and gain confidence in handling real-life conflicts.

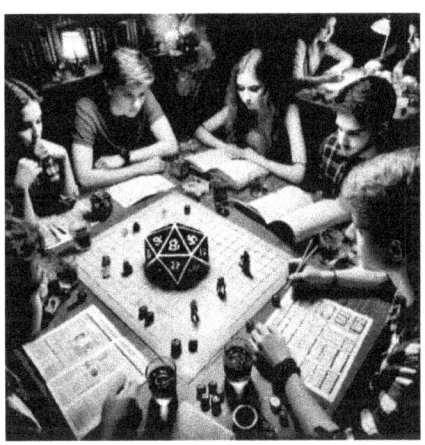

By embracing conflict resolution principles, you transform potential clashes into opportunities for growth and connection. These skills foster healthier relationships and equip you to navigate life's inevitable challenges with grace and wisdom. Conflict doesn't have to be a barrier; it can be a path to deeper understanding and stronger bonds.

1. **Describe the scenario:** What conflict did your group choose to role-play? Who played which roles, and what was the situation about?

_____

_____

2. **Active Listening:** How well did the group members listen to each other? What techniques were used to show active listening (e.g., repeating back, asking clarifying questions, or maintaining eye contact)?

_____

_____

_____

_____

3. **Empathy in Action:** How did each participant demonstrate empathy during the exercise? Did anyone acknowledge feelings or validate perspectives effectively?

_____

_____

_____

_____

4. **What worked well?** What strategies or approaches helped resolve the discussion? Be specific about what contributed to the success.

_____

_____

_____

_____

5. **Challenges and improvements:** What parts of the role-play felt difficult or didn't work as well as expected? What could be done differently next time?

_____

_____

_____

_____

6. **Personal takeaway:** What did you learn about resolving conflicts from this exercise? How can you apply these skills in real-life situations?

_____

_____

_____

_____

Humor and Anger: Laughing it Off

Have you noticed how a good laugh can lighten even the heaviest mood? Humor is a remarkable tool for diffusing anger and tension, offering a fresh perspective on challenging situations. When you are caught in a moment of frustration, a well-timed joke or a funny observation can shift your mindset, easing the intensity of your emotions. It's as if laughter clears the fog, allowing you to see the situation differently. This is because laughter triggers the release of endorphins, those feel-good chemicals that promote a sense of well-being and relaxation. Watching a comedy routine or a funny movie can relieve stress, turning an otherwise tense environment into one that feels more manageable and light-hearted.

Incorporating humor into your daily life can be a healthy way to cope with stress and anger. Consider starting your day with a humorous video or a light-hearted podcast. These moments of joy can set a positive tone for the hours ahead. Sharing jokes with friends or family can reinforce social bonds, creating a shared experience that fosters connection. Even amid a heated discussion, introducing a touch of humor can break the tension and open the door to more constructive dialogue. It's important to remember that humor isn't about making light of serious issues but rather about finding a way to approach them with a bit of levity. When used appropriately, it can transform a conflict into an opportunity for understanding and reconciliation.

However, it's crucial to be mindful of when and how you use humor, as it can sometimes backfire. Jokes that belittle or dismiss someone's feelings can escalate a situation rather than defuse it. Inappropriate humor, especially in sensitive contexts, might come across as insensitive or even hurtful. This is why

timing and context are essential. Using humor as a tool for deflection can also prevent necessary conversations from happening, leaving underlying issues unresolved. It's about striking a balance, knowing when to lighten the mood and when to engage seriously. When handled with care, humor can be a powerful ally in managing emotions and fostering positive interactions.

Countless stories of individuals have effectively used humor to navigate difficult emotions. Take the example of a teacher who noticed their students were agitated during exams. Instead of adding to the stress, they began each session with a funny story or a silly dance. This eased the students' nerves and created a more relaxed and open learning environment. Or consider the story of a parent who used humor to connect with their teenager. During a heated disagreement, they cracked a light joke about the situation's absurdity, and the shared laughter helped bridge the emotional gap. When applied thoughtfully, these anecdotes illustrate how humor can change the emotional landscape, turning potential conflict into moments of connection and understanding.

Humor is invaluable in your emotional toolkit, offering a way to navigate life's challenges with a smile. When you embrace laughter, you invite a sense of relief and perspective that can transform how you handle anger and stress. It's not about avoiding serious issues but about finding a way to approach them that doesn't add to the pressure. As you integrate humor into your life, you'll discover its power to soften hard edges and lighten heavy loads, making each day brighter and more manageable.

As we round off this chapter on practical strategies for managing anger, we've explored various tools—from the grounding power of breathing techniques to the expressive release of creativity and movement. Each plan offers a unique way to channel emotions constructively, equipping you with skills to navigate the complexities of daily life. In the next chapter, we'll delve into building resilience and confidence, crucial elements for sustaining emotional growth and strength.

Chapter 13: Strengthening Relationships

How to Communicate Clearly, Build Trust, and Heal Conflict

Picture yourself in a bustling café, the clatter of cups and the hum of conversation surrounding you. Amid this lively backdrop, you sit across from a friend, eager to share a story that's weighed on you. Your friend's eyes drift to their phone as you speak, nodding absentmindedly at all the wrong moments. Suddenly, you feel like you're speaking to a wall, your words lost in the noise. This scenario highlights a common struggle in our fast-paced world—how often do we truly listen? The art of active listening is a powerful tool that can transform relationships, turning mere exchanges into meaningful connections. When we listen intently, we hear words and the emotions and thoughts behind them, creating a bridge of understanding.

Active listening is more than a technique; it's the cornerstone of healthy communication. It involves paying close attention to verbal and non-verbal cues, ensuring the speaker feels heard and valued. This practice helps reduce misunderstandings and fosters trust, making it an invaluable skill in resolving conflicts. Imagine a heated argument with a sibling or parent, where emotions run high and words are sharp. By employing active listening, you open a pathway for empathy and clarity, shifting the focus from winning an argument to understanding each other's perspectives. It's like diffusing a ticking time bomb with patience and kindness, turning a potential explosion into a calm conversation.

Several techniques can help master active listening. Start with maintaining eye contact, which signals your interest and engagement in the conversation. It's like saying, "I'm here with you," without uttering a single word. Nodding occasionally and using verbal affirmations like "I see" or "Go on" encourages the speaker to continue, knowing they have your full attention. Paraphrasing is another powerful tool. After the speaker finishes, repeat what you've heard in your own words, like a brief summary. This confirms your understanding and gives the speaker a chance to clarify if needed. Reflective listening, where you acknowledge the speaker's emotions, adds another layer. For instance, saying, "It sounds like you're feeling really overwhelmed," shows empathy and validates their feelings.

Body language plays a crucial role in effective listening. It's not just about what you say but how you present yourself. Leaning slightly forward, keeping an open posture, and avoiding distractions like your phone make the speaker feel valued. Non-verbal cues can often speak louder than words, conveying a sense of warmth and sincerity. Imagine a friend pouring their heart out, and you respond with crossed arms and a wandering gaze. Your body language might tell a different story even if your words are supportive. Aligning your verbal and non-verbal signals ensures that your message of support and understanding is loud and clear.

Interactive Element: Active Listening Role-Play Exercise

Gather with friends or family and take turns sharing a story or concern. Practice active listening by maintaining eye contact, paraphrasing, and reflecting feelings. After each story, provide feedback on the listener's strengths and areas for improvement. This exercise helps solidify active listening skills in a supportive environment.

Incorporating active listening into daily interactions strengthens bonds and enhances communication. Whether it's a casual chat or a deep discussion, this practice transforms how we connect with others, fostering relationships built on empathy and understanding. Active listening is a gift we give to those we care about, turning simple exchanges into meaningful moments of connection.

Active Listening Role-Play Exercise

Engage in an interactive group activity to sharpen your active listening skills! Gather with friends or family and take turns sharing a story, concern, or personal experience. The listener's role is to practice active listening by:

- Maintaining eye contact

- Showing attentive body language

- Paraphrasing key points to show understanding

- Reflecting the speaker's emotions

After each story, the group provides feedback to the listener. Highlight what they did well and suggest ways they can improve. This fun and supportive exercise is perfect for strengthening communication skills, building empathy, and fostering deeper connections.

Notes for Feedback

Speaker's Story or Concern:

_____

_____

Listener's Strengths:

_____

_____

Areas for Improvement:

_____

_____

Try it out and see how much better you can listen!

Effective Communication: Saying What You Mean

Imagine a world where everyone said exactly what they meant, where words carried the weight of sincerity and clarity. Communication, at its most effective, is clear and direct. It's not about shouting to be heard but about expressing thoughts and feelings honestly and respectfully. This approach not only fosters understanding but also builds stronger connections. Think about a time when you were misunderstood. Perhaps you felt frustrated or even hurt. Effective communication can prevent these scenarios by ensuring that your message is received as intended. One powerful tool for achieving this is using "I" statements. Instead of saying, "You never listen to me," which can be accusatory, try, "I feel ignored when I'm not heard." This simple shift in wording focuses on your feelings rather than blaming the other person, paving the way for a more constructive conversation.

Articulating needs and desires without aggression or passivity is a skill worth cultivating. Assertive communication is about finding that sweet spot where you respect both your own needs and those of others. It involves expressing yourself confidently without being overbearing. Imagine you're at a group meeting, and your ideas are overshadowed. Instead of withdrawing or bulldozing over others, you might say, "I'd like to share my thoughts on this topic." This communicates your desire to contribute while respecting the group dynamic. Assertiveness is like playing a well-tuned instrument; it allows your voice to be heard harmoniously within the ensemble. It's about standing your ground gracefully, ensuring that your message is neither lost in silence nor overwhelmed by noise.

How we say things — our tone and word choice — profoundly impacts how our message is received. The tone is like the color in a painting, setting the mood and context for what's being communicated. A gentle tone can soften a difficult conversation,

197

while a harsh one might escalate it unnecessarily. Similarly, word choice is the brushstroke that defines the message. Consider the

difference between saying, "I need you to do this," versus, "Could you help me with this?" The former can sound like a command, while the latter invites cooperation. Choosing words thoughtfully creates a dialogue that invites understanding rather than conflict. This awareness of tone and language transforms everyday interactions, making them more meaningful and effective.

Practice is key to building confidence in communication. Role-playing exercises provide a safe environment to experiment with different approaches. Imagine a scenario where you need to discuss curfew with your parents. Practice expressing your viewpoint using "I" statements and assertive language. Role-play with friends or mentors who can offer feedback on your delivery and help you refine your approach. This exercise builds your confidence and equips you with the skills to handle real-life conversations with poise. As you practice, you'll notice a shift in how you express yourself, moving from tentative whispers to confident, clear communication.

Effective communication is a skill that opens doors to deeper understanding and connection. By expressing yourself clearly and directly, you invite others into your world, sharing not just words but the emotions and thoughts behind them. It's about creating a space where everyone feels heard and valued, where conversations become bridges rather than barriers. As you navigate the complexities of relationships, remember that your words have the power to connect, heal, and bring people closer together.

Empathy in Relationships: Walking in Their Shoes

Empathy acts like a bridge, connecting people across the chasm of misunderstanding. It's the ability to step into someone else's shoes, to see the world through their eyes, and feel their emotions as if they were your own. When you practice empathy, you're not just hearing words but also understanding the emotions and experiences behind them. This understanding can transform relationships, turning surface-level interactions into deep, meaningful connections. Imagine a friend sharing their struggles at home, and instead of merely nodding

along, you truly grasp the weight of their words. By acknowledging their pain and responding with compassion, you create a space where they feel supported and valued. It's like offering a hand to someone who's stumbling, helping them find their footing again.

Developing empathy is a skill that can be nurtured through practice. Perspective-taking is a powerful exercise that encourages you to consider situations from another's viewpoint. Picture a scenario where your sibling is upset over something you find trivial. Instead of dismissing their feelings, try to understand why it matters to them. Ask yourself, "How would I feel in their position?" This shift in perspective can open your eyes to their reality, fostering compassion and patience. Empathetic response practice is another technique to hone this skill. It involves actively listening to someone's concerns and responding in a way that reflects understanding and support. For instance, rather than saying, "You'll get over it," try, "That sounds really tough. How can I help?" These exercises help you develop a more nuanced understanding of others, strengthening your ability to connect on a deeper level.

It's important to distinguish between empathy and sympathy, as they play different roles in relationships. Sympathy often involves feeling pity for someone else's situation seeing their struggles from a distance. It's like watching a storm from the safety of your window. Empathy, on the other hand, is about stepping out into the rain, sharing in the experience and understanding the intensity of the storm. While sympathy can sometimes feel condescending, empathy builds a connection rooted in shared experiences and emotions. This distinction is crucial in relationships as it guides how you respond to others' feelings and challenges.

Reflecting on personal experiences of empathy can offer valuable insights into its impact. Think about a time when someone truly understood what you were going through. Maybe it was a friend who sat with you silently when words felt too heavy or a parent who listened without judgment as you poured out your worries. How did it make you feel? Chances are, it provided relief and comfort, knowing

you weren't alone. These moments highlight the power of empathy to heal and connect, reinforcing its importance in relationships. Encourage teens to reflect on these experiences, considering how they felt understood and how it influenced their interactions with others. This reflection helps solidify the value of empathy, motivating them to practice it more consciously in their daily lives.

Interactive Element: Perspective-Taking Reflection

Take a moment to write about a recent situation where you felt misunderstood. Now, flip the script and consider how the other person might have felt. What might they have been thinking or experiencing? Reflect on how this new perspective changes your understanding of the situation. This exercise helps cultivate empathy by encouraging you to explore different viewpoints.

1. **Reflecting on Your Experience**

- Describe the situation where you felt misunderstood.

_____

_____

_____

- What emotions did I feel during this situation (e.g., frustration, sadness, confusion)?

_____

_____

_____

- Why do I think I was misunderstood? What was I trying to communicate?

_____

_____

_____

2. **Flipping the Script: The Other Person's Perspective**

- How might the other person have been feeling during this situation?

_____

_____

_____

- What could they have been thinking or experiencing that influenced their response?

_____

_____

_____

- Were there any external factors or personal struggles that may have shaped their perspective?

_____

_____

_____

3. Gaining Insight from a New Perspective

- How does considering the other person's perspective change my understanding of the situation?

_____

_____

_____

- What lessons can I take away from this reflection about communication and empathy?

_____

_____

_____

4. Moving Forward

- How might I approach similar situations differently in the future to avoid misunderstandings?

_____

_____

_____

- What steps can I take to foster better relationship understanding and connection?

_____

_____

_____

Trust Building: The Foundation of Strong Bonds

Trust is like the bedrock of any relationship. Without it, even the strongest connections can crumble. Do you know how you need a solid foundation when building something? Trust is the foundation of relationships. It allows you to feel safe, knowing you can rely on someone, whether a friend, a parent, or a partner. Trust creates an environment where honesty and openness thrive, and misunderstandings are less likely to cause lasting damage. The glue holds people together, making navigating life's ups and downs easier.

Building trust isn't something that happens overnight, however. It requires consistent effort and commitment to specific behaviors that reinforce reliability. Actions like being honest, keeping promises, and showing up when you say you will all contribute to a culture of trust. Think about it—when someone consistently does what they say they'll do, it's easier to believe in them. Consistency builds confidence, and confidence breeds trust. It's like watering a plant; regular care leads to growth and strength. Every time you follow through on a promise, no matter how small, you nurture the trust between you and the other person.

But what happens when trust is broken? It's a challenging situation, for sure, but not an impossible one. Rebuilding trust takes time, patience, and, perhaps most importantly, accountability. Admitting when you're wrong and taking responsibility for your actions is the first step to repair the breach. It's like acknowledging that a storm has passed; now it's time to clean up the mess. Open dialogue about what happened and why it hurt is crucial. This isn't just about saying sorry; it's about understanding the impact of your actions and showing a genuine willingness to make amends. Forgiveness exercises can play a vital role here, helping both parties overcome the hurt and rebuild what was lost. Forgiving isn't about forgetting but about letting go of resentment to allow healing.

Maintaining trust is an ongoing process, a constant effort to keep the lines of communication open and clear. It's about being transparent about your intentions and feelings, ensuring that misunderstandings don't have a chance to take root. Think of it like tending to a garden; regularly check for weeds and nurture the plants to keep them healthy. Regular check-ins with those you care about can help reinforce trust, making sure everyone feels heard and understood. This doesn't have to be formal—just a simple "How are we doing?" can work wonders. It's a way to stay connected and ensure trust remains strong and intact.

Apology and Forgiveness Exercise

Take a moment to reflect on a time you may have broken someone's trust. Write a letter (that you don't have to send) expressing your understanding of the situation, your feelings, and how you plan to make amends. Then, write a second letter to yourself, forgiving your mistakes and acknowledging your growth. This exercise encourages accountability and self-compassion, two key elements in rebuilding trust.

Apology and Forgiveness Exercise

Reflect on a moment when you may have broken someone's trust. This exercise is about fostering accountability and self-compassion as you work through the experience.

1. **Write an Apology Letter**

Compose a letter (that you don't need to send) to the person involved. In the letter:

   o   Acknowledge what happened and your role in the situation.

   o   Express your feelings about the impact it may have had on them.

   o   Share how you plan to make amends and prevent a similar situation.

2. **Write a Forgiveness Letter to Yourself**

Next, write a letter to yourself. In this letter:

o   Recognize your mistakes with honesty.

o   Acknowledge your steps to grow and learn from the experience.

o   Offer yourself forgiveness and kindness as you move forward.

These letters are for your eyes only. They are a safe space to process emotions and reflect on your growth.

Notes for Reflection

Apology Letter

- **What happened and your role:**

_____

_____

Impact on the other person:

_____

_____

- **Plan for making amends:**

_____

_____

Forgiveness Letter to Yourself

- **Recognized mistakes and lessons learned:**

_____

_____

- **Steps taken for growth and self-improvement:**

_____

_____

- **Words of self-compassion:**

_____

_____

This practice allows you to process emotions and rebuild trust with others and yourself. Take your time, and let the writing guide your healing journey.

Setting Boundaries: Respecting Yourself and Others

Setting boundaries is like drawing a map of your personal space, marking where you feel comfortable and safe. Imagine it as having an invisible fence that safeguards your emotional well-being and promotes mutual respect. These boundaries are crucial because they define your limits, helping others understand how to interact with you. They can be emotional, physical, or digital. Emotional boundaries relate to your feelings and energy, defining what you're willing to share and how you expect to be treated. Physical boundaries involve your personal space and physical contact, ensuring you're comfortable with how others interact with you. Digital boundaries pertain to your online presence, such as who can contact you and what personal information you want to share on social media. Establishing these boundaries is vital for maintaining healthy relationships and ensuring that interactions remain respectful and fulfilling.

Articulating your boundaries can sometimes feel challenging, especially if you're not used to asserting yourself. However, it's essential to communicate them clearly and respectfully. This means using straightforward language that leaves no room for ambiguity. For example, if you need time alone to recharge, you might say, "I need some quiet time right now. Can we talk later?" or if someone is pressuring you to share something personal, you might assert, "I'm not comfortable discussing that at the moment." The key is to express your needs without aggression, clarifying why these boundaries are important to you. This approach protects your well-being and teaches others how to respect your limits, paving the way for healthier interactions.

Equally important is respecting the boundaries of others. Just as you have your personal space and limits, so do those around you. Mutual respect is the cornerstone of any healthy relationship. When someone sets a boundary, it's crucial to honor it, even if you don't fully understand or agree. This respect shows that you value their needs and are willing to try to maintain a healthy relationship. For instance, if a friend tells you they need time alone, respect their request without taking it personally. Doing so demonstrates a level of maturity and understanding that strengthens your bond. It's saying, "I respect you enough to honor your needs," which fosters trust and mutual respect.

Practicing boundary negotiation can be valuable, especially in scenarios where boundaries might conflict. Role-playing is an effective way to get comfortable with this process. Picture a scenario where you and a sibling share a room and need to negotiate personal space. Practice expressing your needs, like saying, "I need a quiet space to study from 7 to 9 PM," while listening to their needs. This exercise encourages open dialogue, teaching you to navigate situations where compromise is necessary. It's about balancing both parties' boundaries, ensuring everyone feels heard and respected. The more you practice, the more natural it becomes to assert your boundaries in real-life situations.

Boundaries are about creating a safe space for yourself and others. They're not walls meant to shut people out but guidelines encouraging healthier interactions. Setting and respecting boundaries fosters an environment where everyone feels valued and understood. This practice is integral to maintaining emotional well-being and building strong, respectful relationships.

Repairing Relationships: After the Storm

When relationships hit rough patches, it can feel like you're standing in the aftermath of a storm, unsure where to begin picking up the pieces. Reconciliation starts with understanding the root cause of conflict. Disputes often arise from misunderstandings, unmet expectations, or deeper issues brewing beneath the surface. Identifying these core issues is crucial. It's like peeling back layers to reveal what's driving the discord. This might involve reflecting on past interactions and considering how each party's actions and words contributed to the tension. Sometimes, it helps to step back and ask yourself what is fueling the disagreement. Is it a specific incident, or are there underlying feelings of resentment or hurt that must be addressed? Understanding the trustworthy source of conflict lays the groundwork for healing and moving forward together.

Once the root cause is identified, the next step is directly addressing the issue, using conflict resolution strategies that foster healing. Mediation can be particularly effective, especially in situations where emotions run high. This involves having a neutral third party facilitate the discussion, ensuring both sides are heard and understood. It's like having a referee who can guide the conversation constructively, helping to keep emotions in check and focus on solutions. Negotiation exercises are another valuable tool, where both parties come together to discuss their needs and work towards a compromise. Picture a scenario where siblings disagree over shared responsibilities at home. They can find a resolution that respects both their needs by sitting down and negotiating a fair division of tasks. These strategies promote collaboration, turning conflict into an opportunity for growth and understanding.

Forgiveness plays a pivotal role in the healing process. It's about letting go of grudges and resentment, allowing space for renewal and connection. Forgiving others and yourself is not about forgetting past hurts but acknowledging them and choosing to move past them. It's like releasing a heavy weight you've been carrying, freeing yourself to embrace the present with an open heart. This process requires patience and understanding, both from those who have been hurt and those who have caused hurt. It can be helpful to engage in forgiveness exercises, where you reflect on the situation, acknowledge the pain, and consciously decide to let it go. This act of forgiveness is integral to rebuilding trust and ensuring the relationship can flourish again.

Repairing relationships also demands ongoing communication and consistent effort. Healing doesn't happen overnight; it's a continuous rebuilding process that strengthens the once-strained bonds. Regular check-ins provide open dialogue, allowing both parties to express their feelings and progress. Imagine touching base with a friend after a disagreement, discussing how things have been and any lingering concerns. This ongoing communication fosters transparency, ensuring that minor issues are addressed before they become more significant conflicts. It's like tending to a garden; regular care and attention help it thrive. By committing to this effort, you reinforce the commitment to the relationship, showing that it's worth investing in.

As you work through these steps, remember that repairing relationships requires a genuine desire to heal and reconnect. The effort you invest in mending broken bonds can lead to deeper, more meaningful connections. It's a reminder that even after the storm, there's always a chance for renewal, growth, and a stronger foundation. The journey of reconciliation can be challenging, but it also offers an opportunity to learn, grow, and strengthen the ties that matter most.

Chapter 14: Navigating Social and Academic Pressures

Balancing Expectations, Self-Worth, and the Stress of Teen Life

P icture yourself sitting at your desk, a pile of textbooks to one side, a laptop open to your latest assignment, and a calendar filled with sticky notes reminding you of looming deadlines. It's a familiar scene for many teens, a silent reminder of the academic pressures that can feel overwhelming. The expectations of juggling homework, preparing for exams, and maintaining good grades can weigh heavily on your shoulders, sometimes leaving you gasping for air. It's not just about the grades but the anxiety that creeps in during exam periods, turning your nights restless and your days stressful.

Test anxiety is a real challenge that many face. The pressure to perform well can lead to sleepless nights and a racing heart as you enter the exam room. It's like standing on a stage, knowing all eyes are on you, and your mind suddenly goes blank. This anxiety can affect your ability to concentrate and recall information, making exams more daunting than they need to be. Coupled with the ever-growing mountain of homework, the stress can feel insurmountable, like trying to climb a peak that keeps growing taller with every step.

Time management becomes your best ally in conquering these academic stressors. It involves organizing and prioritizing tasks to use your time effectively. A daily study schedule can help you allocate specific time slots for different subjects or projects, ensuring you cover everything without feeling rushed. It's like having a roadmap that guides you through your day, reducing the chaos and providing a sense of control. The Eisenhower Box is another effective tool, helping you prioritize tasks based on urgency and importance. By focusing on what truly matters, you can avoid the trap of procrastination and make steady progress.

Setting up a conducive study environment is equally important. Imagine focusing in a cluttered room where every item competes for your attention. A tidy, well-organized space can significantly enhance your focus and productivity. Keep your desk free of distractions, with only the essentials within reach. Good lighting and a comfortable chair also make a difference, turning your study area into a haven for concentration. It's about creating a space that invites focus and minimizes interruptions, allowing you to dive deep into your work.

Study aids and resources are like the secret weapons in your academic arsenal. Flashcards and online quizzes can reinforce what you've learned, making it easier to retain information. They offer a fun and interactive way to test your knowledge, breaking the monotony of traditional study methods. These tools are invaluable for visual learners, who benefit from seeing information laid out in a clear, concise manner. By incorporating these aids, you can transform your study sessions from a chore into an engaging experience.

Interactive Element: Personal Study Space Checklist

Use the checklist below to evaluate and optimize your study space. Includes elements such as lighting, organization, and comfort. Adjust and enhance your environment for better focus and productivity.

Navigating the pressures of school requires a blend of strategy, organization, and self-care. By managing your time effectively, creating a supportive study environment, and utilizing study aids, you arm yourself against the stressors of academic life. These skills help you succeed academically and build resilience and confidence, preparing you for the challenges ahead.

Personal Study Space Checklist

Use this checklist to evaluate and optimize your study space for better focus and productivity.

---

1. Lighting

- Is the lighting bright enough to prevent eye strain?

- Is there access to natural light during the day?

- Are there adjustable lamps for evening study sessions?

- Are there any harsh glares or shadows that might distract me?

---

2. Organization

- Are all my study materials (books, pens, notebooks) within easy reach?

- Do I have designated spots for essential items (e.g., chargers, calculators)?

- Is the space free of unnecessary clutter?

- Do I have shelves, drawers, or organizers to keep things tidy?

- Can I quickly find the materials I need without wasting time?

---

3. Comfort

- Is my chair supportive and adjustable for proper posture?

- Is my desk at a comfortable height for writing or typing?

- Do I have a cushion or back support if needed?

- Is the room temperature comfortable for extended periods of focus?

- Are there distractions (e.g., noise, uncomfortable surfaces) I need to address?

---

4. Technology

- Is my computer, laptop, or tablet set up ergonomically?

- Are all necessary devices fully charged or near an outlet?

- Do I have reliable internet access?

- Are study apps, timers, or digital resources ready to use?

- Have I minimized notifications or digital distractions?

---

5. Atmosphere and Personalization

- Is the space inviting and motivational (e.g., posters, quotes, plants)?

- Do I have a way to play soft background music or white noise if needed?

- Are there personal touches that make the space feel comfortable?

- Is there a balance between being visually interesting but not overwhelming?

---

6. Time Management Tools

- Do I have a clock or timer to help manage my study sessions?

- Is my planner or calendar accessible to track tasks and deadlines?

- Have I set up a to-do list or schedule for the day?

---

7. Break and Self-Care Essentials

- Is there water or healthy snacks nearby to stay hydrated and energized?

- Do I have a comfortable spot for short breaks?

- Have I set a timer or reminder to take regular study breaks?

- Are there relaxation tools (e.g., stress ball, fidget spinner) if I need them?

---

8. Bonus: Quick Tips to Enhance Your Study Environment

- Clear your desk before and after each study session.

- Keep only what you need for the task at hand.

- Test your setup regularly to adjust.

Social Media Savvy: Navigating Online Interactions

Today's social media is like a bustling city square where everyone has something to say. For many teens, it's the place to catch up with friends, share life's highlights, and sometimes seek validation. The impact of likes and comments can profoundly shape how you view yourself. A single post can generate a cascade of likes, offering a fleeting boost of confidence or sitting unnoticed, casting a shadow of self-doubt. This rollercoaster of emotions is familiar, as online interactions often become a mirror reflecting a curated image of self-worth. But it's crucial to remember that self-esteem shouldn't be tied solely to digital approval. Finding a balance where online feedback complements self-worth rather than defines it can be a liberating shift.

Understanding digital literacy and critical thinking is key to navigating this online world effectively. It's about knowing how to evaluate what you see and recognizing reliable sources from misleading ones. Think of it as developing a filter that helps you sift through vast information. When you encounter an article or post, ask yourself: Who wrote this? What's their motive? Is there evidence to support their claims? By questioning the credibility of sources, you become an informed participant in the digital landscape. Understanding digital footprints is essential—every click, share, and like leaves a trace. Awareness of this can guide you in making conscious choices about what you share, knowing it contributes to your online persona.

Maintaining healthy online relationships involves more than just liking and commenting. It requires setting boundaries that protect your privacy and well-being. Start by adjusting privacy controls on your social media accounts. Decide who can see your posts, who can contact you, and what information is visible to others. This safeguards personal details and creates a space to interact more comfortably. Strategies for dealing with cyberbullying are equally important. If you encounter negativity, remember it's okay to block or mute users who make you uncomfortable. Don't hesitate to contact trusted friends, family, or school counselors for support. Engaging positively online means fostering connections that uplift and inspire rather than diminish.

Balancing online interactions with offline experiences is critical for a well-rounded social life. While social media connects you with friends far and wide, real-world connections nurture more profound, meaningful relationships. Make time for activities that don't involve screens, like meeting up with friends for a hike or attending a local event. These offline interactions around you remind you of the joys of face-to-face conversations and shared experiences. They offer a respite from the digital buzz, allowing you to be present in the moment. In this blended world, cultivating a balance between online and offline connections ensures you enjoy the best of both realms.

Interactive Element: Online Self-Reflection Exercise

Reflect on your social media habits. Consider which interactions uplift you and which drain your energy. Use this insight to create a digital space that aligns with your values, fostering positive connections that enhance your self-image and well-being.

Navigating social media with awareness and intention can transform how you interact with the digital world. By cultivating critical thinking, setting boundaries, and fostering real-world connections, you create a balanced social experience that supports your growth and happiness

Online Self-Reflection Exercise: Social Media Habits

Take a moment to reflect on your social media use. Use the following prompts and lines to journal your thoughts:

1. Reflecting on Your Habits

- How much time do I spend on social media daily or weekly?

_____

_____

_____

- What emotions do I typically feel after using social media (e.g., joy, envy, frustration)?

_____

_____

_____

2. Identifying Positive Interactions

- Which accounts or interactions uplift, inspire, or make me feel positive?

_____

_____

_____

- How do these positive interactions contribute to my self-esteem or personal growth?

_____

_____

3. **Recognizing Negative Influences**

- What types of content, accounts, or interactions drain my energy or negatively impact my self-image?

_____

_____

_____

- Why do I continue engaging with these accounts or content, and what steps can I take to limit exposure?

_____

_____

_____

4. **Aligning Your Digital Space with Your Values**

- What are my core values, and how can my social media habits better align with them?

_____

_____

_____

- What steps can I take to curate a digital space that fosters positivity and self-growth?

_____

_____

_____

5. **Action Plan for a Healthier Relationship with Social Media**

- What boundaries can I set for social media use (e.g., time limits, specific apps)?

_____

_____

_____

- What kind of connections or communities do I want to foster online?

_____

_____

_____

Peer Approval vs. Self-Approval: Finding Balance

Imagine walking into school, the halls buzzing with chatter, and feeling that familiar tug—the need to fit in. It's a natural feeling, especially during the teen years, when being part of a group can seem like the most important thing. Peer approval often feels like a ticket to acceptance, a way to blend in and avoid standing out as different. This desire to fit in can sometimes lead to social conformity, where choices are influenced more by what others think than personal beliefs. You might dress a certain way, listen to specific music, or alter your behavior to align with the group. While this can provide a sense of belonging, knowing how it affects your behavior and decisions is crucial.

However, while fitting in can seem important, it's equally vital to nurture self-approval. This means cultivating a sense of self-worth and confidence that isn't dependent on external validation. Self-acceptance and personal integrity are the cornerstones of a fulfilling life. When your actions align with your values, it's like finding a compass that guides you through life's twists and turns. Consider the benefits of living authentically: less stress from trying to please everyone, more confidence in your decisions, and a deeper understanding of who you are. Aligning your actions with your values creates peace and satisfaction, allowing you to stand firm even when external pressures try to sway you.

Resisting peer pressure is a skill that can be developed with practice. It requires the ability to maintain individuality while still fostering healthy relationships. One effective method is role-playing scenarios where you practice saying no. This exercise can be as simple as imagining a situation where friends pressure you to do something uncomfortable. Practice responding firmly and calmly, using clear language to express your boundaries. Rehearsing these scenarios builds the confidence to assert yourself in real-life situations. It's about standing your ground and staying true to yourself, even when it feels challenging. This doesn't mean isolating yourself from others but finding friends who respect your choices and encourage your growth.

Self-reflection is a powerful tool for personal growth and self-discovery. It involves taking the time to set individual goals that reflect your true self. These goals should be based on your interests, passions, and values rather than what others expect of you. Consider what makes you happy and fulfilled, and use that as a foundation for setting your objectives. Regularly checking in with yourself to assess your progress and make necessary adjustments is key. This practice helps you grow as an individual and strengthens your ability to navigate life's complexities with confidence and clarity. By focusing on your personal growth, you create a life that resonates with your authentic self, free from the constraints of external approval.

Striking a balance is crucial in this intricate dance between peer approval and self-approval. It's about embracing your uniqueness while connecting with others meaningfully. This balance empowers you to live authentically, making choices that reflect your identity. As you cultivate self-approval, you build a solid foundation of self-worth and confidence that supports you in all aspects of life. Ultimately, this journey of self-discovery leads to a deeper understanding of yourself and the world around you, allowing you to thrive amidst the ever-changing landscape of adolescence.

Extracurricular Overload: Prioritizing Passions

Imagine diving into a pool of endless possibilities where every club and team calls your name. At first, being involved in sports, drama, band, and debate is exhilarating. But soon, what seemed like a sea of opportunities can turn into a whirlpool of commitments, each pulling you in different directions. The thrill of being active and engaged in multiple extracurricular activities is undeniable. They offer a platform to hone skills, make friends, and explore interests beyond academics. But there's a flip side. Juggling too many activities can lead to burnout, where the joy of participation gets overshadowed by the stress of over-commitment. It's like trying to keep a dozen plates spinning at once—eventually, something's bound to crash.

Balancing sports, clubs, and academics becomes a high-wire act. Each demands time and energy, and when stretched too thin, you risk losing the spark that drew you to them in the first place. It's important to recognize when you're taking on too much. This realization is the first step towards creating a healthier balance. Think of your commitments as a garden. Initially, you might plant various seeds, eager to see what grows. But as time passes, you learn which plants thrive and bring you joy and which require more effort than they're worth. Prioritizing your passions helps you focus on what truly matters, allowing you to nurture those interests that align with your long-term goals and values.

One effective way to manage this is by creating a priority list of your extracurriculars. List all your activities and rank them based on how much they fulfill you and how they contribute to your future aspirations. This exercise helps clarify which activities deserve more time and which might be pruned back. It's about making conscious choices that serve your well-being. Once you've identified your priorities, the next step is to implement time management strategies. Schedule specific times for each activity, ensuring you allocate enough time for rest. Downtime is crucial. It's not wasted time but an opportunity to recharge and reflect. Just as athletes need rest days to perform at their best, you need moments of calm to maintain your enthusiasm and energy.

Encouraging the exploration of new interests is also vital. It's easy to fall into a routine, sticking with activities simply because they're familiar. But stepping out of your comfort zone can lead to unexpected discoveries. Trying new things can reveal hidden talents and passions you never knew you had. Maybe you've always assumed you wouldn't enjoy painting, but a workshop at your local community center sparks a newfound love for art. Or perhaps volunteering at a local shelter introduces you to a passion for helping others. These explorations can be refreshing and invigorating, offering new perspectives and opportunities for growth.

The key to avoiding extracurricular overload lies in balance and self-awareness. You create a fulfilling and sustainable schedule by understanding your limits and prioritizing your passions. It's about finding harmony between doing what you love and maintaining your well-being. Remember, it's okay to say no sometimes. Deciding to focus on fewer activities doesn't mean you're missing out; it means you're making room for what enriches your life.

Handling Bullying: Standing Up for Yourself

Bullying is a term often thrown around, but its impact can be profoundly personal and lasting. It's not just about the physical confrontations that may come to mind first; bullying can take many forms, each with its own set of challenges. Physical bullying involves any form of physical aggression, from pushing to more severe acts of violence. Verbal bullying, on the other hand, includes taunts, threats, and hurtful words that can leave invisible scars. Then there's cyberbullying, a more modern menace, where the anonymity of the internet allows bullies to harass their victims with words and images that can spread quickly and linger online. Recognizing cyberbullying can sometimes be tricky since it doesn't happen in plain view and can manifest through consistent negative comments, exclusion from online groups, or the spread of false information. These various forms of bullying all share a common trait: they can profoundly affect your emotional well-being, leading to feelings of isolation, fear, and helplessness.

Empowering yourself to address bullying starts with understanding the importance of assertive communication. This doesn't mean responding aggressively but standing firm in your own space and expressing your feelings and boundaries clearly. Imagine planting your feet on solid ground, unshaken by the storm around you. When confronted by a bully, you might say, "I don't appreciate your comments; please stop," using a calm yet firm tone. This approach

224

communicates that you will not tolerate disrespect without escalating the situation. In severe cases, reporting bullying to authorities, whether a teacher, school counselor or even law enforcement, is another critical step. It's not about tattling; it's about ensuring safety and support. Schools often have protocols to handle such situations, and reaching out can lead to understanding and action that might not happen if bullying is kept hidden.

Support networks are lifelines in these situations. Friends, family, and mentors can provide the understanding and encouragement you need to face bullying. They offer a listening ear, advice, and sometimes even intervene on your behalf. Imagine your support network as a circle of strength around you, helping to buffer the impact of bullying. Talking to someone you trust can also help you process your emotions, making the burden a little lighter. It's about knowing you're not alone and that others care about your well-being. Reaching out to a trusted adult can sometimes feel daunting, but it's a step toward creating a safe environment where you feel valued and protected. These connections can remind you of your worth and potential, offering hope and perspective when things feel overwhelming.

Building resilience and self-confidence is crucial in overcoming the challenges posed by bullying. Resilience is the ability to bounce back from adversity and rise after being knocked down. It involves developing a strong sense of self-worth and belief in your abilities, which can act as armor against the negativity of bullies. Engaging in activities you excel at or enjoy can help build this inner strength. Whether it's sports, arts, or academics, finding something that makes you feel accomplished can boost your confidence. Surrounding yourself with positive influences affirming your values can bolster your self-esteem. These supportive relationships can act as mirrors, reflecting the qualities that make you unique and valuable. Remember, resilience isn't about never falling but about having the courage to stand up each time you do.

Future Focus: Planning Without Panic

Imagining the future can feel like standing at the edge of a vast, uncharted ocean. The possibilities stretch out before you, endless and sometimes overwhelming. Getting caught up in the uncertainty of what lies ahead is easy, but setting goals can offer a sense of direction and purpose. Think of goal-setting as plotting a course on a map; it helps confidently guide you through the unknown. When you know where you're headed, the journey becomes less daunting and more like an adventure waiting to unfold. Creating a vision board can be a fun and inspiring way to visualize your aspirations. Collect images, quotes, and symbols representing your dreams, and arrange them on a board to keep your goals in sight. This visual reminder is a daily nudge to stay focused and motivated, even when the path seems uncertain.

The SMART framework is a powerful tool for crafting inspiring and achievable goals. SMART stands for Specific, Measurable, Achievable, Relevant, and Time-bound. Start by setting short-term goals as stepping stones toward your larger aspirations. For example, if your long-term goal is to become a veterinarian, a short-term goal could be volunteering at an animal shelter. Make sure your goals are clear and measurable so you can track your progress and celebrate small victories along the way. This approach breaks down the bigger picture into manageable pieces, making it easier to stay on track and avoid feeling overwhelmed. It's like climbing a mountain one step at a time; each step brings you closer to the summit.

Uncertainty is a natural part of life; learning to cope with it is crucial for your well-being. Mindfulness practices offer a way to anchor yourself in the present moment, reducing anxiety about the future. When you practice mindfulness, you focus on what you can control right now rather than worrying about what might happen later. Simple techniques like deep breathing, meditation, or even a mindful walk can help clear your mind and bring a sense of calm. This clarity allows you to adapt more quickly to changes and unexpected challenges, making you more resilient in the face of uncertainty. It's about finding peace in the present, even when the future feels unpredictable.

Exploring career and educational options is an exciting part of planning for the future. It's a chance to discover what truly interests and excites you. Start by researching different fields and talking to those working in those areas. Internships, job shadowing, and informational interviews can provide valuable insights into potential careers. Consider your strengths and passions and consider how they align with various paths. This exploration isn't about making a final decision immediately but gathering information to make informed choices. It's like sampling different flavors before deciding on your favorite ice cream; each experience adds to your understanding of what you enjoy and excel at.

As we conclude this chapter, remember that planning for the future is not about having all the answers right now. It's about laying a foundation for growth and discovery. Setting goals, embracing uncertainty, and exploring new opportunities create a roadmap that guides you forward. This journey of self-discovery and planning is crucial to building a life that reflects your values and dreams. In the next chapter, we'll delve into building resilience and confidence, essential tools for navigating the twists and turns of life with grace and strength.

Chapter 15: Building Resilience and Confidence

Bridge the Gap, Build Understanding, and Work Together

Have you ever watched a tree bend in the wind, its branches swaying yet never breaking? That's resilience in action. It's the capacity to withstand and recover quickly from difficulties, much like that tree that stands tall and rooted despite the storm. Resilience isn't just about enduring; it's about thriving in adversity. Challenges come at us from every angle—school pressures, social dynamics, and family changes. Bouncing back is crucial for surviving these storms and emerging stronger and wiser. Emotional fortitude is the inner strength that helps you navigate these challenges without being overwhelmed. It's like having a mental toolkit filled with strategies for coping with whatever life throws your way.

Resilient individuals often share specific characteristics that set them apart. Adaptability is one of those traits. Life is unpredictable, and those who can adjust to new situations without losing their footing are better equipped to handle change. Think of adaptability as your internal GPS, recalculating the route when you hit a roadblock. Persistence is another key quality. It's the determination to keep going, even when the path gets tough. Picture someone climbing a steep hill; each step is difficult, but each is also progress. Optimism, the ability to see potential good in every situation, fuels this persistence. It's the light that guides you when the way forward seems dark. Together, these traits form a robust foundation for resilience, enabling individuals to face challenges confidently and gracefully.

Cultivating resilience offers numerous benefits, particularly for mental health and overall life satisfaction. Resilient people tend to experience lower levels of stress and anxiety because they have the tools to manage their emotions effectively. This improved mental health leads to a greater sense of life satisfaction, as individuals feel more in control and capable of handling whatever comes their way. Resilience also promotes a positive outlook, encouraging you to view setbacks as growth opportunities rather than failures. This perspective shift can transform how you approach challenges, turning them into learning experiences that contribute to personal development and well-being.

Developing resilience involves practicing certain habits that strengthen your ability to cope with life's ups and downs. Practicing gratitude is a simple yet powerful method. By focusing on the things you're thankful for, you shift your attention from what's going wrong to what's going right, fostering a positive mindset. Try keeping a gratitude journal, jotting down three daily things that bring you joy. Positive thinking also plays a crucial role. It's not about ignoring problems but approaching them with a mindset toward solutions. Engaging in problem-solving exercises can enhance this skill. When faced with a challenge, break it into smaller, manageable parts and brainstorm potential solutions. This approach builds confidence in your ability to tackle problems and reinforces the belief that you can overcome obstacles.

Interactive Element: Resilience Reflection Exercise

Take a moment to reflect on a recent challenge you faced. Write about how you handled it and what you learned from the experience. Consider the traits of resilience—adaptability, persistence, optimism—and how they played a role in your response. What could you do differently next time? This exercise helps you recognize your resilience in action and identify areas for growth.

Resilience is a skill you can cultivate over time, much like a muscle that strengthens with use. Focusing on gratitude, positive thinking, and problem-solving builds a foundation that supports emotional fortitude and adaptability. These practices empower you to navigate life's challenges confidently, turning setbacks into stepping stones for growth and learning. Resilience doesn't make life easier, but it makes you stronger, equipping you with the tools to face adversity and emerge even more capable than before.

Positive Self-Talk: Rewriting Your Inner Dialogue

Have you ever thought, "I'm just not good enough," after a bad day? That internal chatter, or self-talk, plays a massive role in how you see yourself and the world around you. Positive self-talk is like having a cheerleader in your mind, boosting your confidence and motivation. Conversely, negative self-talk can be a relentless critic, eroding your self-esteem and outlook. Imagine waking up to a day filled with possibilities, only to have your inner voice say, "You'll never be able to do it." It sets the tone for how you tackle challenges, often making them seem insurmountable before you've even begun.

Recognizing when negative self-talk creeps in is the first step to transforming it. These thought patterns often hide in plain sight, surfacing in moments of stress or self-doubt. Start by listening to your inner dialogue during challenging situations. Is it supportive, or does it default to criticism? Identifying these negative thought triggers can be as enlightening as uncomfortable, but it's necessary for change. Once you're aware, you can reframe these thoughts with positive affirmations. Instead of "I can't handle this," try saying, "I have the strength to figure this out." It sounds simple, but this shift can make a world of difference. You gradually retrain your brain to adopt a more positive, encouraging stance by consistently replacing negative thoughts with affirmations.

Treating yourself with kindness is crucial. Self-compassion means acknowledging that everyone, including you, has off days and makes mistakes. It's about giving yourself the same understanding and patience you'd offer a friend. When you fall short of your expectations, instead of being harsh, remind yourself that imperfection is part of being human. Think of self-compassion as a soft place to land after a hard day. It doesn't mean ignoring areas where you can improve but not beating yourself up. This practice nurtures resilience and fosters a healthier relationship with yourself, making it easier to bounce back from setbacks.

To make positive self-talk a habit, establish a routine of daily affirmations. You might start each morning by writing encouraging statements on sticky notes and placing them where you see them—like your mirror or computer screen. These affirmations should be personal, reflecting what you need most. For example, "I am capable" or "I am worthy of success" can be daily reminders of your strengths and potential. Crafting personalized affirmation lists is empowering, giving you ownership over your narrative. As these affirmations become a regular part of your day, they help reinforce self-belief and confidence.

Interactive Element: Affirmation Creation Exercise

Set aside time to create a list of personalized affirmations. Consider areas where you need encouragement and write statements that resonate with you. Reflect on them each morning and evening, noticing how they influence your thoughts and feelings over time.

Rewriting your inner dialogue through positive self-talk isn't about ignoring reality; it's about changing your perspective to see challenges as opportunities rather than obstacles. By shifting your self-talk, you cultivate a mindset that supports your growth and well-being. This isn't a quick fix but becomes a powerful tool for building self-confidence and resilience with practice. As you continue this practice, you'll find that the way you speak to yourself becomes more encouraging, helping you to face each day with renewed optimism and strength.

Daily Affirmation Practice Guide

This guide will help you incorporate affirmations into your daily routine, fostering positivity, resilience, and growth. Use it every morning and evening for consistent practice that rewires your inner dialogue.

Step 1: Set Your Intentions

Start by choosing affirmations that resonate with your personal goals and challenges. Below are examples you can use or adapt:

Morning Affirmations

- **Self-Worth:** *"I am worthy of success and happiness."*

- **Resilience:** *"I can handle anything that comes my way today."*

- **Growth:** *"Today is an opportunity to learn and grow."*

- **Gratitude:** *"I am grateful for this fresh start and the opportunities ahead."*

Evening Affirmations

- **Reflection:** *"I am proud of my efforts today, no matter how small."*

- **Emotional Balance:** *"I release today's worries and welcome peace."*

- **Gratitude:** *"I am thankful for the positive moments I experienced today."*

- **Strength:** *"I trust my ability to improve and move forward."*

Step 2: Personalize Your Affirmations

Take a moment to write affirmations tailored to your current needs.

Use the space below:

- Morning Affirmations:

_____

_____

_____

- Evening Affirmations:

_____

_____

_____

Step 3: Create a Daily Routine

Use the following routine to integrate affirmations into your life:

1. Morning Reflection (5–10 minutes):

- Find a quiet space.

- Read your morning affirmations aloud with intention.

- Take a few deep breaths, visualizing a joyous, productive day.

2. Throughout the Day:

- Place affirmations where you'll see them: mirrors, desks, or phone screens.

- When facing challenges, repeat an affirmation that encourages resilience.

3. Evening Reflection (5–10 minutes):

- Sit in a calm space and reflect on your day.

- Read your evening affirmations aloud.

- Write a brief journal entry about how your affirmations influenced your thoughts or actions.

Step 4: Track Your Progress

Use the prompts below to reflect weekly on your affirmation practice:

- Which affirmation resonated with me the most this week?

_____

_____

- How have my thoughts or feelings shifted since starting this practice?

_____

_____

- What challenges did I face, and how did affirmations help me?

_____

_____

- What new affirmations can I add for the upcoming week?

_____

_____

Bonus Tips for Success

- **Consistency is key:** Commit to this practice daily, even for a few minutes.

- **Believe in your words:** Speak affirmations confidently, even if they initially feel unfamiliar.

- **Celebrate progress:** Acknowledge small shifts in your mindset and behavior.

Setting Realistic Goals: Steps to Success

Imagine standing at the base of a mountain, looking up at the peak. It seems daunting, right? That's what life's challenges can feel like without a plan. Setting realistic goals is like mapping out a trail to that summit. It provides direction and motivation, making the climb less intimidating. Goals act as guideposts, leading you step by step toward your destination. They're crucial because they give you something to aim for, something tangible to achieve. Short-term goals are like the rest stops along the way, providing quick wins and keeping your spirits up. Think of getting a passing grade on a quiz, which boosts your confidence for the final exam. Long-term goals, on the other hand, are the peak itself. They require more time and effort, like aiming for a college scholarship or mastering a musical instrument. Both types of goals are important. They work together, creating a path that guides your journey.

The SMART goals framework is a powerful tool for making these goals more effective. SMART stands for Specific, Measurable, Achievable, Relevant, and Time-bound. It's a method that transforms vague intentions into clear, actionable plans. Let's break it down: A specific goal identifies precisely what you want to achieve, leaving no room for ambiguity. For instance, instead of saying, "I want to do better in math," you might say, "I will improve my math grade by one letter by the end of the semester through weekly tutoring." Measurable goals allow you to track progress, providing feedback on how close you are to your target. Achievable goals are realistic, pushing you just enough without setting you up for failure. Relevance ties the goal to your broader life objectives, ensuring it contributes to your long-term vision. Finally, time-bound goals have deadlines, creating a sense of urgency and focus.

Breaking down significant goals into smaller tasks can make them more manageable. It's like dividing the mountain into smaller hills. Each hill conquered adds to your momentum, eventually leading you to the peak. Start by creating a step-by-step action plan. Let's say your goal is to write a novel. Begin with a timeline for drafting, revising, and editing. Break that timeline into daily or weekly writing targets, such as writing 500 words a day or a chapter a week. Each task should feel achievable, giving you a sense of accomplishment with every completion. This approach keeps you organized and reduces the feeling of being overwhelmed by a massive goal. The key is to celebrate each small victory; it fuels your determination to keep going, even when the going gets tough.

Flexibility is an essential part of goal setting. Life is unpredictable, and sometimes, things don't go as planned. Being adaptable means you're open to adjusting your goals as needed. Maybe you experience a setback, like an injury that disrupts your training schedule or a family emergency that demands your attention. Instead of abandoning your goals, consider revising them. Perhaps you need to extend your timeline or adjust your expectations. Flexibility doesn't mean you're giving up; you're navigating the changes with resilience. Your goals should serve you, not the other way around. You keep moving forward by staying adaptable, even if the path looks different from what you originally envisioned.

Setting realistic goals is a dynamic process. It requires a balance of ambition and practicality, vision and adaptability. When you approach goal setting with this mindset, you unlock a powerful tool for personal growth. It's a way to chart your course, one step at a time, as you climb toward your dreams.

Celebrating Small Wins: Building Momentum

In a world that often feels like it's spinning too fast, it's easy to overlook the small victories. Yet, these small wins are like the stepping stones that lead us across the river of life. They might seem insignificant initially, but acknowledging these achievements can fuel your motivation and confidence. Celebrating small accomplishments isn't about patting yourself on the back for every little thing but recognizing your progress. Each step forward brings you closer to your larger goals, no matter how minor. Think of it like climbing a mountain; each foothold you secure is a triumph, making the summit feel possible and inevitable.

Tracking your progress is a powerful way to keep your momentum going. A success journal can become your record of achievements, big and small. Each entry serves as a reminder of what you've accomplished and the effort it took to get there. It might be as simple as jotting down that you finally spoke up in class or managed a difficult conversation with a friend. Over time, this journal becomes a testament to your growth, a resource you can turn to when self-doubt creeps in. Another effective method is creating a reward system for reaching milestones. This doesn't mean splurging on something extravagant whenever you check off a task. It's about giving yourself something to look forward to—a favorite snack, a movie night, or extra time spent on a hobby you love. These rewards reinforce the idea that hard work pays off, encouraging you to keep pushing forward.

Positive reinforcement is more than just a psychological concept; it's a practical tool for self-improvement. When you reward yourself for achieving a goal, your brain releases dopamine, a chemical that makes you feel good. This positive feedback loop boosts your self-esteem and motivates you to continue the behaviors that led to success. It's like giving your brain a high-five for a job well done. Over time, this process can transform your mindset, making challenges feel less daunting and more like opportunities to prove what you can do. By consistently acknowledging and rewarding your progress, you tell yourself that your efforts matter and are worth celebrating.

Adopting a continual growth mindset means viewing each success as a stepping stone to more significant achievements. It's about understanding that every small win is part of a more extensive journey toward personal development. This mindset encourages you to keep learning and improving, no matter how much you've achieved. It's like being a gardener, nurturing each plant with care, knowing it will blossom one day. Encouraging this mindset in teens is crucial. It helps them see that the path to success isn't a straight line but a series of small steps, each building on the last. By focusing on growth rather than perfection, they learn to appreciate the process as much as the outcome.

Interactive Element: Daily Success Tracker

Create a simple chart with columns for the date, the task or goal completed, and a space for reflection on how it felt to achieve it. Please take a moment to complete it daily, acknowledging even the most minor accomplishments. Reflect on how these successes contribute to your larger goals and consider sharing them with friends or family to build a supportive community around your growth.

Recognizing progress and celebrating achievements isn't just about feeling good at the moment. It's about building a solid foundation for future success. Each small win is a building block, contributing to the larger structure of your dreams and aspirations. As you continue to acknowledge and celebrate these steps, you foster a sense of confidence and motivation that propels you forward, ready to tackle whatever comes next.

Learning from Failure: Embracing Mistakes

Have you ever felt the sting of failure, like when you didn't make the team or bombed a test you prepared for? It's easy to think of failure as a dead end, but what if we saw it differently? What if failure was simply feedback—a way to learn and grow? This perspective shift can turn setbacks into powerful opportunities for personal growth and resilience. By analyzing what went wrong, you can identify areas for improvement. Maybe you didn't prepare as thoroughly as you thought or need to change your approach. This analysis isn't about dwelling on mistakes; it's about extracting valuable lessons to guide you toward success.

Consider Thomas Edison, who famously failed thousands of times before successfully inventing the lightbulb. Each attempt taught him something new, a critical knowledge that eventually led to his triumph.

Edison's story is a testament to perseverance and the power of learning from failure. Similarly, J.K. Rowling faced numerous rejections before a publisher took a chance on "Harry Potter." Her journey to success was paved with setbacks, yet she persisted, believing in her story's potential. These examples remind us that failure isn't a reflection of our worth but a stepping stone to achieving greatness. They show that even the most successful individuals encounter obstacles, but their response to those challenges sets them apart.

Processing and learning from mistakes involves a methodical approach. Begin with a post-failure analysis. Reflect on what happened, considering every angle. Ask yourself: What went wrong? What could I have done differently? This reflection isn't about self-blame but understanding the situation more clearly. It's like reviewing a game tape to see where you can improve for next time. Once you've identified the missteps, consider how to apply these insights moving forward. Maybe it's adjusting your study habits, seeking feedback from others, or trying a new strategy altogether. The goal is to use failure as a catalyst for growth, transforming it into a learning experience that enriches your skills and knowledge.

Encouraging a growth mindset is vital in this process. A growth mindset is the belief that abilities and intelligence can develop through dedication and hard work. It's about seeing challenges as learning opportunities, not threats to avoid. Embrace the idea that the brain is like a muscle—it strengthens with use. When you approach failure with this mindset, you view it not as a setback but as an integral part of the learning process. It's a chance to stretch your capabilities and discover new ways to overcome obstacles. This perspective fosters resilience, empowering you to face difficulties with confidence and determination.

As you navigate life's challenges, remember that failure is not the end. It's a natural part of the journey toward achieving your goals. By redefining failure as a learning opportunity, you unlock the potential for growth and transformation. Each misstep becomes a stepping stone, guiding you toward more tremendous success and fulfillment. Embrace your mistakes, learn from them, and let them propel you on your path to personal and academic achievement.

Support Systems: Leaning on Your Squad

Imagine standing on a stage, about to give a speech. Your heart is racing, and your palms are sweaty, but you see your best friend and family cheering you on in the front row. That support makes all the difference. A strong support network can be a lifeline, offering the emotional backing you need to face life's challenges. Friends, family, and mentors provide more than just a shoulder to cry on; they are the pillars that help you stand firm when everything else feels shaky. Close friends offer emotional support, listen to your troubles, and celebrate your successes. They're the ones who know when you need a pep talk or just a quiet moment together. With their unconditional love, the family provides a sense of belonging and security. They are like the roots of a tree, grounding you even when the winds of change blow hard. Mentors, whether teachers, coaches, or older siblings, offer guidance and wisdom. They share their experiences, helping you navigate life's complexities more clearly. These relationships are crucial for building resilience and confidence, reminding you that you're not alone in your struggles.

Building and maintaining these support networks requires effort and intention. It's about creating meaningful relationships that enrich your life, not just collecting acquaintances. Start by engaging with community groups or clubs that align with your interests. Whether it's a sports team, a drama club, or a volunteer group, these communities offer a space to connect with like-minded individuals and form lasting bonds. Reach out to people who inspire you, and don't hesitate to ask for advice or mentorship. It's okay to seek help; it's a sign of strength, not weakness. By asking for guidance, you learn from others and show them that you value their insight. Maintaining these relationships means being present and available and offering support in return. It's a two-way street where giving is just as important as receiving.

Reciprocal support strengthens these bonds, enhancing resilience. When you support others, you create a network of care that uplifts everyone involved. Imagine a group project where each member plays to their strengths, helping each other succeed. The collective effort not only achieves the goal but also builds a sense of camaraderie and trust. This reciprocity fosters an environment where everyone feels valued and empowered, knowing they have a reliable network to lean on. It's like weaving a safety net; each thread represents a relationship that holds you up when you falter.

Encouraging teens to reach out for support is crucial. It's common to feel hesitant, fearing judgment or rejection. But seeking help is a courageous act that opens doors to growth and understanding. It's about recognizing that everyone needs a little help sometimes and that asking for it doesn't make you weak; it makes you human. Start by sharing your challenges with a trusted friend or family member. They might have faced similar issues and can offer valuable advice. Building a support network takes time, but the benefits are lasting. It's about creating a circle of trust where you can be yourself fully and authentically.

As we wrap up this chapter, remember that support systems aren't just beneficial; they're vital. They provide the foundation for resilience, confidence, and growth. With a strong network, you can face challenges with courage and assurance. Next, we'll explore how to navigate social pressures, equipping you with tools to maintain your well-being in a connected world.

Chapter 16: Engaging Parents and Guardians

Keep Growing, Stay Grounded, and Own Your Story

Imagine standing on a bridge over a wide river, the water rushing below and the banks stretching apart on either side. The bridge symbolizes the connection between generations, linking the experiences and values of parents and teens. Yet, sometimes, the bridge feels shaky, swaying with misunderstandings and miscommunication. This generational gap space is filled with different perspectives shaped by unique historical, social, and technological contexts. As teens, you might find it easy to text or post a quick story while your parents remember when face-to-face conversations were the norm. This digital divide can create tension, as parents may struggle to keep up with the rapid pace of technological change, leading to friction in communication styles. Recognizing these differences is the first step in building a stronger connection, like reinforcing the bridge to withstand the currents below.

For many parents, raising teens today presents challenges that previous generations might not have faced. Technology plays a massive role, not just in communication but in parenting itself. The constant connectivity of smartphones and social media can be overwhelming for parents who grew up without such instant access. Imagine the anxiety of trying to understand a world where likes, comments and online interactions carry as much weight as face-to-face conversations. Economic pressures compound these challenges as parents juggle work, finances, and family responsibilities. These pressures can influence family decisions, from budgeting for necessities to planning vacations. Understanding these struggles can foster empathy, helping teens appreciate the complexities parents navigate daily. It's about seeing beyond the surface and recognizing that behind every decision lies a web of considerations and constraints.

Open conversations about differing viewpoints can transform misunderstandings into opportunities for growth. It's like opening a window in a stuffy room, letting in fresh air and perspectives. One effective strategy is using family dialogue prompts—questions or topics that encourage sharing and listening. These prompts can be simple yet powerful, like asking, "What's something you wish I understood better about your world?" or "How can we better support each other?" Such questions invite honesty and reflection, creating a space where both teens and parents feel heard and valued. These conversations aren't about winning an argument but exploring each other's realities with curiosity and respect. It's like weaving threads into a tapestry, where each story adds richness and depth.

Appreciating parental wisdom can be a game-changer in approaching life's challenges. Parents bring a wealth of experience, often learned through trial and error, that can guide you in making informed decisions. Imagine having a map with routes marked by someone who's walked the path before you. By valuing their advice, you tap into this reservoir of knowledge, avoiding pitfalls and embracing opportunities. It's about recognizing that while the world has changed, certain truths remain timeless—like the importance of integrity, kindness, and resilience. These conversations can enhance personal growth as you learn to integrate your parents' insights with your vision of the future.

Interactive Element: Generational Perspective Exercise

Set aside time for a conversation with your parents using the guide below. It starts off with "Share a challenge you faced as a teen and how you overcame it." Listen actively and then share a similar challenge from your own life. Reflect on the similarities and differences and consider how their experience might inform your approach.

Understanding and bridging the generational gap requires patience, empathy, and dialogue. It's about building a partnership where both sides learn from each other, strengthening the bonds that hold families together. This chapter invites you to walk that bridge and engage with the unique perspectives that shape your family's story.

Conversation Guide: Bridging the Generational Gap

This guide will help you engage in a meaningful dialogue with your parents, fostering connection, understanding, and empathy. Use this framework to explore challenges, share stories, and reflect on your shared experiences.

Step 1: Prepare for the Conversation

1. **Set the Stage:**

- Choose a quiet, comfortable time and place to talk without distractions.

- Let your parent(s) know you'd like to have a reflective conversation.

For example: *"I'd love to hear about your experiences as a teen and share some of mine. Could we talk sometime soon?"*

2. **Be Open and Curious:**

- Approach the conversation with a genuine interest in learning from their experiences.

- Remind yourself to listen without judgment and reflect before responding.

Step 2: Start the Conversation

Use this prompt to begin:

- **Prompt:** *"Can you share a challenge you faced as a teenager and how you overcame it?"*

Step 3: Actively Listen

While they share their story:

1. Practice Active Listening:

- Make eye contact, nod, and show you're engaged.

- Avoid interrupting or jumping in with your own experiences right away.

2. Ask Open-Ended Questions:

- "How did that experience make you feel?"

- "What was the biggest lesson you learned from that challenge?"

- "Did you have anyone supporting you through it?"

Step 4: Share Your Experience

Once they've finished, respond with gratitude:

- "Thank you for sharing that with me. It's really inspiring to hear how you overcame that."

- Then, share your own story:

- "I faced a similar challenge when I was younger. Here's what happened…"

- Include:

- The context of your challenge.

- How did you feel at the time?

- The steps you took to overcome it (or what you're still working on).

Step 5: Reflect Together

- Explore the similarities and differences in your experiences:

- "It's interesting how we both dealt with [insert similarity]."

- "I hadn't thought about [their approach] before—it gives me a new perspective."

- "Our situations were different in [insert difference], but I can see how your approach might work for me."

Step 6: End on a Positive Note

- Thank them again: "I really appreciate you sharing that—it helps me see things in a new light."

- Express what you've learned: "This conversation reminded me of how resilient we both are, and it's given me some great ideas for tackling challenges in the future."

Step 7: Reflect on the Conversation

Take time after the discussion to journal or think about:

- What insights did I gain from their story?

_____

_____

- How does their experience inform my own challenges?

_____

_____

- What surprised me about their perspective or approach?

_____

_____

Tips for Success

- **Be Patient:** Allow the conversation to unfold naturally. Don't rush or pressure them to share.

- **Stay Empathetic:** Remember that their challenges were shaped by a different time and context.

- **Celebrate the Connection:** Acknowledge the value of learning from one another and strengthening your bond.

Family Meetings: Creating a Safe Space for Dialogue

Imagine the living room as a stage, where the whole family gathers regularly, not for a performance, but for genuine conversation. Family meetings are like setting up a consistent date with your loved ones—when everyone can share thoughts, discuss concerns, and celebrate successes. Establishing a regular schedule for these meetings is key. It's like marking a recurring event on the calendar, making sure everyone knows when to show up and what to expect. The sense of routine helps create a comfortable atmosphere where dialogue flows naturally over time. These meetings become a safe harbor in the week's storm, a place to anchor conversations and strengthen connections.

Conducting effective family meetings requires structure but not rigidity. Start by creating an agenda, a simple list of topics to guide the discussion. This isn't about strict adherence but rather about giving the conversation a clear direction. Think of it like a road map; it helps you navigate the meeting without getting lost in tangents. Setting ground rules is equally important, ensuring everyone knows the norms—like taking turns to speak or listening without interruptions. Rotating roles for meeting facilitation can also be beneficial. Allow each family member to lead a meeting, take notes, or keep time. This rotation keeps the process dynamic and empowers everyone to contribute equally. A shared agenda encourages collaboration, making it a collective effort rather than a top-down lecture.

Creating an inclusive environment is vital. Everyone should feel comfortable expressing their thoughts without fear of judgment or dismissal. It fosters a sense of safety where all voices are valued and respected. Imagine the meeting as a circle, where each person's perspective adds a piece to the whole picture. This non- judgmental space

250

encourages openness and honesty, allowing for deeper understanding and connection. It's not just about hearing words but about truly listening and understanding the emotions and intentions behind them. This atmosphere of acceptance is like fertile soil, nurturing ideas and solutions that might not emerge elsewhere.

Family meetings can cover many topics, from the mundane to the meaningful. Discussing upcoming family outings or activities is a great way to start. Planning a weekend hike or a movie night can spark excitement and collaboration. It's an opportunity to share interests, discover new activities, and create shared experiences. These planning moments can lead to cherished memories, strengthening the bonds that unite everyone. Addressing concerns, like household chores or school challenges, can also be constructive. It's about finding solutions collectively, where everyone's input is considered and valued. These discussions can transform potential conflicts into opportunities for growth and understanding, like turning rough stones into smooth pebbles.

Regular family meetings are more than just a scheduled chat; they are an investment in relationships. They provide a platform for everyone to express themselves, fostering a culture of communication and mutual respect. Over time, these meetings can become a cherished tradition, a cornerstone of family dynamics that supports emotional well-being and unity. Whether planning the next family

vacation or discussing a recent disagreement, these meetings offer a space where everyone can be heard, understood, and appreciated.

Negotiation Skills: Finding Middle Ground

Imagine a bustling kitchen on a Saturday morning: everyone's clattering about, bumping into each other, and arguing over who's supposed to clean up and who's making breakfast. It's a familiar scene in many households, where balancing responsibilities can feel like a tug-of-war. Negotiation skills are the key to turning these chaotic moments into smooth operations. In family dynamics, negotiation is not just for resolving conflicts; it's about meeting the needs of everyone involved and creating a harmonious environment where each member feels heard and valued. Consider household responsibilities, for instance. Negotiating who does what can transform a dreaded chore into a shared task. It's like turning a solo performance into a duet, where each person plays their part for a collective win.

Negotiation begins with active listening and empathy, often overlooked but compelling skills. When you truly listen, putting aside your agenda, you open the door to understanding another's perspective. It's about hearing not just the words but the emotions behind them. Empathy allows you to step into someone else's shoes, feel their feelings, and respond with genuine understanding. These skills are the foundation of any successful negotiation, turning potential conflicts into opportunities for connection. Identifying shared interests is another crucial step. It's about finding that sweet spot where everyone's needs overlap and creating a solution that benefits all parties involved. Think of it as finding a shared goal, like planning a family movie night where everyone can choose a film on rotation. It's not about winning or losing but creating a scenario where everyone walks away satisfied.

Flexibility is a vital component of effective negotiation. It's the willingness to bend without breaking, to adapt as the conversation unfolds. Parents and teens can benefit from remaining open-minded and ready to explore alternative solutions if the initial plan doesn't work. This flexibility requires a mindset shift, moving from rigid positions to a space where creativity and compromise thrive. Imagine negotiating the destination for a family vacation. Instead of insisting on a single location, explore multiple options, each offering something for everyone. This approach reduces tension and enriches the experience, allowing for unexpected discoveries and shared memories.

To practice these negotiation skills, try role-playing different family scenarios. Create a situation, like deciding on the family vacation destination, and take turns negotiating each person's preferences. This exercise provides a safe space to experiment with different strategies and test out what works and doesn't. It's a bit like a rehearsal, where you can refine your skills without the pressure of real-world consequences. Through these practice sessions, everyone learns to articulate their needs clearly, listen actively, and find solutions that respect everyone's viewpoints. These skills, once honed, become invaluable tools in navigating the complexities of family life. They transform everyday interactions, making them more collaborative, respectful, and fulfilling.

Negotiation is a lifelong skill that extends beyond the family dynamic into friendships, work, and community interactions. It fosters a culture of mutual respect and understanding, where each voice is valued and each needs to be considered. By mastering negotiation, families can create a home environment that thrives on cooperation and harmony. Potential conflicts are turned into opportunities for growth and connection, laying the foundation for stronger relationships and a more peaceful home life.

Joint Activities: Building Bonds Through Shared Experiences

Picture this: the kitchen is filled with the rich aroma of spices and the sizzling sound of onions hitting the pan. You and your family are gathered around the counter, each person adding their touch to a beloved family recipe. Cooking meals together is more than just an exercise in culinary skills—it's a way to weave memories into the fabric of everyday life. As you mix, chop, and stir, stories flow as freely as the laughter that fills the room. These shared moments in the kitchen become a canvas for connection, where each ingredient is a brushstroke that paints a picture of togetherness. Preparing a meal becomes a ritual that strengthens family bonds, creating a sense of unity and accomplishment everyone can savor, both in taste and spirit.

Beyond the kitchen, the world offers various activities catering to diverse interests and abilities. Imagine the family lacing up their hiking boots, ready to explore a nearby trail. Nature walks are a perfect opportunity to disconnect from the digital world and reconnect with each other. As you wander through the woods, conversations flow naturally, inspired by the beauty of the surroundings. It's a chance to share observations, marvel at the wonders of nature, and enjoy the simple pleasure of each other's company. For those who prefer the comfort of home, a family game night can be just as enriching. Gather around the table for a game of cards or a challenging puzzle, where the competition is friendly, and the laughter is contagious. These activities cater to different skill levels, ensuring everyone can participate and enjoy, regardless of age or ability.

Regular quality time is the glue that holds family relationships together. It's like watering a garden; the more you nurture it, the more it blooms. Consistent participation in shared activities fosters a deeper understanding and empathy, allowing family members to see each other in new and meaningful ways. These moments offer a break from the routine, a pause to appreciate the people who mean the most to you. They remind you that even in the hustle and bustle of daily life,

there's always time to connect, listen, and love. It's these shared experiences that create a tapestry of memories woven with threads of laughter, joy, and sometimes even a little chaos.

Creativity is the key to keeping these activities fresh and exciting. Families are encouraged to think outside the box and explore new experiences and traditions that reflect their unique interests and values. This could be as simple as starting a family scrapbook, where each member contributes photos, drawings, or writings about their adventures together. The scrapbook becomes a living document, a testament to shared experiences and memories. The project invites everyone to contribute, fostering a sense of ownership and pride in the family's story. The possibilities are endless, whether trying a new sport, visiting a local museum, or even embarking on a DIY home project. Each new activity is an opportunity to learn, grow, and discover something new about each other, strengthening the bonds that make your family a cherished part of your life.

Encouraging Independence: Trusting Your Teen

Imagine a bird learning to fly. At first, it hesitates, unsure if its wings will hold. It takes a few cautious flaps, then soars with confidence. This is much like the process of encouraging independence in teens. As a parent, the instinct to protect is strong, yet allowing your teen the freedom to make decisions is crucial. It's about finding that spot between guidance and autonomy, where teens learn from their choices but with a safety net below. Gradually increasing responsibilities is one way to support this growth. Start small, perhaps by managing chores or planning their schedule. As they show responsibility, they introduce more complex tasks, like handling personal finances. This progression builds competence and self-assurance, like adding weights to a barbell to build muscle.

The benefits of fostering independence extend far beyond adolescence. Each decision made and responsibility handled prepares teens for the complexities of adulthood. Consider personal finances as a prime example. Teaching teens to budget, save, and even manage

a small bank account can instill lifelong skills. It's not just about managing money; it's about understanding the value of resources and making informed choices. When teens learn to rely on themselves, their confidence grows. They begin to see themselves as capable individuals, ready to tackle the world's challenges. This self-reliance is empowering, providing a foundation of confidence supporting all life areas.

Building trust is a two-way street. It starts with consistent communication and mutual respect. Open discussions about expectations are key to fostering this trust. Sit down with your teen and discuss what you both hope to achieve. Discuss boundaries and responsibilities clearly, ensuring everyone is on the same page. This transparency removes ambiguity and sets a framework for accountability. Please share your thoughts, but also listen to theirs. It's about creating a dialogue, not a monologue. When teens feel heard, their willingness to trust and be trusted increases. This mutual respect strengthens the parent-child relationship, creating a partnership where both sides feel valued.

Parents often find themselves balancing the roles of mentor and controller. However, acting as a mentor rather than a controller can significantly enhance a teen's growth. Mentors guide, advise, and support without dictating every move. They empower teens to take ownership of their choices, encouraging them to learn from successes and failures. This approach fosters independence while providing a safety net. Imagine a coach on the sidelines, offering advice and encouragement but ultimately allowing the player to make decisions on the field. This empowers teens to navigate their path, knowing they have someone to turn to for guidance. By acting as mentors, parents help teens develop critical thinking skills and resilience, preparing them for the diverse challenges of adulthood. It's about stepping back just enough to let them soar, knowing you're always there if they need a steady hand.

Professional Help: When to Seek Counseling

Imagine feeling trapped in a room where the walls seem to be closing in, with no apparent way out. This is what persistent mood changes or academic decline feel like for some teens. It's more than just having a bad day or struggling with a tricky subject at school. When these feelings persist over time, they might be signs that professional intervention could be beneficial. You might notice your teen withdrawing from activities they once loved or their grades slipping despite their efforts. These behaviors can signal underlying emotional challenges that need more than a parent's loving support.

Seeking professional help through counseling provides a framework for teens and families to navigate these challenges. Counseling is not about fixing someone but equipping them with tools to understand better and manage their emotions. It's like learning a new language—one that helps articulate feelings, identify triggers, and develop coping strategies. Through therapy, teens can explore their emotions in a safe space, guided by someone trained to listen without judgment. For families, counseling offers insights into dynamics that might contribute to stress, helping everyone learn to communicate more effectively and support each other more fully. It's a proactive step towards building emotional resilience, like strengthening muscles to prevent injury.

Approaching the counseling topic can be sensitive, especially if your teen already feels vulnerable. It's essential to frame counseling as a positive, proactive choice rather than a sign of failure. Start by openly conversing, expressing concern and care rather than blame. You might say, "I've noticed you've been feeling down lately, and I want to ensure you have all the support you need." Emphasize that seeking help is a strength, not a weakness, and that it's okay to reach out when things feel overwhelming. Encourage them to ask questions and express any reservations they might have. This approach fosters a sense of partnership, showing that you're in it together, ready to support them every step of the way.

Choosing the right counselor is crucial for ensuring a positive experience. It's not just about finding someone with the proper credentials but someone who aligns with your family's values and your teen's needs. Start by considering what type of counseling might be most beneficial—individual therapy, family therapy, or perhaps group sessions. Research different professionals, considering factors like their specialization, approach, and availability. Some teens might feel more comfortable with a counselor of a particular gender or age, so consider these preferences. It can also be helpful to schedule a meeting with potential counselors to see how your teen feels in their presence. This initial meeting is like a test drive, allowing one to gauge comfort levels and establish rapport. The goal is to find someone who makes your teen feel understood and supported, creating an environment where they feel safe to explore their emotions.

Counseling can be a pivotal step in a teen's journey toward emotional well-being. It offers a path to understanding and growth, where challenges become opportunities for learning and resilience. By recognizing when professional help is needed, framing it positively, and carefully selecting the right counselor, families can ensure their teens receive the support they need to thrive.

Red Flags Indicating a Teen May Need Help or Counseling

1. **Drastic Changes in Behavior**

   - Sudden withdrawal from family, friends, or activities they once enjoyed.

   - Acting out in ways out of character, such as aggression or defiance.

2. **Significant Academic Decline**

   - Poor performance in school despite previous success.

   - Skipping classes or losing interest in education altogether.

3. **Mood Swings or Emotional Instability**

   - Persistent sadness, anxiety, or irritability.

   - Unexplained outbursts or difficulty managing emotions.

Social Isolation

   - Avoiding social interactions or spending excessive time alone.

   - Struggling to maintain friendships or connect with peers.

4. **Changes in Sleep Patterns**

   - Sleeping too much, struggling with insomnia, or experiencing frequent nightmares

   - Complaints of constant fatigue or low energy.

5. **Appetite or Weight Changes**

- Noticeable weight loss or gain.

- Skipping meals, overeating, or developing unhealthy eating habits.

6. **Risky or Self-Destructive Behavior**

- Experimenting with drugs, alcohol, or unsafe sexual activity.

- Engaging in dangerous activities without regard for consequences.

7. **Physical Signs of Self-Harm**

- Unexplained cuts, burns, or bruises.

- Wear long sleeves or clothing to cover up injuries, even in warm weather.

8. **Expressions of Hopelessness or Low Self-Esteem**

- Frequent statements like "I'm a failure," "I don't belong," or "What's the point?"

- A sense of worthlessness or feelings of being unloved.

9. **Talk of Death or Suicidal Thoughts**

- Talking or joking about death or suicide.

- Searching online for ways to harm themselves.

Next Steps

If you observe any of these red flags:

- **Approach with Compassion:** Have a nonjudgmental conversation about what they're experiencing.

- **Seek Professional Support:** Contact a school counselor, therapist, or trusted professional for guidance.

- **Stay Involved:** Regularly check in, listen, and offer ongoing support.

Chapter 17: Sustaining Emotional Growth

Sustaining Emotional Growth – Nurturing the Skills for Lifelong Success

Imagine standing in a garden that's been meticulously tended over the years. Every plant and flower reflects the care and effort put into nurturing it. Your emotional growth is much like that garden—it requires regular attention and dedication to flourish. Emotional growth is not a one-time event but a continuous journey, demanding commitment just like tending to a garden does. It's easy to assume your work is done once you've learned a few techniques. However, emotions are dynamic and ever-changing, much like the seasons. They require you to adapt and learn constantly. This ongoing process ensures that your emotional skills remain sharp and ready to tackle whatever life throws your way.

Engaging in workshops and seminars on emotional intelligence can be incredibly beneficial. These sessions provide a space to learn from experts and fellow participants, gaining insights into how others manage their emotions. They offer a chance to practice new skills in a supportive environment, like a rehearsal before a big performance. Consider attending events focusing on emotional intelligence to immerse yourself in the latest research and strategies. They can provide knowledge and practical exercises to incorporate into daily life, helping you better understand and manage your emotions.

Beyond workshops, there are numerous resources available for ongoing self-education. The vast world of books, podcasts, and online courses offers countless opportunities to deepen your emotional skills. Books like "Emotional Intelligence" by Daniel Goleman provide foundational knowledge, while podcasts such as "The Happiness Lab" offer regular insights into emotional well-being. Online courses from Coursera or edX can also provide structured learning, allowing you to explore topics ranging from mindfulness to communication skills. These resources are tools in a toolbox, each offering unique strategies to help you navigate your emotional landscape. Dive into these materials with curiosity and an open mind, and you'll find that there's always something new to learn.

Curiosity plays a crucial role in emotional growth. It's the spark that drives you to explore new ideas and approaches. Imagine approaching your emotions with the same wonder and openness as a child discovering the world. This mindset encourages you to experiment, question, and reflect, leading to deeper self-awareness and understanding. Curiosity allows you to see mistakes not as failures but as opportunities for growth. It invites you to ask questions like, "Why did I react that way?" or "What can I learn from this experience?" By staying curious, you keep your emotional skills sharp and ready for whatever challenges come your way.

Developing a personal growth plan can provide structure and direction for your emotional education. Start by setting clear, achievable goals that align with your values and interests. These goals

could be as simple as practicing mindfulness for five minutes each day or as ambitious as completing a course on emotional intelligence. Outline the steps needed to achieve each goal and consider scheduling regular check-ins to track your progress. This plan serves as a roadmap, guiding you toward emotional maturity. A structured approach ensures that you remain focused and motivated, helping you build resilience and confidence.

Interactive Element: Personal Growth Plan Template

The personal growth plan below will help you list three emotional skills you want to improve. Write down specific actions you'll take to develop each skill, such as attending a workshop, reading a book, or practicing a new technique. Set a timeline for achieving these goals and include regular check-ins to assess your progress. This template will serve as a guide, helping you stay on track and measure your growth.

Emotional growth is a lifelong pursuit. You ensure your emotional skills remain vibrant and compelling by continuously learning, exploring new resources, nurturing curiosity, and creating a personal growth plan. This ongoing commitment to self-improvement enhances your emotional intelligence and enriches your relationships and overall well-being.

Personal Growth Plan: Enhancing Emotional Skills

Use this template to identify and develop three emotional skills. Follow the steps below to create actionable goals, set a timeline, and track progress.

1. Emotional Skill #1: (Example: Managing Stress and Anxiety)

- **Specific Actions:**

1. Practice mindfulness or meditation for 10 minutes daily.

2. Read a book on stress management (*e.g.*, *"The Anxiety Solution"* by Chloe Brotheridge).

3. Attend a local or online stress management workshop.

- **Timeline:**

1. Begin mindfulness practice today.

2. Complete the book within 4 weeks.

3. Attend a workshop within 2 months.

- **Check-In Points:**

1. Weekly: Journal on how mindfulness has impacted your stress levels

2. .Monthly: Reflect on how techniques from the book/ workshop have improved your coping strategies.

---

2. Emotional Skill #2: (Example: Improving Communication Skills)

- **Specific Actions:**

1. Take an online course on effective communication (*e.g.*, *via Coursera or Udemy*).

2. Practice active listening by summarizing what others say before responding.

3. Engage in weekly conversations with a trusted friend or mentor to apply new skills.

- **Timeline:**

1. Enroll in an online course within 1 week.

2. Begin practicing active listening daily.

3. Schedule weekly conversations starting this week.

- **Check-In Points:**

1. Weekly: Reflect on how communication techniques are applied in real-life conversations.

2. End of course: Assess your growth and areas needing more attention.

---

3. **Emotional Skill #3: (Example: Cultivating Gratitude and Positivity)**

- **Specific Actions:**

1. Write down three things you're grateful for every evening.

2. Read a book on gratitude (*e.g., "The Gratitude Diaries"* by Janice Kaplan).

3. Volunteer or perform small acts of kindness weekly to foster a sense of contribution.

- **Timeline:**

1. Begin gratitude journaling today.

2. Finish the book within 6 weeks.

3. Commit to weekly acts of kindness starting this weekend.

- **Check-In Points:**

    1. Weekly: Reflect on how gratitude journaling and acts of kindness have influenced your mood.

    2. Monthly: Assess how gratitude has shifted your outlook and mindset.

Tracking and Reflection

1. Use this space to log your progress for each emotional skill:

Skill 1 Progress:

_____

_

Skill 2 Progress:

_____

_

Skill 3 Progress:

_____

_

- **Questions for Reflection:**

  o What successes am I seeing in my personal growth?

  _____

  o What challenges am I facing, and how can I overcome them?

  _____

  o How have these changes impacted my emotional well-being and relationships?

  _____

  _____

Conclusion By continuously learning, exploring new resources, and nurturing curiosity, you ensure your emotional skills remain vibrant and compelling. Use this journal as a living document to guide and measure your personal growth. Commit to self-improvement, and watch as it enriches your relationships, emotional intelligence, and overall life satisfaction.

Reflective Practices: Regular Check-Ins with Yourself

Imagine standing before a mirror, not just seeing your reflection but truly looking within. Regular self-reflection is like holding that mirror up to your emotions and actions, allowing you to track your progress and pinpoint areas for growth. It's a valuable practice that can reveal patterns in your behavior, helping you understand why you react the way you do. Think of it as a personal check-in, a dedicated time to pause and ask yourself, "How am I doing?" This kind of introspection is more than just thinking about your day. It's about digging deeper, exploring your emotional responses, and identifying what might hold you back or propel you forward.

One way to engage in effective self-reflection is through weekly self-assessment exercises. Set aside time weekly to sit with your thoughts and evaluate your emotional journey. Ask yourself questions like, "What went well this week?" or "What challenges did I face, and how did I handle them?" This practice isn't about criticizing yourself but rather understanding your emotional landscape. It's like reviewing a map before setting out on a road trip, ensuring you know where you've been and where you're headed. By consistently engaging in these exercises, you gain a clearer picture of your emotional health and can adjust as needed.

Techniques such as journaling, meditation, or self-questioning can facilitate this introspection. Journaling lets you capture your thoughts and feelings on paper, providing a tangible record of your emotional experiences. Use reflective journaling prompts to guide your writing. For instance, consider prompts like "Describe a moment this week when you felt most at peace" or "What triggered strong emotions, and how did you manage them?" These questions encourage you to explore your inner world and gain insights into your behavior. Meditation offers another path to reflection, where you focus inward, observing your thoughts without judgment. It's a chance to quiet the noise and listen to your inner voice. Self-questioning, too, can be a powerful tool. It involves asking yourself targeted questions, like, "What am I grateful for today?" or "What could I have done differently in that situation?"

Integrating these practices into your daily or weekly routine ensures consistent reflection. It might be a few minutes before bed each night or a more extended session on a Sunday afternoon. The key is to make it a regular habit, something you look forward to as a time for personal growth. Consider blocking this time off your calendar, treating it as an essential appointment with yourself. This dedicated space allows you to step back from the busyness of life and focus on what truly matters—your emotional well-being.

Tracking emotional changes over time can lead to greater self-awareness and growth. Observing patterns in your responses, you begin to notice what triggers certain emotions and how you typically react. Perhaps you realize that stress at school often leads to irritability at home or that spending time with friends lifts your mood. These observations empower you to make informed choices. You might incorporate stress-relief techniques or prioritize activities that bring you joy. With time, you'll see how small changes in your routine or mindset can significantly improve your emotional health.

Interactive Element: Reflective Journaling Prompts

Use the list of reflective journaling prompts below to guide your introspection. These prompts include questions like, "What was a highlight of my day?" and "What lesson did I learn this week?" Use these prompts as a starting point for journaling sessions, allowing you to delve deeper into your thoughts and emotions.

Embracing reflective practices as part of your life enriches your understanding of yourself. It's not just about looking back but also about looking forward, using the insights gained to shape a more emotionally aware and resilient future.

1. Daily Highlights

- What was the highlight of my day?

_____

_____

_____

- What made me smile or feel grateful today?

_____

_____

_____

_____

2. Emotional Check-In

- How am I feeling right now?

_____

_____

_____

- What emotions did I experience most strongly today, and why?

_____

_____

_____

3.. Growth and Lessons

- What lesson did I learn this week?

_____

_____

_____

- How did I step out of my comfort zone recently?

_____

_____

_____

_____

4. **Gratitude and Positivity**

- What are three things I am grateful for today?

_____

_____

_____

- Who or what made me feel supported this week?

_____

_____

_____

5. **Challenges and Problem-Solving**

- What challenge did I face today, and how did I overcome it?

_____

_____

_____

- How can I approach this problem differently in the future?

_____

_____

_____

_____

6. Personal Aspirations

- What is one goal I want to focus on this week?

_____

_____

_____

- How am I progressing toward my long-term goals?

_____

_____

_____

7. Self-Care and Balance

- Did I care for myself physically, emotionally, and mentally today?

_____

_____

_____

- What can I do to recharge and nurture myself tomorrow?

_____

_____

_____

_____

8. **Relationships and Connections**

- Who made me feel valued and loved today?

_____

_____

_____

- Is there a relationship in my life I want to nurture more?

_____

_____

_____

9. **Mindfulness and Awareness**

- What is something I noticed today that I usually overlook?

_____

_____

- How present was I in my interactions and activities today?

_____

_____

_____

_____

10. **Dreams and Creativity**

- What have I been dreaming about but haven't pursued yet?

_____

_____

_____

- How can I incorporate more creativity or passion into my life?

_____

_____

_____

Giving Back: Helping Others Manage Their Emotions

Imagine standing at the front of a room, with voices buzzing around you as you prepare to lead a discussion. Your heart quickens, not with fear, but with excitement. You're about to guide your peers through a conversation about managing emotions—a topic you've been exploring deeply. It's a moment where everything

you've learned begins to flow outward, transforming your life and those around you. Supporting others on their emotional journeys is like looking into a mirror: your understanding deepens as you teach and mentor. You reinforce your skills whenever you help someone else manage their feelings. It's an empowering realization that your experiences and insights can impact others, prompting you to grow even more.

Volunteering as a peer counselor or mentor provides a meaningful avenue for this kind of growth. Picture yourself sitting across from a friend, offering a listening ear and gentle guidance. In these moments, your empathy and patience are invaluable. These skills, honed over time, become essential tools in creating a supportive environment where others feel safe to express themselves. As a mentor, you're helping someone else navigate their emotions and learning to navigate your own with more remarkable finesse. Consider getting involved in school or community programs that focus on peer support. These roles offer a chance to build connections, develop leadership skills, and make a tangible difference in the lives of others.

Opportunities for emotional support roles are plentiful. Think about leading a support group or club dedicated to emotional well-being. Imagine the impact of creating a space where teens can come together to share their struggles and triumphs. This kind of leadership requires empathy and active listening, which are crucial for supporting others effectively. When you actively listen, you offer your full attention, creating a sense of validation and understanding. It's about being present and truly hearing what the other person is saying beyond just their words. This approach fosters trust and encourages open communication, laying the foundation for meaningful connections and emotional growth.

Community service projects also provide an excellent platform for promoting emotional well-being. You may volunteer at a local shelter, school, or community center, engaging in uplifting and inspiring activities. Through these projects, you contribute to the community and cultivate a more profound sense of purpose and fulfillment. Think about organizing workshops on stress management or mindfulness, providing practical tools for emotional health. These projects offer a unique chance to connect with individuals from diverse backgrounds, broadening your perspective and enhancing your empathy. As you work alongside others, you realize the power of collective effort in fostering positive change.

In giving back, you discover a profound truth: helping others manage their emotions is reciprocal. Each interaction, every shared experience, becomes a learning opportunity, allowing you to refine your emotional skills. You find yourself more attuned to your feelings and more aware of your strengths and areas for growth. This cycle of support and learning creates a ripple effect, extending beyond individual encounters to impact entire communities. As you continue to engage in these roles, you gain confidence in your ability to make a difference in your life and those around you.

Staying Inspired: Finding Motivation in Others

Imagine the feeling of discovering a story that resonates so profoundly that it lights a fire within you. That's the power of inspiration—it's contagious and transformative. Learning from the stories and achievements of others can be a catalyst for your personal growth. Consider the biographies of emotionally intelligent individuals, where real-life narratives showcase resilience, empathy, and determination. These stories serve as roadmaps, illustrating how others have navigated their paths with grace despite challenges. By absorbing their experiences, you can gain insights into your journey, find motivation in their triumphs, and learn from their setbacks.

Sources of inspiration are all around us, waiting to be discovered. Influential figures such as Malala Yousafzai or Nelson Mandela offer profound lessons in courage and empathy. Books like "Becoming" by Michelle Obama or "The Power of Now" by Eckhart Tolle invite you to explore new perspectives and deepen your understanding of yourself and the world. Podcasts like Brené Brown's "Unlocking Us" or TED Talks on emotional intelligence can ignite a passion for self-improvement. These resources are more than just words; they are seeds of inspiration, ready to grow into meaningful change in your life. By immersing yourself in these stories and ideas, you open yourself to new possibilities and expand your emotional horizons.

Surrounding yourself with positive influences is another way to sustain your growth. Imagine building a network of supportive friends, mentors, and role models who inspire you to be your best self. These individuals become your safety net, offering encouragement and guidance when needed. They help you see your potential, even when you doubt yourself. You create an environment where emotional growth can thrive by spending time with people who uplift and challenge you. This network is not just about receiving support;

it's also about giving back, creating a cycle of inspiration and empowerment that benefits everyone involved.

Finding mentors who exemplify emotional intelligence can provide invaluable guidance. A mentor doesn't have to be a famous figure; they could be a teacher, coach, or family friend. What matters is their ability to guide you with empathy and wisdom. A mentor can offer a fresh perspective on challenges, helping you navigate complex emotions and situations. They are like a lighthouse, providing direction and reassurance as you chart your course. Seeking out mentors is an active process involving reaching out and building relationships based on trust and mutual respect. In doing so, you gain access to a wealth of knowledge and experience, enriching your journey toward greater emotional understanding.

Inspiration fuels sustained growth, driving you to explore new heights and overcome obstacles. By engaging with stories of resilience and surrounding yourself with positive influences, you create an environment where emotional growth can flourish. These connections and lessons remind you that you are not alone in your pursuit of self-improvement. Instead, you are part of a larger community of individuals striving to grow and positively impact the world.

Adapting to Change: Embracing New Challenges

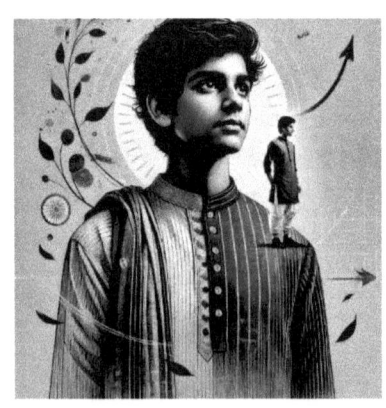

Change is one of life's few constants, impacting us all uniquely. Change can be both unsettling and invigorating, starting with moving to a new city, starting at a different school, or adjusting to a new family dynamic. Imagine the first day at a new school: unfamiliar faces, other classrooms, and a new schedule. It might feel overwhelming, but it's also a fresh start, a blank page waiting to be filled with new experiences and friendships. Adapting to change is a vital part of building emotional resilience. It allows you to navigate life's unpredictable nature with grace and confidence. Embracing change means recognizing it as an opportunity rather than something to fear. It's about acknowledging the discomfort that comes with newness while seeing the potential for growth and learning.

So, how do you embrace change with open arms? One powerful approach is adopting a "growth mindset." This concept, popularized by psychologist Carol Dweck, is about believing that abilities and intelligence can be developed with effort and time. Instead of viewing challenges as insurmountable obstacles, a growth mindset encourages you to see them as chances to improve and learn. It's the difference between thinking, "I can't do this," and "I can't do this yet." Shifting your perspective opens you to possibilities you might not have considered. This mindset doesn't eliminate fear but helps you move through it, knowing that each challenge is a stepping stone to greater understanding and capability.

The emotional benefits of adaptability are vast. When you're open to change, you invite new experiences and insights into your life. It's like broadening your horizon, allowing you to see beyond the immediate and familiar. This openness leads to personal growth, as each new experience teaches you something about yourself and the world. Adaptability also builds resilience, equipping you to easily handle future changes and less stress. Picture yourself as a tree that bends with the wind rather than breaking; each gust makes you stronger and more flexible. By embracing change, you expand your comfort zone and increase your capacity for joy and discovery.

Setting goals that push you beyond your comfort zone is an excellent way to embrace change. These goals should challenge you, sparking both excitement and a little bit of nervousness. It could be joining a new club, trying out for a sports team, or starting a creative project you've always wanted to explore. These goals encourage you to enter the unknown, where actual growth happens. They offer a chance to develop new skills and meet people who inspire and support

you. As you pursue these challenges, you'll find that your confidence grows with each step you take. The more you push your boundaries, the more you realize what you can achieve.

Embracing change is about more than reacting to life's shifts—it's about actively seeking growth and embracing the unknown. By developing a growth mindset, remaining adaptable, and setting ambitious goals, you cultivate an environment where personal and emotional development can flourish. Remember, change is not something to be feared but embraced as a constant companion on your path to self-discovery and resilience.

Crafting Your Narrative: Owning Your Story

Imagine your life is a book for a moment, and you write a new page daily. The story is yours, filled with your values, goals, and experiences. This is your narrative, a powerful tool that shapes how you see yourself and how others see you. Teens often feel like they're living stories written by others—parents, teachers, or peers—but the truth is, you are the author of your own life. Crafting your narrative means taking control of your story and ensuring it reflects who you are. It's about deciding what is important to you and what you want your life to be about. Writing a personal mission statement can help with this process. Think of it as your life's North Star, a guiding principle that keeps you focused on what matters most. It's a statement that captures your core values and aspirations, reminding you of your purpose even when life gets chaotic.

To begin crafting your narrative, consider engaging in activities that encourage self-expression. Storytelling workshops or exercises can be beneficial. These activities create a space to explore your past, reflect

on your present, and envision your future. You might start by writing short stories or poems about pivotal moments in your life, those times when you learned something new about yourself or overcame a challenge. Sharing these stories can be empowering and enlightening, helping you identify themes and patterns that resonate with your mission. Creating a vision board or timeline can visually map your goals and achievements, visually representing your journey. These exercises are creative outlets and opportunities to articulate your life story and uncover insights into your identity.

Owning your story means embracing your experiences, both the triumphs and the setbacks. It's about accepting your past and using it as a foundation to build your future. When you take control of your narrative, you empower yourself to lead an authentic life. You begin to see that your story is not just a series of events but a reflection of your choices and values. This realization can be incredibly liberating. It allows you to break free from the expectations and labels others might place on you. You start living on your terms, making decisions that align with your true self. This authenticity leads to greater self-confidence and a deeper connection with others as you attract people who appreciate and support the real you.

Sharing your story with others can have a profound impact. It's a way to connect and inspire, showing everyone has their unique path. When you share your journey with peers, you create a space for understanding and empathy. Others might see parts of themselves in your story, realizing they are not alone in their struggles. This connection can foster a sense of community, where individuals support and uplift one another. It's like weaving a tapestry of shared experiences, each thread adding to the richness of the whole. By opening up about your narrative, you encourage others to do the same, creating a ripple effect of authenticity and empowerment that extends beyond your immediate circle.

As you craft and own your narrative, remember that it's a living document that evolves as you grow and change. Your story is not set in stone but is shaped by the choices you make and the experiences

you embrace. By actively participating in this process, you cultivate a sense of ownership over your life, guiding it in your desired direction. This chapter is just the beginning, setting the stage for the next phase of your emotional journey. As you continue to explore and define your narrative, you build a foundation for a life filled with purpose and connection.

Family Games

Here are five engaging family games designed to help teens with anger management while fostering communication, emotional regulation, and positive family bonding:

1. Feelings Charades

Objective: Improve emotional awareness and expression.

How to Play:

Write different emotions (e.g., frustration, joy, embarrassment, anger, excitement) on slips of paper

Players take turns acting out the emotion without speaking while others guess.

After each round, discuss ways to manage or express the emotion healthily.

Benefits: Helps teens recognize emotions, develop empathy, and explore strategies to manage feelings.

---

2. Calm Down Relay

Objective: Practice calming techniques under pressure. How to Play:

Create stations with calming activities (e.g., deep breathing, squeezing a stress ball, coloring a mandala, or naming five things they see).

Players race to complete the calming tasks at each station.

The focus is on completing the tasks mindfully rather than speed.

Benefits: Introduces teens to calming strategies when feeling angry or stressed.

---

3. The "What If?" Game

Objective: Encourage problem-solving and perspective-taking.
How to Play:

Pose hypothetical anger-inducing scenarios (e.g., "What if your sibling takes something without asking?").

Each player shares how they might react and brainstorm alternative ways to handle the situation calmly.

Discuss the best strategies as a group.

Benefits: Teaches teens to think before reacting and consider alternative approaches to anger.

---

4. Emotion Jenga

Objective: Facilitate discussion about emotions and coping techniques.

How to Play:

Write questions or prompts on Jenga blocks (e.g., "What helps you calm down when you're angry?" or "Describe a time you handled anger well.").

Players answer the prompt on the block they pull before adding it to the stack.

Benefits: Promotes self-reflection and emotional expression in a fun, interactive format.

---

5. **Gratitude & Growth Board Game**

Objective: Shift focus from anger to gratitude and problem-solving. How to Play:

Create a simple board game with spaces that prompt players to share things they are grateful for or challenges they've overcome.

Include spaces encouraging deep breathing or recounting positive moments from the day.

Benefits: Encourages positive thinking and fosters a supportive family environment.

Conclusion

As our journey together comes to a close, it's essential to reflect on the core purpose of this book: to empower you with practical tools to manage anger and emotions, to enhance your self-awareness, and to build meaningful, lasting relationships. Throughout these pages, I have aimed to provide a compassionate and supportive guide for you, the teens, and your parents and guardians. It's about creating an understanding environment where emotional challenges become pathways to growth, self-awareness, and deeper connections.

We started by diving into the roots of anger in Chapter 1, exploring the science behind emotions and how family dynamics, past experiences, and social pressures can influence how you feel. Understanding these aspects helps you see that emotions are natural and manageable. Then, in Chapter 2, we moved on to recognizing emotional triggers and building self-awareness. Here, you learned about identifying the patterns in your responses, which is the first step toward controlling them. We also introduced mindfulness practices and journaling as tools for gaining clarity and perspective.

Chapter 3 focused on practical strategies to manage anger, such as breathing techniques, physical activity, and creative expression. These are immediate tools when emotions run high. Chapter 4 emphasized the importance of strengthening relationships through active listening, effective communication, and empathy. These skills are vital in turning conflicts into discussions and building trust with those around you.

Chapter 5 focused on navigating the pressures of school and social life, discussing managing academic stress, balancing peer approval with self-approval, and handling bullying. Chapter 6 explored building resilience and confidence, highlighting how positive self-talk and celebrating small wins can boost self-esteem and help you bounce back from setbacks.

For parents, Chapter 7 provided insights on bridging generational gaps and fostering open communication, emphasizing the importance

of collaboration and understanding in family dynamics. Finally, Chapter 8 encouraged ongoing emotional growth, reflecting on how embracing change and crafting your narrative can empower you to own your story.

The key takeaways from this journey are simple yet powerful. Emotional intelligence is your ally, helping you navigate life with empathy and understanding. Resilience allows you to turn challenges into growth opportunities, and strong communication skills are the foundation of healthy relationships. These are skills worth nurturing, as they can profoundly impact your life and the lives of those around you.

I encourage you, the teens, to apply what you've learned here. Embrace your emotions and let them guide you to personal growth. Practice the exercises and strategies we've discussed. Don't hesitate to seek support when you need it—whether from friends, family, or professionals. Remember, asking for help is a sign of strength, not weakness.

Your role as parents and guardians is crucial. Continue fostering those open dialogues and supporting your teens' emotional journeys. Your understanding and collaboration can make all the difference in strengthening family bonds and creating a supportive home environment.

This book is just the beginning. I urge you to keep learning and growing. Explore additional resources, participate in community activities, and maintain a mindset open to new experiences and insights. Emotional development is a lifelong journey; there's always more to discover.

Thank you for embarking on this journey with me. Your willingness to learn and grow is inspiring, and I am grateful to have been part of your path toward emotional intelligence and fulfillment. Resources and support are always available, and you are not alone in this journey.

I want to leave you with hope and confidence as we close this chapter. You have the tools to navigate life's challenges and build a future filled with meaningful connections and emotional well-being. Trust yourself and the skills you've gained, and know you can lead a fulfilling and emotionally intelligent life.

References

- ***The Neurobiology of the Emotional Adolescent***. *Retrieved from https://pmc.ncbi.nlm.nih.gov/articles/PMC5074886/*

- ***Puberty: Tanner Stages for Boys and Girls***. *Cleveland Clinic. Retrieved from https://my.clevelandclinic.org/health/body/puberty#:~:text=Hormones%20involved%20in%20puberty%20include,the%20testes%20to%20produce%20testosterone.*

- ***The Role of Family Dynamics in Teen Mental Health***. *Retrieved from https://www.wingswithin.in/article/the-role-of-family- dynamics-in-teen-mental-health*

- ***How Using Social Media Affects Teenagers***. *Retrieved from https://childmind.org/article/how-using-social-media-affects-teenagers/*

- ***Teaching Emotional Intelligence to Teens and Students***. *Retrieved from https://positivepsychology.com/teaching-emotional-intelligence/*

- ***Mindfulness Exercises (for Teens)***. *Nemours KidsHealth. Retrieved from https://kidshealth.org/en/teens/mindful-exercises.html*

- ***The Mental Health Benefits of Journaling for Teens***. *Retrieved from https://tillyslifecenter.org/2022/10/25/journaling-for-teens-mental- health-resources/*

- ***Decoding the Myers-Briggs Type Indicator (MBTI): Evaluating Its Strengths and Limitations***. *Retrieved from https://www.theteenmagazine.com/decoding-the-myers-briggs-type-indicator- mbti-evaluating-its-strengths-and-limitations#:~:text=Teenagers%20are%20in%20a%20constant,strengths%2C%20weaknesses%2C%20and%20motivations.*

- *Breathing Exercises for Stress*. NHS. Retrieved from https://www.nhs.uk/mental-health/self-help/guides-tools-and-activities/breathing-exercises-for-stress/

- *Help Your Teen Get More Exercise*. Mayo Clinic Health System. Retrieved from https://www.mayoclinichealthsystem.org/hometown-health/speaking-of-health/teens-and-exercise

- *14 Engaging Art Therapy Ideas for Teens to Unlock Healing*. Retrieved from https://occasion.app/blog/art-therapy-activities-for-teens

- *Teens and Social Media Use: What's the Impact?* Mayo Clinic. Retrieved from https://www.mayoclinic.org/healthy-lifestyle/tween-and-teen-health/in-depth/teens-and-social-media-use/art-20474437

- *How to Practice Active Listening: 16 Examples & Techniques*. Retrieved from https://positivepsychology.com/active-listening-techniques/

- *The Root of Teen Empathy Begins with Secure Relationships*. CNN. Retrieved from

  https://www.cnn.com/2021/07/15/health/teen-empathy-secure-family-relationships-wellness/index.html

- *10 Trust-Building Exercises for Kids and Teens*. Healthline. Retrieved from https://www.healthline.com/health/parenting/trust-exercises-for-kids

- *Creating Safe Boundaries for Teens to Push Against*. Retrieved from https://parentandteen.com/creating-safe-boundaries/

- *13 Practical Time Management Skills to Teach Teens*. Retrieved from https://lifeskillsadvocate.com/blog/13-practical-time-management-skills-to-teach-teens/

- *Social Media and Youth Mental Health*. HHS. Retrieved from https://www.hhs.gov/surgeongeneral/priorities/youth-mental-health/social-media/index.html

- *How to Resist Peer Pressure & Stand Up for Yourself*. WikiHow. Retrieved from https://www.wikihow.com/Resist-Peer-Pressure

- *Stress Management and Teens*. AACAP. Retrieved from https://www.aacap.org/AACAP/Families_and_Youth/Facts_for_Families/FFF-Guide/Helping-Teenagers-With-Stress-066.aspx

- *Resilience: 5 Ways to Help Children and Teens Learn It*. Harvard Health. Retrieved from https://www.health.harvard.edu/blog/resilience-5-ways-to-help-children-and-teens-learn-it-202202242694

- *The Impact of Positive Self-Talk on Teen Confidence and Motivation*. Retrieved from https://teencoachacademy.com/blog/teen-confidence-and-motivation/

- *SMART Goal Setting for Students*. Retrieved from https://www.asvabprogram.com/media-center-article/65

- *8 Famous People Who Overcame Obstacles*. Familius. Retrieved from https://familius.com/8-famous-people-who-overcame-obstacles/?srsltid=AfmBOorPQuCRyev4lWlu_fefrVcbfXw2y8cItQ3TcNkMGtV9dZWhPPU4

- *How Does the Generation Gap Affect Relationships?* Retrieved from https://mindbodycounselingreno.com/blog/relationships/generation-gap/

- ***10 Tips for Successful Family Meetings***. *Colorado State University Extension. Retrieved from https://extension.colostate.edu/topic-areas/family- home-consumer/10-tips-for-successful-family-meetings/*

- ***Negotiation with Your Children: How to Resolve Family Conflicts***. *Harvard. Retrieved from*

  https://www.pon.harvard.edu/daily/conflict-resolution/negotiating-with-your-children-2/

- ***The Benefits of Family Bonding Activities***. *Retrieved from https://www.pontchartrainpediatrics.com/the-benefits-of-family-bonding- activities*

- ***Peer-to-Peer Mental Health Support***. *Retrieved from https://www.schoolhealthcenters.org/resources/student-impact/peer-support/*

- ***Lucy Hone: 3 Secrets of Resilient People | TED Talk***. *Retrieved from https://www.ted.com/talks/lucy_hone_3_secrets_of_resilient_people?language=en*

Leave a Review!

Thank you for reading *Anger Management for Teens: Mad to Calm*! We'd love to hear your thoughts if you found the strategies helpful, the exercises insightful, or the examples relatable. Your feedback helps us grow and helps others discover tools to manage their emotions and build confidence. Please take a moment to leave a review and share how this book has impacted your journey. Your voice matters!

Website link attach :

Amazon Link Attach: